T0103507

The Messiah According to Judaism

Also by Rabbi Ariel Ben Yaakov:

"The Final redemption and the Ten Tribes"

"The War of Gog and Magog"

To contact the author to purchase the books 'The Final Redemption and the Ten Tribes' or 'The War of Gog and Magog', public appearances, questions or comments:

ArielBenYaakov3@hotmail.com

http://themessiahblog.blogspot.co.il

check blog to confirm email

The Messiah According to Judaism

Ariel Ben Yaakov

PARTRIDGE

ISBN: Softcover 978-1-4828-8011-3
eBook 978-1-4828-8012-0

Print information available on the last page.

To order additional copies of this book, contact
Toll Free 800 101 2657 (Singapore)
Toll Free 1 800 81 7340 (Malaysia)
orders.singapore@partridgepublishing.com

www.partridgepublishing.com/singapore

Who is the suffering servant? This book goes into Isaiah 53's meaning of who is the suffering servant as per the rabbinic commentators and the Midrash.

The author read all available books on the subject of the Messiah and incorporated all the main points of these books as well as other important points that the Torah teaches regarding the Messiah, so as to compile the most comprehensive and authoritative book available on the subject of the Messiah according to the Torah, which is the basis of Judaism.

Endorsements and Approbations

"Rav Ariel Ben Yaakov's work (the three book series on the Messiah according to Judaism, the Final Redemption and the Ten Tribes and the War of Gog and Magog) is a very interesting and informative work on the arrival of the Messiah... and is recommended reading for those interested in this important subject".

Ariel Ben Yaakov is "the most knowledgeable person in the generation on matters of the Moshiah (the Messiah)"-Rosh Yeshivas Mir Nathan Tzvi Finkel (zt'l).

Although not famous, behind the scenes, Ariel Ben Yaakov is "the leader of the Jewish people in Israel"- David Kimche (zt'l), former assistant director of the Mosad.

Ariel Ben Yaakov is a 'genius'- Rabbi Chaim Kramer Shlita author of 'Moshiah Who What Why When Where' as per Aaron Teitelbaum.

Book Approbation by Rabbi Avraham Stern Shlita

בס"ד

Kehillas Ohel Torah 4 Rav Yosef Karo St. Beitar Illit Rabbi Avraham Stern, Rabbi	קהילת אוהל תורה רח' רב יוסף קארו 4 ביתר עילית הרב אברהם שטרן, רב הקהילה

חשון תשע"ו
Cheshvan 5776

Rav Ariel ben Yaakov Spiegelman has compiled a very interesting informative work concerning matters of the arrival of our Messiah.

(He informs me that the renowned Reb Nosson Zvi Finkel zt"l, (Rosh-Yeshiva of Mir) agreed he was the leading expert on the topic.)

Rav Ariel ben Yaacov's work is recommended reading for all those interested in this important subject.

Rav Ariel, who himself has suffered a lot for our people has many deep insights,

With deep respect,

Avrohom Stern.

רב קהילת אוהל תורה

Kehillas Ohel Torah • 4 Rav Yosef Karo St., Beitar Illit 99879 • 99879 קהילת אוהל תורה • רב יוסף קארו 4, ביתר עילית
Phone, Rabbi's study: (02) 580 7410 טל' לשכת הרב 5807410 (02)

Approbation to the author from Rav haTzadik Dov Kook haCohen Shlita

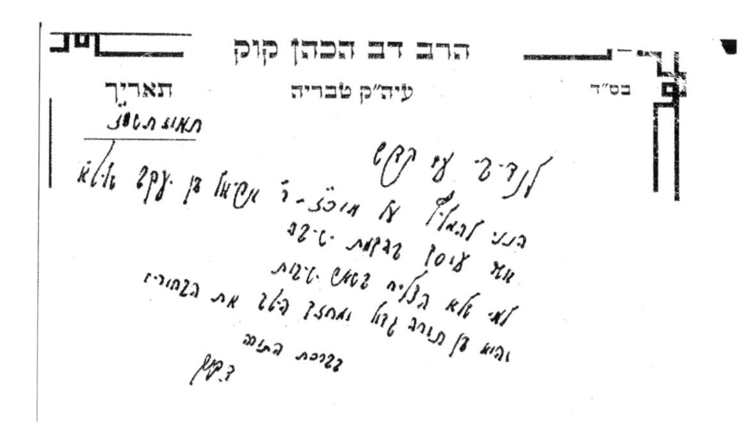
הרב דב הכהן קוק

בס"ד

עיה"ק טבריה

תאריך

BH

Translation of the above Recommendation:

Tamuz 5767

To the generous people of the Holy Nation:

I hereby recommend that

Rav Ariel Ben Yaakov Shlita

establish a yeshiva to those who hadn't succeeded in other yeshivas (due to those peoples' moral purity and goodness),

as he is big in Torah and

a good strengthener of young men.

With Blessings of Torah

Rav Dov HaKohen Kook Shlita

Blessing His People Israel with Love

The Holy City Of Tiberius

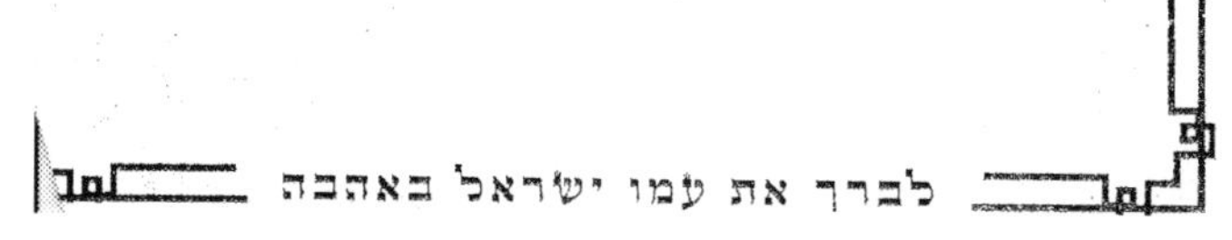

Dedication

Honor and thanks to Hashem, my father Maestro Joel Warren Spiegelman, my mother Mrs. Gail Voelker Barrnett (z'l), my sisters Maia Hunter and Katia Lief; my cousins Harry Hunter, Eli Lief and Karenna Lief; my grandparents including Dr. Harry and Jennie Spiegelman (z'l), Ceil Gilden Spiegelman and Mr. Edward (z'l) and Francis Voelker (z'l), my whole family, my many friends and Rabbis especially Cantor Ira Fein Shlita, the Rebbe (zt'l), the Baba Sali (zt'l), Yaakov David Tress, Rav Moshe Feinstein (zt'l), Rabbi Menahem Listman Shlita, Rav haDayan Yitzchak Goldstein Shlita, Rav Yosef Trachman Shlita, Hananya Ehrman, Zahave Green, Rav haMikoobal Yitschak Kadoori (zt'l), Rabbi J. Center Shlita, Rav Perets Ohrbach Shlita, Rav haGadol Avroham Greenbaum Shlita, Rabbi Beresht Zlotnick Shlita who taught by his righteous actions alone (not words), the Shtleipler Rebbe (zt'l), Rav haGadol haDor Yosef Shalom Eliyashev (zt'l) and Rav haGadol haDor haTzadik haKadosh Avraham Stern Shlita, all my friends, martial arts and music teachers, Dr. Leah Gold Fein (z'l) who gave me direction to Hashem, singing teacher Judy Hages who gave me my voice, Rabbi Emmanuel Gentlecore Shlita, Rav haTzadik Yom Tov Glaser Shlita (the surfing Rabbi) all of the people of Israel, all the Righteous Gentiles, all of the people who ever existed and who ever might have been born, and all of the Creations as G-d loves us all

Edition One (July 8, 2015 Tamuz 21 5775)

May Hashem's Honor, the honor of the Holy Torah, the honor of the Holy Rabbis, the House of David, the fully rebuilt Jerusalem, the Sanhedrin, all the people of Israel, the Noahide laws & the Temple All return and Be Speedily Rebuilt in Our Time

The first book of a comprehensive three book series on the Messiah, his identifying traits, how to bring the real Messiah, the final Redemption, the Ten tribes of Israel, the war of Gog and Magog, Gog, Amalek, Armilus (the 'Anti-Christ'), Edom, the fourth beast.

Based on traditional Jewish and authoritative ancient Torah Sources

Compiled, translated from original ancient Hebrew texts, interpreted, correlated, copyrighted, edited and written *in the Name of Heaven with great assistance from Heaven* From 1995 (Hebrew year 5755) until 2015 (5775) by Rabbi Eric Irving Ariel Ben Yaakov Spiegelman Shlita born September 29, 1962 Rosh HaShana 5723 from Monsey Kaal Yaakov, Jerusalem (Mea Shaareem, Beit viGan (AKA 'David Gross'), Har Tzion, Tsfat, Beitar Illit, Yeshivas Ohr Sameah (Monsey and Jerusalem), Kol Yaakov (Monsey), Diaspora, Machon Meir, Tzemach Tzedek, Bircat Torah, Tiferet, Mir (Jerusalem), Adereth Torah (Rabbi J. Center Shlita), Nahal Novea Makor Chochma, Rabbi Feuer Shlita Kollel of Shaarei Chesed, Kollel Yaakov Meir Krieger (z'l) Beitar Illit circa 1998-2012; AKA American name Eric Irving Ariel Spiegelman AKA stage name Eric Alrich from Brookline, MA; Bronxville, Scarsdale, Yonkers, Manhattan, Franklin School, SUNY Purchase, NY; Hamden, CT; Bergen County NJ (Wyckoff, Oakland, Prospect Park, Paramus, Ridgefield, Lodi, Teaneck); MCL, Anritsu, EMC, Midnight Sun Studio, Raytheon MDS circa 1967-1982/1987-1998; AKA Arik Shpiegleman from kibbutzim Beerot Yitzchak, Maagan Michael, Sdot Yam, the Technion Electrical Engineering Dept, Haifa circa 1982-1987

'Of all the Torah, the Torah that moves from place to place is the greatest Torah of all and is called a River'- Rabbi Avroham Chaim Feuer Shlita of Kollel Shaarei Chesed based on Kabbala. Most Kosher Jews who know him regard the author of this book Rabbi Eric Ariel Ben Yaakov Spiegelman

Note from the author

This book is part of a comprehensive three book series on the Messiah, the final Redemption, the war of Gog and Magog, Gog, Amalek, Armilus (the Anti-Christ), Edom, the fourth beast, and the lost 10 tribes of Israel.

The three books are titled 'The Messiah According to Judaism', 'the final Redemption and the Ten Tribes', and 'the War of Gog and Magog'.

It is recommended to read all three books in order to attain a more complete understanding of each book. 'The Messiah' is a comprehensive book covering all aspects of the Messiah including the personal identifying traits of the Messiah, conditions of the times preceding and during the days of the Messiah, prophesies of the coming of the Messiah, obstacles to the coming Messiah and what hastens his coming, what we must do to bring the Messiah in our times, the names of the Messiah, from where the Messiah comes, the Messiah as a man of war, the suffering and imprisonment of the Messiah, the Messiah as per Isaiah 53, the reasons why Jesu of Nazareth is not the Messiah, the many assimilated Jews among the Palestinian Arabs, the Messiah son of Josef, reestablishing the Sanhedrin today, the building of the third Temple, proof of G-d as the creator, proof of the Divinity of Torah, the Noahide Covenant as the proper way for Gentiles to live, moral for our times, what merits that one will survive. 'The Final Redemption and the Ten Tribes' is a comprehensive book covering all aspects of the Final Redemption of Man and the Ten Tribes including the stages of the final end of days redemption, the location of the ten tribes today, the exile, the prophesies of the final redemption and coming of the Messiah, Edom the fourth beast, the building of the third temple, the resurrection, the days of the Messiah. 'The War of Gog and Magog' is a comprehensive book covering all aspects of the War of Gog and Magog including the identifying traits of Gog, the identifying traits of Amalek, the identifying traits of Armilus 'the Anti-Christ', the Messiah son of Josef, the modern locations of the nations who fight in the war of Gog and Magog.

To Contact the author to purchase the books 'The Final Redemption and the Ten Tribes' or 'The War of Gog and Magog', public appearances, questions or comments:

Ariel BenYaakov3@hotmail.com

http://themessiahblog.blogspot.co.il
check blog to confirm email

Table of Contents

Subjects of the author's second book of the three book series: 'The Final Redemption and the Ten Tribes'

- Concise Relevant Background History of the World Prior to the Redemption
- The Destruction of the First Temple
- The Decline of Jewish and World Civilization as a Result of the Destruction of the Sanhedrin and the First Temple
- The Jewish people are scattered all over the world until the Full Redemption
- The wicked kingdoms of Edom and Aram will rule the world prior to the Messiah
- Edom/Rome/USA/West Serves Righteous Jews
- The concept of the 'Exile of Ishmael'
- Spiritual Darkness will cover the world prior to the coming of the Messiah
- The Redemption is an Evolving Historical Process that Happens in Stages
- The laws of nature don't change during the Redemption
- Auspicious 'times' when the Redemption can occur

- **The Bible Prophesies Foretelling and Describing the Redemption of Israel in the 'End of Days' or 'End Time'**
- Wars mark the different stages of Redemption and preclude its Beginning
- The Beginning of the Redemption Period
- The Jewish People Return to the land of Israel from the captivity of exile

- Ingathering of the Exiles to the land of Israel One Person by One, Not in Groups
- The Messiah Doesn't Lead the Jewish People Back to the Land Israel
- The Heresy all over the world prior to the coming of the Messiah
- People will search for the Word of Hashem but will not find it
- Unrepentant Sinners of the Jewish people will be destroyed
- The House of David will be Re-established and The Jews will inherit Edom
- The righteous king Messiah
- The End of all War: Peace on Earth

- **<u>The Chronological Order of Stages of Redemption according to Ezekiel</u>**
- The Land of Israel is Desolate Prior to the Redemption of the People of Israel
- When is the Beginning of the Redemption?
- First the Ten Tribes Return to the Land of Israel
- Hashem Sanctifies His Name that was desecrated in the Exile
- More Jews come to the land of Israel
- The Jewish People Return to Living by the Torah
- The Jewish people get a 'Heart of Flesh' from a 'Heart of Stone'
- The Jewish Return to Fulfilling Torah Commandments
- The Jewish Peoples Faith in G-d Will Strengthen
- The Jewish People Will Increase in our Vigilance against Sin
- Israel Will be agriculturally Self-Sufficient
- The Jewish People Will Be Disgusted with Ourselves for our Past Sins
- The Nations will see that Hashem has Rebuilt, Repopulated and Replanted Israel
- The Jewish people in Exile are spiritually rejuvenated from their 'Valley of Dry Bones'
- Reunification of the Ancient Division between Judah and Josef
- Another Wave of Jewish Emigration to the Land of Israel
- The Messiah son of Josef becomes king of Israel in order to pave the way for the Messiah son of David
- Yet another deeper level of repentance for Israel
- The Power of Repentance to Rectify Your Past and Turn Past Sins into Merits

Subjects of the author's third book of the three book series: 'The War of Gog and Magog'

- Introduction and Overview
- Who is Gog?
- Who is Amalek (may their memory be erased)?
- *Possible* real life scenario of how Gog may operate
- Where are the nations of the army of Gog an Magog currently located?
    - Magog
    - Tubal/Tuval
    - Meshech
    - Tiras/Paras
    - Gomer
    - Cush
    - Put
- Prophesy of the forces of Gog and Magog that are gathered for destruction
- Gog and Magog is a continuation of the war from king Hezekiah's time
- Prophesy that Smart Missiles that 'find their target on their own' will be used in Gog and Magog
- Converts living in Israel will Abandon the Torah in the war of Gog and Magog
- The War of Gog and Magog lasts Twelve Months
- Up to two thirds of mankind or Israel may perish by the time of the war of Gog

To Contact the author to purchase the books 'The Final Redemption and the Ten Tribes' or 'The War of Gog and Magog', public appearances, questions or comments:

ArielBenYaakov3@hotmail.com

http://themessiahblog.blogspot.co.il
check blog to confirm that email address is current

Preface

The subjects of the Messiah, the final Redemption, the ten tribes of Israel, Gog, the war of Gog and Magog, Edom, the fourth beast, Amalek (may their memory be erased) and Armilus (the 'Anti-Christ') are learned from the ancient teachings called 'the Torah'. Therefore, we must relay upon the original Torah sources to know and understand these subject's true authoritative definitions. Ideas without accurately interpreted Torah sources are nonsense and have no bearing on the reality of what the Messiah and the related subjects of these books really are. I found that there are many incorrect beliefs, falsehoods, and misunderstandings in society about these subjects, so I wrote this book series to correct and educate the society regarding what the Torah really teaches about these subjects, what the real truth is, and what are the sources of each real truth, since information is only as valid and authoritative as is the source. This book series is also needed to educate the Rabbinate and even the biggest rabbis of the generation so that the Messiah can come in our generation. Without this book series there is little chance. With this book series, particularly my book titled 'The Messiah According to Judaism', it is possible.

The book series is written for Jewish people of all beliefs and is permissible for Gentiles who live by the Noahide laws to read as well (as per 'The Path of the Righteous Gentile' by Chaim Clorfene and Jacob Rogalsky). This permissibility according to Torah includes all 24 books of scripture and writings other than the Talmud and Jewish laws that apply exclusively to Jews alone such as Sabbath, the holidays, Tefillin, Mezooza and Torah that applies only to the Jewish people (ibid). It is written that Jews and righteous Gentiles have a place in the Heaven (Talmud Bavli Avoda Zara 10b, 18a) and Talmud Bavli Avoda Zara 3a and Sanhedrin 59a teach that a Jew as well as a Gentile who occupies himself in the study of Torah (that pertains to him) is worthy of respect like that of the Cohen Gadol. But, I must warn that it is strictly forbidden to idol worshipers to read this book series (ibid citing Rambam Laws of kings chapter 10:9). I must say this warning from the beginning of the book. This is a Torah based book series and just as learning Torah that is permissible to one gives him blessing, learning Torah that is forbidden to one can damage one's soul and can bring dangerous judgments from G-d including death if not adhered to (ibid citing Rambam Laws of kings chapter 10:9,10). I understand that the widespread permissibility to Gentiles to read my Torah books is allowed because "*Rav Chiya Bar Abba said in the name of Rav Yohanan that Gentiles outside the land of Israel are not idol worshippers. Rather it is a custom of their fathers that is in their hands*" (Talmud Bavli Chullin 13b). That was in the year 280 AD. ArtScroll notes there that this means that the Gentiles don't really have ideological devotion to idolatry. This seems to still be the case to this day, especially considering that the Great Knesset removed the evil inclination for idol worship from the world in ancient times (Talmud Bavli Yoma 69). Therefore most people today are really not idol worshipers so it's safe to read my book series, and even a Mitzva, to market this book in the Gentile markets, where incidentally, Jews will also find the book so it can help the serve G-d properly too. But, if the reader really is a true idol worshiper (May G-d have Mercy on your soul), then you must read only the first chapters of the book titled 'G-d Loves All People', 'G-d Created and Sustains the World', 'The Divinity of Torah', 'The Noahide Covenant' and 'Christianity and the G-d of Israel's Infinite Mercy, Grace and Forgiveness'. If after reading these chapters you will accept the Noahide laws then you may read the other chapters of the book series further. If not, then give or sell the book to a Jew or a Noahide Gentile and you will be rewarded by Heaven for your good deed. I was told by Rabbi Emanuel Gentilcore Shlita that in the past, Rav Nahman Bulman (z'l) made a Heshbone (deliberated judgment of considerations), or 'psak' (Torah judgment ruling on law) so to speak, and set the current precedent when he permitted selling Torah books meant for Jews in markets where Goyim (Gentiles) would buy them as well.

The book series is based on traditional Jewish and authoritative Torah sources such as the Tanach (the original version of the Bible in Hebrew including the Bible prophets), Chumash (the five books of Moses), Talmud (the parts of the Torah that were orally transmitted from Mount Sinai), Midrash (the parts of the Torah that were orally transmitted) and accepted Jewish sages such as Rashi, Rambam, Radak, and the Arizal, and recent modern orthodox Jewish Rabbis as well. To resolve a tragic misunderstanding espoused by misinformed misnagneem in the Lithuanian community, I must teach something now.

On one occasion, when I spoke with the recent Gadol haDor (Biggest Rabbi of the generation) Rav Yosef Shalom Eliyashev (zt'l), circa 2003 in Mea Shaareem where we lived, he referred me to the Breslov Rabbi Yaakov Meir Shechter Shlita, so from this I understood that Breslov Torah is Kosher for the Lithuanians. The letter of approbation for the Breslov Rebbe Odesser that was given by Rav haGadol haDor Moshe Feinstein (zt'l), mentioning 'the petek hapela-ee (not understood)', to support the distribution of Breslov works, already showed this acceptance as well. There is also a book in Breslov called 'Shivho shel haTzadik' that quotes the Gidoleem of the Lithuanian Rabbis; such as the Steipler (zt'l), the Hazon Eesh (zt'l), the Chefetz Chaim (zt'l), Rav Kahanaman (zt'l) and more; all of whom support Breslov as kosher Torah. I thus quote Rav Nahman of Breslov in this book as well as other reliable traditional sources, and include some current great orthodox Rabbis, living Torahs, who are still alive. So, if you are a Lithuanian Jew, rest assured that this book is kosher limihadreen for you to learn. Also, everything I say gives a Torah source. To deny the words of this book would be kfira (Hashem Yirachem).

The Torah, written in ancient Hebrew, is the ancient scripture of the Jewish people that was given by G-d on Mount Sinai (circa 1500 BCE) to the Jewish people and is divided into the written Torah (AKA the five books of Moses) and the oral transmission from Mount Sinai that was eventually written down in the Talmud (Circa 500AD). The Torah is the foundation of Judaism which is not only the most ancient still existing religion in the world, but also the most ancient one of all religions, since parts of the Torah come from the Garden of Eden in Man's original first tongue; ancient Hebrew. A more comprehensive explanation of what Torah is can be found in Rabbi Arie Kaplin's (zt'l) handbook of Jewish thought.

A number of good books were written on the Messiah, but not so much on many of the other subjects of this book series. This book series brings the sources of the best of the other books that were written on the subjects, and in addition, brings many important and even essential new sources that were not included in the other books written on these subjects, particularly that of the Messiah. Upon distributing essays on the Messiah, the Redemption of Israel and the war of Gog and Magog in Jerusaelm during 2003 to 2005 to various Rabbis and colleagues, Rabbi Nathan Tzi Finkel (of blessed memory), the head of the Mir Yeshiva in Jerusalem, said that I am 'the most knowledgeable person in our generation on the subject of the Moshiah (the Messiah) and related matters'. The book series shows that this statement is true to the best of our knowledge. I would like to add that this book series focuses on Nigla and has self censored some essential nister of which I only give over orally to those who are appropriate and worthy receivers of the Kabala.

I wrote this book series because I saw a need to educate and clarify to Torah scholars and the public these subjects which are generally not understood, misunderstood, rife with misconceptions and false information, and generally obscure to the general public and even great Torah scholars who would really like to understand these subjects, but just simply don't have the time of thousands of hours that I took to write this work to gain the elevated understanding that HaShem has given me with great Siata Dishmaya (Assistance from Heaven).

The book series is also written for kiruv (bringing people closer to G-d) and musar (morals) in addition to Torah education for the scholars and general public. The book series was also written with the express intent to teach the world the greatness, immense wisdom and Holiness of the ancient Talmud. Rav haGadol Avraham Greenbaum said that all the heretical sects are based on denial of the Talmud, so bringing the Talmud to proof as the truth has the impact of showing that the many heretical sects of the world are just simply not true.

The book uses Rabbinic scholarship to bring an interpretive elucidation of the subjects, based on Torah sources, and to bring as simple and truthful an understanding as is possible to the reader. Although the traditional Yeshiva Rabbinic scholarship tends to involve quoting as many sources as possible, sources that often seem to contradict one another, especially among the later Rabbis (Ahroneem) in this subject matter, some of which even seem to contradict primary sources, I have thus chosen to base the book on the undisputed primary sources, as much as possible, so as to keep the matter as clear and well founded on undisputed primary sources, as much as possible. Otherwise the reader would just walk away confused with a barrage of seemingly contradictory and obscure information. This book is meant to clarify the matter in the deep simple meaning in concise terms as possible ('the pshat Rashi'), and not to show off Rabbinic scholarship with masses of sources which would only leave the reader confused. There is already enough confusion in these matters. This book clarifies the issues covered with the main essential basic primary sources that are not even cited in the other books on the subject.

I have received approbation from Rav haTzadik Dov Kook Shlita, the in law of Rav Yosef Shalom Eliyashev (zt'l) and a copy of it is in the beginning of this book. My approbation is to teach Torah but is not to make legal decisions of halacha ('psak') so any ideas or statements in this book that may seem to be psak are to be taken only as teaching Torah reasons and logic of judgments and not psak halacha. The Gidoleem and Poskeem are the only Torah authorities allowed to decide the psak halacha. As the Rosh Yeshivas Mir recognized me as the Gadol haDor on Moshiah, then maybe I am the posek on these issues, as my book series indicate. I have passed copies of the book to many of my Rabbis and colleagues such as Rav haGadol haTzadik Avraham Stern Shlita (who studied under Rav Matityahoo Solomon at Gates head Yeshiva, Rosh Yeshiva Mir Nosan Tzvi Finkel (z'l)), and was mishameash Rav Eliyashiv (zt'l)), Shmuel David Ellis, Yerachmiel Fogel, Rabbi Yonathan Beitz Shlita and Rabbi Gentilcore Shlita. I thank them for their criticism and support of this work. At least thirty other Rabbis have also seen this work. Many military generals and planners use my book series as a reference manual for the actuality of future and current wars that they must plan for. Former deputy director of the Mosad, David Kimche (zt'l), recognized the author as the leader of the Jewish people, as opposed to one of the leaders of the non Jewish Erev Rav system of the State of Israel that is currently for the time being in power, discussed in my book titled 'The Messiah According to Judaism'. This is coming to an end and the royal House of David (Beith David) under the leadership of Moshiah Ben David will take over soon with G-d's Help.

A piece of information is only as reliable and authoritative as its source. Since the subjects of Messiah, the final Redemption and the war of Gog and Magog all originated from and are learned from the ancient scriptures collectively known as Torah, I use the Torah sources upon which to base the book, for these sources explain and define authoritatively what these topics really are. Other man made religions claim to be sources but are really false and only the Torah is from g-d and tells the real truth about these subjects and all other subjects as well. The primary Torah sources include the 'five books of Moses' (in Hebrew called the Chumash), the Prophets, the Writings, the Talmud, Midrash, Zohar, the accepted classic Jewish sages (i.e. Rashi, Rambam, Ramban, Malbim, the Gaon of Vilna, Arizal, etc.) and some currently living Rabbis Shlita, who knew all these sources and can therefore explain them with great insight, wisdom, knowledge and understanding. In the book I give reference to the sources by giving the source and page number after the source's statement such as: "*statement* (source page number)". Throughout the book I put quotes of sources in italics and interject comments of my own in parenthesis in the middle of the quotes of sources. Information based on Ruah HaKodesh has been censored out of this revision of the book series. Only one Rabbi who I have met has the competence to accept the validity of the Ruah HaKodesh of the author. As he is a popular advisor to many, he requested that his name is not given so as to avoid controversy by the ignoramuses on these subjects, which unfortunately includes many Rabbis who know nigle well, but not nister, and certainly not in any experiential capacity as the author has been given as a great gift from Hashem many years ago when he was moser nefesh for clal Yisrael and thus merited Ruah HaKodesh (Midrash Raba on Parshat Biholeteacha).

In Honor of G-d, this book series is a rectification of the foundation of the world (in Hebrew called a 'Tikoon Yesod Olam') by pointing out the falsehoods that people in modern society believe regarding these highly misunderstood subjects and correcting them with the eternal truths of Torah. The books may even help people to make the right choice to live by the ancient Torah truths contained here in about the subjects. Those who support the book series will be supported by Heaven, bring blessing to the world and be blessed themselves.

In this book I do my best to teach Torah. I know that I will be judged by G-d for writing this book, its truthfulness, *my* motives, how much I *really* wrote it 'in the Name of Heaven', how much it brings people closer to G-d, and how much it brings people closer to the real truth. I try to be respectful of everyone and not to offend anyone and apologize if I inadvertently did so. In addition to my being scholar who writes, my father Maestro Joel Spiegelman also wrote a hilarious book called "the road to Shmagegee' and my sister, Katia Leif (AKA Kate Pepper), who is an amazingly talented professional writer, wrote many excellent popular suspense novels like 'Waterbury', 'Vanishing Girls' and 'You're Next' and it's German translation 'the Domino Killer' that is very popular in Germany.

A Mitzvah is a Torah commandment commanded from G-d that we are obligated to do. It is a Mitzvah for a Jewish person to learn Torah and to teach the Gentiles the Noahide laws (Shulhan Aruch Codes of Jewish law and Rambam). It is forbidden for a Gentile to learn the Torah that applies only to Jews but a Mitzvah for the Gentile to learn his Noahide Torah which includes much of the Torah works (see the chapter of this book on the Noahide Laws and for more detail see 'The Path of the Righteous Gentile' by Chaim Clorfene and Jacob Rogalsky). I wrote this book series mainly for Jews but with the understanding that some Gentiles may read it too. The book series is kiruv for Gentiles as well as Jews. Therefore, I must state that one of the highest and greatest things that a man can do in this world is to learn the Torah that applies to him; the Jew learning his Torah and the Gentile learning the Noahide Torah that applies to him, which is the seven laws of the Noahide Covenant and other Torah understandings that apply to him as well. The best book on the Noahide Laws that I have seen is 'The Path of the Righteous Gentile' by Chaim Clorfene and Jacob Rogalsky and is recommended for all. It is a Mitzva for Jews and Gentiles to teach this to Gentiles. The Noahide Covenant is what the Jewish faith believes is what Gentiles are obligated to abide by in their lives. That is why I included in this book a short essay on the Noahide Covenant in this book series; to bring Gentiles to their Noahide Torah that they must learn according to the Torah. It is obligatory for Gentiles to know and abide by the seven laws of the Noahide Covenant and their lives may depend on it in the end of days as well as now, so thus it is a matter of life and death for Gentiles to know these laws and therefore I teach them for their benefit in case they read this book series. Again, I wrote this book series mainly for people who are Jewish but with the understanding that some Gentiles may also read the book series as well so that is why I teach the Noahide Covenant here, to help Gentiles know their Noahide Torah that will help them serve G-d properly and merit Heaven. This is what G-d truly wants of them.

This Noahide education may also help the Jewish people, by converting Muslims, Atheists and Christians who are Gentiles, to Noahides, who will then stop proselytizing, oppressing, slandering, persecuting and terrorizing Jews by their man made religions. This will help stop the subjugation and anti-Semitic attacks of these religions against the Jewish people, and bring the Jewish people to their proper place of respect and nobility that is viewed by the Gentiles as 'the light unto the nations' (Isaiah 49:6, 42:6), a 'kingdom of priestly ministers' (Exodus 19:6), chosen by G-d to be a 'kingdom of priestly ministers' who teach the Gentiles their Torah laws, and are a guiding light to them, not a subject of derision; 'a despised nation' (Ezekiel 36) as we are now to many Gentiles and even self hating Jews (may Hashem have Mercy). Let us all rise together through love and light.

Someone is Jewish if his mother is Jewish (codes of Jewish law- Shulhan Aruch). The book series may also help Jews who are Muslims, Atheists or

Christians return to their ancestral faith of Torah Judaism which is also called Orthodox Judaism. This is what G-d truly wants of them, to live by the Torah alone, with G-d alone. Many aspects of the Messiah, the final redemption and the war of Gog and Magog may apply to the Gentile's Noahide Torah as well as Jewish people's Torah since the Gentiles will be affected by these issues as well. The kiruv of this book is a matter of saving Gentiles' lives as well as Jew's lives. I also included a short essay on the Divinity of Torah to explain to atheistic readers and academics that this book is not just an academic work but an explanation of the Word of G-d as given by the Holy Torah (the ancient scriptures of the Jewish people believed to be given by G-d and thus the absolute truth and obligatory for us to follow). In this light I hope that this book will return honor to the G-d of Israel, the people of Israel and return the ancient Torah, including the Talmud, to the people of Israel as well as give practical information on how to define and qualify what is and who can actually be the Messiah. My book The Messiah According to Judaism shows people how to identify who is the Messiah son of David. Without this book you don't stand a chance of identifying the Messiah unless you know all the Torah perfectly by memory and understand it too. That's not a reality for most people. Learning and disseminating this book may help bring the real Messiah and redeem Israel and G-d's Divine Mystical Presence (the Shichina) out of exile, as well as redeeming the Gentiles and the entire world. May we merit to actualize the book series' relevant precepts into spiritual and material reality in our time. Those who do so may be counted among those who uphold the world with Torah learning and teaching, fight G-d's wars and hasten the coming of the Messiah and redemption of Israel possibly before the final time. In any case, in addition to knowing more about the subjects at hand, I hope that we all grow from this book series in our service of G-d, humility and compassion.

Torah learning *attaches one's mind to G-d* even stronger than it was before he learned the new G-dly things of the Torah that he learned (The Tanya). Aside from a few major points about the Messiah that cannot be understood otherwise, in this book I don't teach many Kabalistic aspects of the Messiah because they are forbidden to teach to Gentiles and non observant Jews and can damage them if done so. In addition, I want to add that true Kabbalists who really know Kabbala and abide by the Torah law of teaching as a general rule don't translate Kabbala (as quoted in his book 'Faith and Folly' by Rabbi Yaakov Hillel Shlita). Kabbalists teach that by learning Kabbala people can be seriously hurt by evil *and even good* angels that *will* attack them *merely for saying their names* while studying Kabbala unless 'Hashem ('Hashem' is Hebrew. It means 'the Name' of the G-d of Israel) protects the fool' (as Rabbi Yaakov Hillel states in his book called 'Faith and Folly' which discuses occult practices and fake Kabbalists; a good book to read if one wants to learn more).

Although this book series is essential to understanding the subjects of the Messiah, the Redemption of Israel and the war of Gog and Magog to any believer or academician of any religion, this book series was written for Jewish people who believe in the Torah or want to learn because they love truth, seek the truth, and want more truth, in particular about the subjects discussed here in, and believe that the Torah is the real ultimate truth. It is also written for Gentiles to help them return to the Noahide laws.

I cite current events such as the world trade center bombings and hurricane Sandy for purposes of musar (moral) and to illustrate points of how G-d acts in the world as He is a Living G-d.

I try as much as possible to express in this book series the point of view of the ancient Torah that is required for every generation to learn with also focus on guidance for this generation. The Torah does not make concession to modern values and is not always politically correct, and I therefore apologize to anyone who may be offended or dismayed by the Torah or what it has to say. I and the Torah respect everyone and G-d loves everyone, even 'sinners'. In any case, what ever you thought, I want you to truly understand and know fully that G-d loves all people whoever you are and I want that to be remembered by the reader throughout the book series. I hope the teaching here is Torah true to be accepted by Heaven to be timeless for all generations and will help you get closer to G-d in your understanding and practice of Torah.

The Redemption and in particular the war of Gog and Magog can be terrifying and dangerous to those who don't live by the Torah. I write this book series to save peoples' flesh and souls. In addition to that G-d loves you, I want people to remember that G-d only does good and that every thing is for the best. What you may have thought was evil, before you read this book series, you may then come to realize is really only good and for the best. In addition to educating you about the Messiah, final redemption and the war of Gog and MaGog, may this book bring you closer to G-d, find grace and mercy, and merit us to the speedy coming of the real Messiah in our days.

The need for and approach of this book series

On February 28, 2015, Parshat Titzave, 5775, the Aida Haredit Beith Din; signed by the chief judge Yitzchak Tuvia Weiss Shlita and Av Beit Din Moshe Sternbach Shlita, and many other great Rabbis Shlita and Dayanim Shlita; publicized in Israel a 'Kriath Kodesh' (Holy Calling) calling for the public to support anti Missioanary activists in Israel (Yad liachim) saying that the matter is 'Pikuah Nefesh Mamash' (literally saving Jewish and souls) that justifies Hillul Shabath (Desecration of the Sabbath). This statement alone shows the importance of this book series because this book series not only teaches people what the Messiah really is, which is what Jews and Gentiles need to know, but it is a proof against the Missionaries most of whom are supported from abroad by English speakers. In addition, this book series is very educational in teaching the Gentiles and Jewish people the proper way to serve G-d; the Noahide laws for Gentiles and the Torah for Jews; and is great kiruv rihokeem (bringing people closer to G-d) and musar (moral), while always being respectful to all people, which is what we need today. For those who don't know, a 'Messianic Jew' is a Jew who believes in Yeshua as the Messiah. According to Rabbi Emanuel Gentilcore Shlita, there are some 150 'Messianic Jewish' churches in Israel, 30,000 Israeli Jews who have become Christian and hundreds of thousands of Jews internationally who have become Christian. A leading Messianic Jewish scholar, Dr. Michael Brown, even spoke of 'harvesting' souls in Iran. This book will help stop this problem.

More importantly, this book series is also very much needed for basic Torah education, education about G-d for atheists, and kiruv and musar work for the entire English speaking society which is mostly Christian. It will help Gentiles and Jews of all beliefs come closer to G-d and their Noahide and Jewish Torahs; respectively. The book series is a direct connect to G-d to people who are very lost and have fallen into a very deep dark place in life; in all religions.

I don't think that Christianity is our biggest problem though. Western culture, the culture of Eisav, which is often non-Christian and even anti-Christian, even highly anti-Christian (the Nazis and Romans killed Christians and even Yeshua himself), is a bigger problem. Modern 'secular' Eisavian Western 'morals' is far more wicked and this is seen by that the Rabbis have banned the Internet, along with TV, in the orthodox community for the damage that is has caused to many orthodox Jews and families. Christianity holds by many Torah values that Western culture rejects in its belief in 'freedom' (casting off the yoke of Heaven and Torah laws). Christianity adheres to morals, ethics and responsibility. They believe in G-d, the Bible scripture and going to Heaven. Christians in America now feel boxed in and under attack by immoral and unethical beliefs and laws of the Eisavian establishment as they are witnesses to the punishing wrath of G-d Almighty's Divine retributions striking America with hurricanes, floods, tornadoes, and plagues (i.e. AIDS). They witnessed the Oklahoma City Federal building and World Trade Center buildings being blown up by its own citizens and government as part of that Retribution. They know that G-d is punishing us for our sins. They know the society is in a downward spiral and is going off the rails of a crazy train. Two American senators even came out in 2014 and said that "America is going down the tubes. Only the Jewish Messiah can save us". The American Christians (particularly the Bible belt and Evangelists) have aligned themselves with Israel and the religious Jews; as a protective group solidarity of self defense in this assault on them by Edom in America and the West. The Christians are basically good people who back Israel, morality and G-d and I believe will mostly end of in Heaven at some point. This book series will help level rise to their higher level of Noahide and Torah Covenants.

The bigger problem we face, in my opinion, is Western civilization (see chapters on Edom; the values of Eisav; in my book the final Redemption and the Ten Tribes); which isn't really that Christian any more, is opposed to Torah values, and is essentially Eisav/Roman in morality and ethics. Eisav fakes being Christian in order to appear good and get Christian votes. Christianity is usually a guise that Eisav wears to deceive people into thinking he is righteous in terms of what they are tricked into believing is righteous.

Another big problem is the lack proper Torah education in world society at large, particularly Israel, and the lack of Media publicity of the real Torah leaders who are righteous, humble, wise, and pure. These people are supposed to be the leaders guiding the society but there is a media blackout on them. This is evil and part of the darkness that covers the world before Moshiah comes. I hope this book series brings America to back G-d, Torah and Israel; which will help bring the Messiah son of David to be king. The Torah education of this book series will help make the Messiah a concrete reality as a real king of the world and not just an abstract religious belief that no one understands how this thing could ever really happen or what we are supposed to do to make it a concrete reality in our times.

I will explain further.

In society at large, and the Torah world as well, there is a huge amount of misunderstanding, confusion, misinformation and ignorance regarding the topics of the Messiah, the final Redemption of Man, the ten tribes and the war of Gog and Magog. The esoteric nature and difficulty of these subjects, the education system and organized religion are largely responsible for this misunderstanding, confusion, misinformation and ignorance.

The purpose of this book series is to educate people and rectify the misunderstandings and misinformation about the Messiah (originally called the 'Moshiah' in the original Hebrew), the Biblically prophesied final Redemption of Israel, the ten tribes and the war of Gog and Magog. The book series is written so that people ranging from a ninth grade education to the level of university professors and the most advanced Torah scholars of the generation will be able to understand the book and learn much from it as well. The book series attempts to explain the deep simple meaning of these topics in as clear and concise a manor as possible, while presenting the Torah sources that elucidate the topics, but not too many sources so as to confuse the reader. The work is an interpretive elucidation of the Torah sources meant to clarify the subjects based on primary sources that are not in dispute by scholars. I considered writing the book series in Hebrew but decided to write it in English so that it would be accessible to more people. I have taught this book in Yeshivas in Hebrew and English and published summaries of it in Hebrew as well as English. I hope it will be translated into Hebrew so that it will be made accessible to the Israeli population and Torah scholars who don't read English since these topics are highly relevant in modern Israel. I also hope that it is translated into all the languages as a guide to people of all nations so that they can understand these critical topics.

I want to clarify here, from the beginning of this book series, that the book series exposes many values that the Torah considers as truths that people of different beliefs today may not used to hearing and may even find uncomfortable or even seem offensive. The book series is in no way meant to disparage any individual, group of people, other religion or belief at all. Hashem (Hashem is the Hebrew word meaning 'the Name' as in 'the Name of the G-d of Israel') loves *all* people of all religions and beliefs, even sinners and the misguided. G-d understands and has mercy, compassion and forgiveness for all people; even those that may be thought of as 'evil' or unforgivable. Hashem *hates the sin but still loves the sinner which includes all the people that He Created*; even with our many sins and imperfections.

This book series is not meant to hurt nor disrespect people who have sinned or who according to the Torah are wrong in their beliefs, but to enlighten them, free them from the falsehoods under which they are currently enslaved, and to connect them with the G-d Who Created them and still really *loves them no matter how far they have strayed*. As the sages of Israel have said in Ethics of the Fathers '*The world stands on three things: Truth, Upholding the Torah Judgments, and Peace*'. This book series attempts to be a pillar of Truth; the real Truth according to the eternal Torah; not false modern values that change with the times. It is meant to free people from falsehood through Torah education. This book series is meant to save the reader's life by giving him the Torah he needs to live as it is written that 'a man without Torah is like a fish out of water; as soon as men separate themselves from Torah and commandments they perish' (Talmud Bavli Avoda Zara 3b). The book series teaches the Torah that you need to save your life and soul, in addition to teaching the Torah's Messianic prophesies. Don't be afraid. It won't hurt you. It will only help you to be more loved by G-d than you already are.

The great classic Torah sage authority, the Rambam (remembrance of the righteous is for blessing), whose authority we hold by, gives a brief yet thorough commentary on the Messiah, final Redemption and the war of Gog and Magog at the end of Mishna Torah, laws of kings. There he says that '*these things cannot be known how they will be until they will happen*'. He said this statement some 900 hundred years ago. Today, many of '*these things*' in the redemption *have* already started to happen in our times, such as the ingathering of the exiles and building of the Jewish cities in the land of Israel, which marks the beginning of the multi-stage process of the Redemption period of history, as this book series shows. Therefore, unlike the Rambam's time when he wrote this statement, learning these subjects is relevant to us in our times as we can see ancient prophesies unraveling before our eyes. This book series contains much information which the Rambam did not include in his short summery of the Messiah, but none the less the Rambam is absolutely authoritative according to the Torah, and, of course, the Rambam holds true with no contradiction to the Torah passages cited here in this book series whatsoever. This book series probes much deeper and with more detail into these subjects than the Rambam took the time out to do in his authoritative book Mishne Torah. The Rambam says that one shouldn't make these matters the '*main part*' of his Torah study because they wont increase Reverence for Heaven, but *now that these things are actually happening in our days, at this point in society, they do increase our love and Reverence for Heaven*, for all levels of Torah scholars, from beginner to advanced, and therefore are relevant for us to study at this point in time and now it is a Mitzva to learn my book series well, as two Roshei Yeshivas and a Gadol in Israel have already had me teach my book to them in their institutions. The Rambam's definition of chezkat haMoshiah (laws of kings 11:4) where the Mashiah compels all of Israel to live by the Torah can not be achieved until the Mashiah is appointed king by the Sanhedrin and a Navi (prophet) (ibid 1:3) and controls the media, music industry, education system and legal system. Therefore the Mashiah can only be identified by the pre-kingship traits outlined in my book here. Otherwise, there is as much a chance of Moshiah being identified and the later 'coming' as there is someone learning out the halachoth of how to make a kosher mezooza or Tfillin directly from the gemoora without rishonim. I would thus re-address peoples' misquoting the Rambam by saying that he is discouraging the learning of these subjects as the main part of study and say that the Rambam does want us to learn these subjects, but just not as the main part of our study. The chapter on misquoting the Rambam explains this more deeply. In any case, since these subjects are now more relevant then ever, it is now a Mitzvah to learn my book and they will now help increase our Reverence for Heaven. Thus, I write this book series.

I received Rabbinic approbation ('smeecha') to teach Torah from Rav (a Rav is a Rabbi) haTzadik Dov Kook haCohen Shlita of the Holy city of Tiberius. He is not that well known by the bulk of Ashkenazi Jews (other than big scholars) but Sephardim and Middle Eastern Jewish communities recognize that he is a Tzadik (a righteous man who thus is esteemed by G-d) and great Rabbi. Rav Kook Shlita was an 'Ilooee' (genius) at the Ponevitch Yeshiva and is now a Rosh Yeshiva and well respected Tzadik and Rabbi in his own synagogue and Beith Midrash in Tiberius, Israel, where he leads a Kehila (congregation). There he teaches Torah and answers halcahic questions as well as being known for being a Kabbala Mikoobal and Tzadik from whom people come to ask for blessings. He is also known to elongate his prayer in the Shimona Esrei Tfila (eighteen prayers formulated by the great Knesset some two and a half thousand years ago) and to pray extra to make tikooneem (rectifications) as part of his Avoda (convocation) of Holiness. Rav Kook Shlita often prays much of the day in his Synagogue to save Israel, to the point of exhaustion that he risks his own health. He is moser nefesh (giving over of his soul) in his service of Hashem. On the Sephardic 'Eish Matzliah Mahadoora Riveeth' sidur (prayer book), fourth edition, Rav haTzadik Dov Kook Shlita gives his approbation to the sidur along with the great recognized Rabbis of the generation such as Rav Ovadia Yosef (of blessed memory), the Rishone liZion Rav Shlomo Amar Shlita and Rabbi Shmuel HaLevi Woelber Shlita who the Ashkenazim recognize greatly, so he is obviously recognized as a Rabbinic authority by the Sephardim and Middle Eastern Jewish communities. As an Israeli Rav, he speaks Hebrew, not English, and is the grandson of the brother of Rabbi Avraham Isaac Kook (zt'l), the first Ashkenazi Rabbi of the State of Israel, as well as being the in law of the recognized biggest Ashkenazi Rabbi of the recent generation, former Gadol haDor haRav Shalom Yosef Eliyashev (remembrance of the righteous is for blessing). Unfortunately, most English speaking Anglo-American Ashkenazi Jews in this generation don't know who he is. Neither did I when I was living in Tsfat from 2006 until 2008, and first saw his picture in 2007 on the cover of a booklet by Rabbi Bengamin Goldman of Har Nof, encouraging the people to repent regarding problems in the Israeli Jewish society. When I asked Rabbis about him I was told he is a big Tzadik and Rabbi so I took the bus to Tiberius and met Rav Kook Shlita. While waiting in his Beith Midrash to speak to him he graciously sent me a health drink brought by one of his servants so I saw he was a man of kindness to guests, as well as being well respected in Tiberius where he lives. We discussed Torah issues and he read some of my Divrei Torah (Torah essays). After that we got to know each other as scholars and after some time and seeing that I am authoritative in my knowledge of Torah he gave me written approbation to be a Rosh Yeshiva (a head of a Torah academy) to teach Torah there. He accepted me and gave me approbation to be one of the Israeli Rabbis of the land of Israel, of which I am proud to be.

As an indication of Rav Kook's greatness for truth with no regard for scrutiny, one of his students from Tel Aviv produced a video called 'Hotam Emeth' (in Hebrew meaning 'Stamp of Truth') about his experience of dying and being granted by the Heavenly court to come back to life on the condition that he begin to keep the Torah commandments after having been non-observant. He is one of the only people in the Jewish people today who had the wisdom, courage, and truthfulness to come out and teach the generation about the very great problem of accusing demons that a person creates against himself by spilling semen in vein. This brought many people to repent and saved many souls. The video shows that when a person dies all the semen that he spilled in vein become partially developed baby spirits that shout at him in accusation in the Heavenly court: 'Wicked one! Wicked one! Look what you did to me! Look what you did to me! Wicked one! Wicked one! Look what you did to me! Look what you did to me! You fathered partially developed humanoid like baby creatures that will never be whole nor complete. Etc. etc.'. 'Hotam Emeth' can be found on the Internet. It is scary in its truth about what happens to a person in his judgment after he dies. It can help a man or boy repent from the sin of spilling seed in vein and thus merits the generation from refraining from doing something which the great Kabalist Hasidic master Rav Nahman of Breslov says 'spilling seed produces husks of spiritual impurity that give power to Edom that keep Israel in exile'. Rav haTzadik Dov Kook Shlita and his student are about Truth; not politics nor money nor power. I also try to be for truth. We try to stand for Hashem's truth and know we will be judged in the next world so we are careful to do things for Hashem and the next world, not this world. I wanted to share this about Rav Dov Kook haCohen Shlita to show that he and those with whom he associates are true servants of Hashem.

Being based on Torah, which is the absolute truth, this book comes from the world of Truth. It will shatter many vessels of impurity and falsehood that now hold much of this world captive in the husks of spiritual impurity of the other side regarding the subjects of this book. By sharing the book with others the dominion of wickedness and falsehood over man will be diminished. G-d's Glory will grow and there will be more light in the world.

Based on Torah essays in Hebrew that I distributed in Jerusalem since 2003, when I studied at the Mir Yeshiva, and gave classes there and at yeshiva

Hovavoth Livavoth, in Mea Shaareem, on the subjects of Messiah, Redemption and the war of Gog and Magog in English and Hebrew, another Torah great of the generation, Rabbi Nisan Tzvi Finkel (of blessed memory), the former head of the Mir Yeshiva in Jerusalem, recognized me as the most knowledgeable scholar on Messiah in the generation and related subjects. His recognition of my expertise on these subjects made me realize my responsibility to educate the generation on these subjects. Thus I write this book. I find Rabbi Finkel's (zt'l) comment very interesting since my parent's names are Joel and Gael (of blessed memory) which in Lashon Kadosh (the Holy Hebrew Tongue) are both spelled by the letters 'Gimel-Aleph-Lamed'. These letters spell 'Goel' which in Lashon Kadosh means 'redeemer' and I was born on Rosh Hashana which is the day on which the Messiah may probably be born as the chapter in my book The Messiah According to Judaism shows. Its not a coincidence that I write this book. It shows that G-d runs the world in every minute aspect.

There are piles of unworthy works on the subjects of this book series, particularly on the Messiah, that are total nonsense and mislead the reader and teach wrong information based on non source or sources that are misquoted, misinterpreted or taken out of context. In addition to weeding through these unworthy works, I have read all of the available serious Torah based works about the Messiah, redemption and the war of Gog and Magog, that are known to me, and with *great assistance from Heaven*, including computer data base searches of Torah (DBS and Bar Ilan University CD data bases of Torah, as well as the huge data base 'Otzar Hochma'), have been *granted from Heaven* an understanding and knowledge that encompasses all these other excellent books. My book series though contains essential sources of important information that these other worthy books left out.

Among the books that I read that are written from my worthy and knowledgeable colleagues in the Rabbinate and also highly recommend that you read and own as well are: 'Moshiah Who What Why When Where' by Chaim Kramer of the Breslov Research Institute, 'Mashiah' by Rabbi Jacob Immanuel Shochat (z'l), 'When Moshiah Comes' by Rabbi Yehuda Chayoon Shlita and 'Hevlei haMoshiah bizmananoo' by Rabbi Rafael Eisenberg HaLevi (of blessed memory). There may be other works with which I am unfamiliar that are also worthy. I also accessed once rare and inaccessible ancient historical documents and information over the Internet that help place some of the modern locations of ancient nations mentioned in the Bible, such as Magog son of Japheth (Genesis 10). These modern locations of the ancient nations that war in the war of Gog and Magog are given in my book on the war of Gog and Magog. I also had the privilege of studying with many fine Rabbis in Monsey, New Jersey, Manhattan, Jerusalem, Tsfat and Beitar Elite, all of whom taught me many things which contributed to this book, and some of whom I quote.

After learning these subjects since 1993 for thousands of hours, and then after submitting Torah essays in Hebrew on these subjects to Rabbis in Jerusalem, particularly Mea Shaareem, where I lived, in 2005 the Mir Rosh Yeshiva (that's Hebrew for 'head of the Torah learning academy'), Rabbi Nathan Tzvi Finkel (z'l), said that I am 'the most knowledgeable scholar in the generation on the subjects of the Moshiah (that's Hebrew for Messiah)" including the redemption (in Hebrew called the 'Gioola') and the war of Gog and Magog. My book series proves that statement conclusively. After reading the other worthy works on these subjects, and researching the subjects for the past twenty years, I decided to write a book on these subjects that includes all the essential main points of these other great works, and, includes many essential sources on these subjects that these other great works overlooked and didn't include. My book includes many new sources bringing out essential points of understanding that are not cited in these other works and are not known to the general public, the orthodox Rabbinate or even many of the wisest and most righteous Rabbis of the generation. One of the wisest and most righteous Rabbis of the generation (but not most popularized), Rabbi haGadol haDor haHasid haTzadik Avroham Stern Shlita, asked me to teach him my book on Moshiah in his morning learning seder instead of 'Nefesh HaChaim', written by a student of the Gaon of Vilna. On the merit of these other great Torah works and computer data bases of Torah that give all the sources of each topic, to the best of my knowledge, and for the sake of the readers and students of these subjects, from the level of the unlearned layman to the greatest Rabbis of the generation, I have done my best to make sure that this book is the most comprehensive book available on the Messiah, the final Redemption, the ten tribes and the war of Gog and Magog, based solely on authoritative Torah sources. The book is an elucidation of the herein subjects based on Torah sources. It is a book that covers all of the points of the other books on these subjects and many more essential points that the other books left out.

This book series is 'a must read' for anyone who wants to know about the Messiah, the final Redemption of Israel, Gog, Amalek, the war of Gog and Magog, Armilus (the Anti-Christ) or the lost ten tribes of Israel. This is no matter who you are, from the beginner to the biggest Rabbi of the generation, and it does not matter what belief or religion you hold as true. If you want to understand these subjects then you must study this book series and own a copy of it for your Beith Midrash or home library.

Being the most comprehensive book series available on the war of Gog and Magog, to the best of my knowledge, people should know this subject as well because this war may not be too far off. This book series also discusses a relevant prophesy about Paras attacking the world which may be relevant to Iran since Paras may be Iran who has threatened Israel, the United States and the world. This book series is relevant to the here and the now of the *modern times in which we live and pertains to us all.*

Being an activist for many years who risked my life many times in pursuit of justice and sanctifying Hashem's name, fighting His wars, and saving Israel, I have also been given great insight into the importance of the main aspect of the Messiah that the prophets talk about, namely his *enforcing justice according to the Torah.* That is why he is referred to in Torah sources as 'Our Righteous Messiah' (in Hebrew called 'Moshiah Tzeedkanoo'). The book series explains some of the aspects of Torah wisdom that explain why Torah justice is so important to society in preparing the foundation of the kingdom of G-d on earth and world peace, which is the foundation of the Messiah's kingdom since justice is a pillar of society. For people who are waiting for true justice to come to the world, the Messiah is the answer. I mention this point here because the issue of justice is *grossly overlooked by religion today*, even though it is the central and most mentioned theme by the prophets regarding the Messiah. Once the courts fall into line with upholding the proper Torah law, then everything else in society will fall into place; including the education system, business and media. The Messiah is part of that process. Establishing Torah justice is a essential part of the final redemption and salvation of mankind.

Every statement in this book that has a Torah source is *authoritative as the Word of G-d.* Insights and interpretive statements that I make or other recent Rabbis quoted herein *based* on the sources may be interpretive or also somewhat authoritative but not necessarily as authoritative as the Torah sources or established traditional Rabbis such as Rashi and the Rambam.

Since this book is based on the Torah, it is good to know a little about how we learn things from the Torah. There are a number of principles regarding how to interpret the Torah properly. One principle is that although a Torah verse has four basic levels of interpretation: the simple meaning, the hinted meaning, the derived law, the Kabalistic secret meaning. The simple meaning always holds true (Talmud Bavli Shabbat 63). Also, there can be a number of reasons that explain the meaning of a verse (Talmud Bavli Sanhedrin 34). The meaning and reason for one verse or statement in the Torah has to correlate with all the other verses and statements in the Torah so that there are NO contradictions on all levels of the understanding of the Torah. Mostly in an agreement with their other authoritative Jewish translations, I translated the Hebrew and Arameic texts of the Bible and Talmud myslef. The Jewish Press and Art Scroll books on the Prophets are also excellent from which to learn. Rabbi Arie Kaplan's handbook of Jewish thought gives a great explanation of how Torah is learned.

Throughout the book that comments on Christianity I refer to the man who Christianity believes to be the Messiah not by his colloquial name but as 'Jesu' or 'Jeshu'. This is because as a Jew I am forbidden by the Torah (G-d's law) to pronounce the name of what some people worship as an idol, or to mislead others to do so (Heaven Forbid), since some people worship the man that Christianity views as the Messiah as a god, and this is idolatry, and I therefore can not pronounce nor lead others to pronounce his name. I mean no offence by this to the many good people who are Christians and respect them as people even though I don't share their point of view of who is the Messiah. Not all Christians worship Jesu as an idol but since some do I cannot pronounce his name nor lead others to do so since some do worship him as an idol. Other than Christianity's Messiah, there have been many claimant Jewish Messiahs in history; some whose influence caused great damage to the Jewish people, like Shabetai Tzvi; and some causing great benefit to the Jewish people and humanity, like the potential Messiahs the Baal haTanya, king Hezekiah, Rebbe and the Rebbe of Chabad Lubavitch, who still has many pious devotees to this day who do great good in the world on a daily basis, and are helping bring the real Messiah.

The Torah defines what the Messiah is, who can be the Messiah, and what are his identifying traits by which we can know who he really is. The Torah research of this book series clarifies many of the misunderstandings regarding what and who the Messiah actually is by giving accurate and reliable Torah sources that define what and who he actually is. Due to the Torah criteria given in this book series of who is qualified to be the Messiah and who is not, this book series, particularly my book titled 'The Messiah According to Judaism', can be used to determine authoritatively who could qualify to be the Messiah, or most likely potential Messiah of the generation, and who is not qualified. It also shows us at what stage in the Redemption period we may now be holding, and how we can make it the final hastened 'end'. The book series shows how it may be possible to *hasten the coming of the Messiah* which most good people would really like to do. It also gives a somewhat revealing description of the final apocalyptic war on earth called the 'war of Gog and Magog' which will bring in the 'days of the Messiah' here on earth (Rambam laws of kings 12). This book series also gives kiruv (bringing people closer to G-d), musar (moral) and gives basic rescue first aid Torah education for a lost and floundering generation. The book series is a *testimony to the Greatness of Hashem*, the G-d of Israel, His Holy Torah, the people of Israel, and the good among the Gentiles, all of whom Hashem loves and really wants the best for us all in this world and the next.

May we merit seeing the coming of the Messiah speedily in our days. Amen.

G-d Loves All People

Since this book series is based on Torah, the foundation of Judaism since ancient times, and being that religion in general and many statements quoted by the Torah prophets in this book series can be judgmental towards people, I want to emphasis from the beginning of the book series that *G-d loves all people despite His judgments of people for our sins. He loves us all* even when we sin even in the most serious ways and He still always *hopes that we will return to Him* and live by His Torah *no matter how far we strayed, Jew or Gentile.* He hates the sin but loves the sinner. He will always love and accept us even when we sin and always desires that we return to living by His Torah commandments no matter how low we have fallen.

We learn from the Torah that 'Repentance' (in Hebrew called '*Tshuva*') was created before G-d created the world because the world would not have been able to survive without repentance since man would have been destroyed for his sins. Thus, *G-d always waits for us to return to His ways* even when we have sinned in the most serious of ways. As king David said: 'There is always hope for G-d to save even when the sword is on your throat (even in the direst of situations)'. As Rav Saadia Gaon (remembrance of the righteous is for blessing) points out in his masterpiece book, 'Emuna and Deoth', even many of the warriors on the side of Gog and Magog; at first fighting against Hashem, the Messiah and Israel; will repent and return to believe in Hashem during the war of Gog and Magog. From here we see that anyone can return to Hashem. This includes even people who sinned and fell to very low places like Hitler, Nebuchadnezzar, Pharaoh, Caesar, etc.. These people were subjugated by very heavily and over powering internal evil inclination forces that dominated their behavior but even they could repent at any time and were loved by G-d. In terms of Jewish history, Nebuchadnezzar is considered to be of the most evil and cruel anti-Semite ever to have lived. He destroyed G-d's Holy Temple. The

Talmud teaches us that when Nebuchadnezzar died the people in hell were afraid that he would become the new boss there. They were more afraid of Nebuchadnezzar than Satan. The Torah teaches us that even Nebuchadnezzar could repent. This teaches us that people can go lower than Satan but can still repent.

No matter who you are, I hope this book inspires you to return to Hashem and live by the Noahide Covenant (see chapter on Noahide laws and Covenant) if you are a Gentile or the Torah if you are Jewish. I know that not everyone who reads this book will do so with the initial intention of serving Hashem or determining what is the real truth. What's important is not from where the person begins but the goals to which he is aiming and how he finishes. This understanding will help get people to Heaven, any one, no matter from where he started. I hope we all make it.

A Gentile once came up to me and told me that he 'hates Jews'. I asked him why he hates Jews and he told me because he 'hates G-d'. I asked him why he hates G-d and he told me 'look what He made me'. Upon telling him that G-d really loves him and that he is truly good and that is why G-d created him, he thought a moment and said 'Do you know what? I don't really hate G-d or Jews at all'. This taught me that if people only knew how much G-d really loves us all then we would have a lot less problems. Our problem is that we forget that G-d loves us we forget how great each and every one of us really is.

Again, I want to emphasis to people reading this book that *Hashem loves all people*, Jews and Gentiles, even when we sin, even in the most serious way. Even when the prophets judge us G-d still always *Hopes that we will return to Him* in living in His Torah Ways, *no matter how far we strayed,* He will accept us. In any case He still loves us. Please remember this when reading the here in quoted judgments of the prophets.

Some people say that love has the power to conquer the world because it can empower people to see the good in themselves and be good and live by their good inclination and can help allot of the people in the world become healthy again but we also need reverence of Heaven to help prevent us from sinning.

G-d Created and Sustains the World

Most people today have been brainwashed by the 'education system' of their Western biology class to believe in the theory of evolution. Usually this theory is just taught that man evolved from apes when a genetic mutation occurred in the DNA gene code of an ape and a baby man was born from the ape. The ape came from a lower mammal, that lower mammal from another lower mammal, etc., that mammal came from a fish that left the water to dry land. The fish came from a multi cellular organism, where that multi cellular organism evolved from a cell. The theory says that living beings including people were created by a long process of biologically based evolutionary steps, where atoms, molecules, cells, tissues, organisms, animals and all of nature, formed spontaneously by random chance in an evolutionary process. The different animals are said to have evolved from one another by genetic mutations that occurred in their DNA gene code to produce similar but different new higher species of animals; like a man from an ape as they say. Think about this statement. Is it really true or even possible that such a thing could happen without an intelligent creator behind it? The theory misses a lot of critical points if one looks at it more carefully than it is given over in biology class. Unfortunately, most students just accept the theory blindly, with out thinking about it, and therefore fail to see the truth that the theory is really just impossible to ever really happen in reality. Belief in evolution is really blind faith. Let's think about the basic points of the theory of evolution to see they really can not be true at all.

For example, if pieces of scrap metal and engine parts are lying around in a junk yard, could a Boeing 747 jet plane form out of them all of the sudden, spontaneously by random chance? Similarly, if one threw a deck of cards up into the air, is it possible for the cards to land in a house of cards spontaneously by random chance? Or similarly, in parallel, as we are taught in science class, can electrons, neutrons and positrons form an atom spontaneously by random chance? More so, as isn't mentioned in science class, could trillions of atoms form spontaneously by random chance all at the same time? The answer to these questions is obviously 'absolutely not'. This is not possible by even a slight chance even if an infinite number of possible chances of such situations in different planets would present themselves over an infinite amount of time. It is impossible. Intelligently designed things don't form spontaneously by random chance. It can not happen; ever; not the Boeing 747 jet plane, not the house of cards, not the atoms, not the molecules, cells, tissues, organisms, animals or any of nature.

Furthermore, if one thinks about the plausibility of evolution, one will see that it is an impossible theory unless it is guided by the Hand of an Intelligent Designer, namely G-d.

Let's look at the theory of evolution more closely in order to see that it is impossible unless it is guided by the Hand of an Intelligent Designer.

What we have to do is to break down the evolution theory of life into its basic stages. Evolution theory says that the world was created by the following process: first, billions of years ago, there was a 'big bang' that created the universe and all its matter and energy 'out of nothing'. Out of this the solar systems, orbiting planets and all matter including atoms formed; all working in perfect harmony, as if by design. On planet Earth there was a land, liquid and gas environment made of these atoms out of which the atoms formed molecules and these molecules formed amino acids due to a spark (Miller's experiment shows this). These amino acids were the building blocks of proteins. Molecules also formed a material called 'coacervates' which formed cell walls and along with proteins formed into cells. These cells formed tissues like bone, muscle, nerves, brain, liver, kidneys, etc. which eventually formed into living beings that have all sorts of many tissues, all working in perfect harmony, as if by design. This is the evolutionary theory of how 'Nature' created men and woman, animals, fish and plants; all spontaneously by random chance since there were billions of planets for the possibility for this to happen, which made the chances of evolution possible.

If we break down this process of 'evolution' and look at it very carefully we can see that *no stage of the process of evolution could have happened on its own at random nor spontaneously no matter how many infinite of such possibilities were manifest.* We can see that every stage of the evolutionary process needs an intelligent Designer and Motivator to make it happen. Think about the following aspects of evolution. For instance:

1) What existed before the 'big bang' and what made it happen? The answer is: G-d who was the Motivator and intelligent Creator of things out of nothing. Only G-d can Create something out of nothing.
2) Could the approximately one hundred and eight different kinds of atoms really have formed by themselves all around the same time spontaneously by random chance? No; never. Could even one atom form by itself from sub-atomic particles like neutrons, positrons and electrons that orbit around the nucleus, spontaneously by random chance? No; never. Could these atoms really have formed into molecules spontaneously by random chance with out an intelligent designer? No; never. What makes the electrons orbit around the nuclei of atoms? Nature as we are told? Who Created nature? What maintains the forces and laws of nature that make the atoms and nature work as they do? Nature? Who Created nature?
3) Could coacervates have formed cells spontaneously at random? No; never.
4) Could cells have formed spontaneously at random and then form into different types of tissues that all work in unison together to make up a higher life form such as an animal or fish? No; never.
5) How is all of nature (Man, animals, plants, weather, air, sea, land, solar system, the universe) maintained in a VERY VERY delicate planet earth eco-system balance without it going out of balance and destroying it-self if it is not being maintained by a Higher power?

All of these questions show us that there must be an intelligent Designer who not only created the atoms, molecules, cells, tissues, fish, plants, animals and universe, with an intelligent design, but this intelligent Creator also maintains the world as well. It also existed before the 'big bang' if there really was one. This intelligent Creator is infinite in time, having no beginning and no end, and is infinite in space, having no beginning and no end. We cannot conceive of its Grandeur and Majesty in our small limited minds. This intelligent Designer is none other than G-d, the Creator and Ruler of all nature and the world.

By observation, people have found that if you pray to 'It', 'It' Listens and can answer you and help you and others. There are no things ever happening in the world by 'random chance' nor 'spontaneously'. Any thing that happens is Guided by this Infinite Being called G-d in English or in Hebrew called 'Hashem'. 'Hashem' means 'The Name', as in the Name of G-d, as His Name in Hebrew is too profound and Big for us to pronounce His Name. That is why we call Him 'The Name', Hashem.

Two excellent books that show the many perplexing and unbelievable wonders of Nature that G-d Created and runs daily are: "Designer World" and "Our Amazing World" by Rabbi Avroham Katz and Tuvia Cohen. These books are highly recommended to see G-d's Greatness in His Creations.

Hashem is Infinite with no beginning in time nor space, Omniscient, All knowing, Omni Present, All powerful, Merciful, Kind, Loving, Righteous, Just, Truthful, Long Suffering, and Rules all worlds as the Everlasting King.

The Divinity of the Torah

> *'I present to you today the blessing and the curse. The blessing that you hearken to the commandments of Hashem your God that I command you this day, and the curse if you do not hearken to the commandments of Hashem your God, and you stray from the path that I command you today, to follow other gods that you did not know'* -Deuteronomy 11:26-28.

Whether or not you believe in the Divine origin of the Torah, in any case, this book acts as a reliable definition and explanation of the Messiah, the redemption and the war of Gog and Magog since it is based on the Torah which defines these subjects.

For the non-believer, who does not believe in the Divine origin of Torah, I will take a short pause here to explain to you that you should recognize that the ancient Torah prophesies could only have been received from Hashem (Hebrew for the Name of the G-d of Israel), and not invented by man, since many of these Prophesies that are over two thousand years old; such as the ingathering of Jewish exiles to the land of Israel, the rebuilding of the Jewish cities in the land of Israel and the rebirth of the state of Israel; have come true in our time. How could man have known the future from over two thousand years ago? This has never happened with any other nation in history other than the Jewish people. Man could only have known this future prophesy if it was revealed by Hashem. Has *any* other ancient people in the entire world history, other that the Jewish people, also known as the people of Israel, retained their religious and national identity since ancient times, and, has returned to their ancient land after thousands of years of exile as Prophesied in their ancient scriptures? The answer is NO. How could this happen? How did this happen? How could this happen unless it was revealed by G-d in ancient times to the

Prophets and then directed by G-d as a Guider of history? The reality is that it could not have happened unless G-d revealed it to the Prophets and then was directing history to make it happen. If you think about it you will realize that the only possibility is that the Torah prophesies of the return of the Jewish people to the land of Israel were revealed by G-d and He is directing history to make the prophesies happen. G-d is not only the Creator as proven in the previous chapter, but He is also the Director of history.

The Torah was received by Moses from G-d on Mount Sinai approximately 1310 BCE (Before the Common Era; BC) as per Talmud Bavli Avoda Zara 10a.

The Torah includes the 'written law', known as the five books of Moses (in Hebrew called the 'Chumash'), and the 'oral law' later to be written down and known as 'the Talmud'. The 'written law' was written down by the Moses and the elders on animal hide scrolls in special black ink and the 'oral law' was transmitted orally, in 1310 BCE, on Mount Sinai, from G-d to Moses, to the elders, from generation to generation, until it was eventually written down, out of fear of forgetting it, circa 500AD and is called 'the Talmud'. Most people call the Talmud the 'oral tradition', but I prefer to call it the 'oral transmission from G-d' so as not to confuse nor diminish its importance as a Sacred Scripture, since anyone can start an 'oral tradition'.

The oral law explains much of the necessary details not given in the written law. For example, Exodus 13 and Deuteronomy 11 command for Jewish men to wear 'a sign' on their arm and 'between their eyes'. What does this mean? Put a 'Stop' sign between your eyes? A 'No Smoking' sign on your arm? Of course not! But, these are the ridiculous type of conclusions and speculations one could arrive at without the oral laws. Without the oral transmission it is impossible to understand what this means. The oral transmission, also called 'a tradition' of the Talmud, explains that these 'signs' are small black leather boxes containing specific scriptural passages that are strapped on to the arm and head with black leather straps. They are called Tfillin and every Jewish man is commanded to wear them. Orthodox Jews keep this commandment to this day; all the details of which regarding how to build them and how to wear them, when to wear them, who can wear them, etc., are explained in the Talmud. There are many examples like this where the oral transmission is needed to explain what is written in the five books of Moses. In fact, all of the written Torah can not be understood reliably without the Talmud. Without the oral laws that were transmitted orally through the elders from Mount

Sinai, generation to generation, the 'written law' would be undecipherable and impossible to understand. This is why people who read the Bible say they cant really understand what the Bible is talking about most of the time; because it is impossible to understand without the Talmud! The Bible lacks the details that the oral transmission explains. The Talmud is one of the primary sources of *this* book *and* the key to understanding of the five books of Moses and the Prophets.

Further more, the Talmud; written down over some one thousand five hundred years ago; 500 AD; knew many things that only in recent modern times has science discovered and were in the dark ages until recently. This proves that much of the Talmud was from Divine origin; other than to the Rabbinic ordinances found in the Talmud that the Rabbis made, but they too were inspired from Heaven or at least Torah wisdom, which is also from Heaven. These recent modern discoveries known to the Talmud include:

1) the lunar cycle is 29.53059 days exactly. This is stated in Talmud Bavli Rosh haShana page 25 but was only recently discovered by NASA; 2) the naked eye can see only eight stars in the Pleiades constellation. Talmud Bavli Brachot page 58 says that the Pleiades constellation includes over one hundred stars. Only in recent modern times with the aid of powerful telescopes did modern science discover that the Pleiades constellation includes over one hundred stars; 3) many ancient peoples, including the most scientifically advanced Edom/Rome, believed the earth is flat, whereas the ancient Zohar (part of the 'secret' level of Torah) on Leviticus 10 says the earth is round. Only modern science and observation from space have proven that the earth is round; 4) Talmud Bavli Megilla page 6 says that if Germany isn't contained it could destroy the entire world. This was written down in the Talmud in 500 CE, and in 1939 CE we saw how Germany almost destroyed the entire world if it wasn't stopped, and at great cost and loss of life in doing so. Missile warfare, invented by Germany, or its absorbed Prussia (in 1936 Germany absorbed Prussia, which may be from Paras, another world super power), is still to this day every modern superpowers method of destroying the world as 'weapons of mass destruction' so in this sense German missiles still could destroy the world; 5) On the scriptural passage Jeremiah 50:9 'His arrows are like a deadly warrior' the Malbim, in the 1800s, said that this refers to '*smart missiles that will find their target on their own*'. This reality that was foretold in the prophesy of Jeremiah 50:9 was fulfilled by modern smart missiles such as Tomahawk

cruise missiles and other satellite laser guided smart bombs that 'find their target on their own'.

How could ancient man have known these things unless they were revealed by G-d? They couldn't have been known unless they were revealed by G-d to ancient man through prophesy direct from G-d Himself. Many of these points, along with many others, are cited by Rabbi Zamir Cohen Shlita in his book called 'Science Out Scienced'.

In addition, could an atom, much less trillions of trillions of atoms, have formed spontaneously by random chance? Absolutely NOT. They needed an Intelligent Creator (G-d) to have created them. If you think about it, you would also realize that they also need G-d to sustain them, along with all the extremely sophisticated workings of all the bio-chemical reactions that go along with the delicate balance of life in the world.

Considering these above arguments, lets face it, there is a G-d, He Created and Runs the world, and, He revealed the entire 'written' Torah including the 'oral transmission', called the Talmud, which includes ancient prophesies and revelations that are coming true and being revealed in our times.

In any case, whether or not you believe in the Divinity of Torah, which is uncontestable as proven in this chapter, this book will explain to you what is the Messiah, the Redemption and the war of Gog and Magog as defined by the Torah which is the only truly valid and primary source that defines these subjects.

The Noahide Covenant

"Religions are man made. The Torah was given by G-d".

Some religions such as Christianity and Islam teach that everyone must follow their religion or else they are damned and must be put to the sword. Judaism is the most ancient 'religion' in the world; older than Buddhism, Christianity, Islam and the new religion of modern secular Atheism.

What does the most ancient 'religion', Judaism, teach us what people must live by?

Judaism does not say that only Jews can be blessed by G-d with Heaven and that Gentiles must convert to Judaism. Judaism says that Gentiles must live by what is called the Noahide Covenant and obey its seven categories of laws known as the seven Noahide laws. What is the origin and development of the Noahide Covenant?

The Torah begins its record of human history with the first man, Adam, in the Garden of Eden. There G-d gave Adam and Eve six commandments to live by in addition to not eat from the tree of god and evil (Talmud Bavli Sanhedrin 56-60). Then human history continued to a man named Noah and his three sons, Shem, Yefeth and Ham. Noah and his three sons were the only survivors after a great flood that wiped out all of man, for their sins, and left Noah and his three sons as the ancestors of all of modern man. The Torah teaches us that after this great flood, in that time, Noah received a seventh commandment not to eat flesh from alive animal, and made a Covenant (agreement) with Hashem that if Noah and all his descendants follow the seven commandments, then Hashem will bless Noah and his descendants with prosperity in this world and then go on to eternal life in Heaven after they pass away from this material world.

These seven commandments are (Rambam Laws of kings chapter 9): 1) not to curse Hashem, 2) not to worship idols, 3) not to steal, 4) not to murder, 5) to be moral, 6) to uphold courts of justice and 7) not to eat living animals or parts of them while they are still alive. The first six of these laws were passed down from Adam and Eve from the Garden of Eden. More detailed information can be learned about these seven categories of laws and their derivation, called the seven Noahide commandments, in a book called "The Path of the Righteous Gentile" by Chaim Clorfene and Jacob Rogalsky. This is highly recommended for Gentiles and even Jews so that they can teach Gentiles the proper path so as to embrace our service of G-d as being a 'light unto the nations' (Isaiah 49:6, 42:6) and 'kingdom of priestly ministers' who teach the Gentiles their Torah laws, and are a guiding light to them.

After the great flood Noah and his sons believed in only One G-d and worshipped Him only. They lived by the seven Noahide commandments and blessed only G-d for all the creations that He had Created including the stars.

As time went on, eventually Noah's descendants would gaze at the stars and instead of worshipping G-d and blessing Him for Creating the stars, they made a 'slight' deviation in understanding, and began worshipping the stars instead of G-d, as if the stars were a deity unto themselves with independent powers out side of G-d Almighty. Rashi on the book of Genesis says that G-d Created the world in such a way that the positions of the stars and their constellations correspond to the events of mankind, but not that the stars guide the events; only G-d is guiding the events and the position of the stars correspond to those events.

Then, after that, the worship of the stars, people strayed from the path even more and would also began worshipping other things like rocks, trees, mountains, seas, the sun and even people, seeing that they too also had some kind of power and should therefore be worshipped, instead of G-d. They had forgotten that G-d was the One Who Created them and is really the One Who rules over them and all of creation. People eventually also forgot about the Noahide Covenant and the seven Noahide laws and started creating their own laws and new religions. This is where we still stand today as well as this was in ancient times. Society has forgotten the Noahide Covenant, the seven Noahide laws and has created new religions and laws by which we live today.

After mankind had already forgotten about G-d and the Noahide Covenant and was rampant with the worship of idols, around 1900 BCE. BCE means

Before the Common Era. The year zero BCE is equivalent to the year zero AD or it's equivalent zero CE (common era) according to the Western Gregorian Solar calendar and is commonly used today and taken as the year in which Jesu of Nazareth was born as a reference point for Western society. A unique man of his kind, named Avraham (in English called 'Abraham'), began to once again recognize G-d, to worship Him and to teach others about Him. Avraham re-established the recognition of the Covenant of Noah and made a Covenant with G-d. Later his son Yitschak (Isaac in English) and Yitschak's son Yaakov (Jacob in English; later called Yisrael or Israel in English) accepted the Covenant and to live by it and were thus the rightful inheritors and bearers of the Covenant.

Avraham, Yitschak and Yaakov were the progenitors of the Jewish people and at that time were obligated to hold by the Noahide Covenant as was all mankind. Later in history around 1310 BCE the 613 commandments of the Torah were revealed to the Jewish people on Mount Sinai for them and their descendants to follow for eternity and the Gentiles were still obligated to live by the Noahide Covenant and NOT the 613 Torah commandments which are an inheritance ONLY to the Jews. The descendents of the Jewish people who stood at Mount Sinai are today called the Jewish people and are still obligated by Hashem (G-d) to live by the Torah and its 613 commandments and are judged by G-d regarding how well they follow the Torah commandments. The Noahide Covenant and the seven Noahide laws still holds true for the non-Jewish people in the world; called the Gentiles (in Hebrew called 'goyim' of the singular form 'goy'); and it is the set of laws by which G-d judges all the Gentiles. The Gentiles are obligated to live by the Noahide Covenant and follow it's seven laws.

Again, the seven Noahide laws include: 1) don't worship idols, 2) Don't curse G-d, 3) Don't murder, 4) Don't steal, 5) be moral, 6) Enforce Justice, 7) Don't eat flesh of living animals or parts of them while they are still alive. Disobeying any one of these laws makes a Gentile liable to the death penalty by decapitation. It is a general Torah rule that one who is not mentally competent and does not have understanding that he violated one of these laws is exempt from punishment. Since people don't know these laws in our times G-d has abundant Mercy in judging people since they don't have understanding that they are violating the seven laws. Again, more detailed information can be learned about these seven categories of laws and their derivation, called the seven Noahide commandments, in a book called "The Path of the Righteous Gentile" by Chaim Clorfene and Jacob Rogalsky; Recommended.

Gentiles (and Jews) must believe in G-d, the Torah and the authority of the kosher orthodox Rabbis. Everyone must have a Rabbi in order to learn the proper laws of what to do and what is right or wrong. It's good to be in contact with your local orthodox Rabbi.

In terms of the prohibition about worshiping idols we learn about what G-d really is from the Torah and any deviation from the Torah is strange worship (in Hebrew called 'avoda zara' -Divrei Yaziv chapter 70). From the Torah we learn that G-d is the Sole, Unified, One Being Who is the Creator and King of the world who rules over everything, all worlds, spiritual and material, is Infinite in time and space with no beginning nor end, All Knowing, Omnipresent, Omniscient, Merciful, Forgiving, Just, Truthful, Humble, Long Suffering, etc (see the thirteen Attributes of Hashem). He is One and can not be divided into parts but includes everything in Creation. By calling or worshiping any one of His Creations, anything or anyone, other than G-d Almighty Alone as One is idol worship and is strictly forbidden by the Noahide Covenent and Torah for both Gentile and Jew, respectively.

The proper way to pray to G-d is directly without any intermediaries, but the Rama says, in Mishna Brura 156, that a Gentile is permitted to do what is called worshipping an idol in partnership (in Hebrew called 'Shitoof Avoda Zara') with G-d. This is believing that G-d gave independent power to a thing or person and worshipping G-d through that thing or person in 'partnership' with it. Jews are forbidden to do Shitoof Avoda Zara though, so we must be careful of this too.

Also, one may reason that since the Torah of Moses is the quintessential scripture that defines G-d, therefore any denial of the Torah of Moses in any way is avoda zara (foreign worship or idol worship) in addition to being a deviation from the proper path to follow G-d; which is the Noahide laws for the Gentiles and 613 Torah commandments for Jews. See the book the Path of the Righteous Gentile by Chaim Clorfene and Jacob Rogalsky for the most comprehensive coverage of the Noahide laws that I have seen available. The book details with traditional Torah and Rabbinic sources the Noahide Covenant and seven Noahide laws which is the proper path and set of G-d given laws for Gentiles.

The G-d of Abraham was and is still defined by the Torah. Anyone who does not accept the Torah fully or denies part of it (as the manmade religions do) does not really believe in the G-d of Abraham. Anyone who is an enemy of Israel or the Jews, the people of the Torah, is not really worshipping the G-d of Abraham which is the real G-d.

Most Rabbis today hold by the Rambam who holds that Islam is not idol worship. In contrast to Rambam who is quoted as regarding that Islam is not idol worship, Rav Yaakov Emden (zt'l) says in his sidur (prayer book) that "Islam is avoda zara (foreign worship) in the name of Hashem" and the Klozenberger Rebbe says that Islam is avoda zara since it's Koran is a denial of the Torah of Moses which defines G-d (Divrei Yatziv chapter 70). According to the Koran, anyone who denies the Koran, that Mohamed is a prophet or is not a Muslim should be killed. These laws and the Muslim's Jihad (Holy War) that they have against all non Muslims constitutes murder and is punishable by death penalty. They should know better. None the less, I want to say that I have met many great people who are Atheists, Muslims and Christians who support Israel and in this sense are friends of G-d as Rashi says 'those who are enemies of the Jews are enemies of G-d', so those who are friends of the Jews are really friends of G-d. These people really believe in G-d. They see the higher truths of the One G-d being the real G-d in spite of the many lies of the rhetorical dogma their man made religions in which they have been imprisoned has tried to brainwash them. I hope this book frees them and they return to Noah's laws because they are really good people and this is their true heritage. Many of these people are good people and will go to Heaven I believe.

Again, "*Rav Chiya Bar Abba said in the name of Rav Yohanan that Gentiles outside the land of Israel are not idol worshippers. Rather it is a custom of their fathers that is in their hands*" (Talmud Bavli Chullin 13b). That was in the year 280 AD. ArtScroll notes there that this means that the Gentiles don't really have ideological devotion to idolatry. This seems to still be the case to this day, especially considering that the Great Knesset removed the evil inclination for idol worship from the world in ancient times. Therefore most people really are not idol worshipers so it's safe, but man made religions trip them up from serving G-d in the full true proper way which is the Noahide Torah.

It is the duty of every man to return to live by the ancient Noahide Torah laws and by doing so he will be blessed and bring blessing and salvation to the world. If he or she is a Gentile, then he or she is really a Noahide and should live by the Noahide Covenent; not and other belief system or ideology. Then he or she may start a Noahide worship group in his town or city and thus bring blessing to the world. The Internet has some and they should grow. Don't be deceived by other religions that say that their religion is the true way. They add to or detract from the Noahide laws or the Torah and thus lead people away from true service of G-d. These other religions were invented by man and often violate the Noahide Covenant and thus mislead people to sin and this sin brings destruction, poverty, sickness and death to them as a result. These religions were invented by man but the ancient way of the Torah and the Noahide Covenant are from G-d. The most ancient of peoples, the Jewish people, lived through all the ancient kingdoms and religions (Egypt, Babylon, Greece, Persia, Rome, etc), and still live today with the ancient Torah that was given by G-d and thus withstood the test of time and other religions that fell by the way in history. Following these ancient Noahide and Torah ways brings blessing, health, prosperity, wealth and eternal life in Heaven for those who follow them. May we all merit this and be blessed in teaching others about this so that they and the rest of the world may be blessed too.

Overview of the book series

Before reading this book series and going into detail regarding the more specific details about the Messiah, the final Redemption, the ten tribes and the war of Gog and Magog, it will help you to understand these matters if you first get a summarized overview of them. That way the book series will be more comprehendible and understandable since you will be able to understand the details within the context of the bigger picture.

For a basic overview of the Messiah, the final Redemption, the ten tribes and the war of Gog and Magog, you must understand that the final Redemption marks the final stage of human history which marks the salvation of mankind when the knowledge of G-d is accepted by mankind. At that point mankind worships G-d alone in His Temple in Jerusalem, lives by His Torah laws as ruled by the Sanhedrin of 71 elders, and the royal House of David is the kingship of the world with the Messiah son of David as king ruling all people of the world from Jerusalem in the Temple area where the Sanhedrin sits and judges all of mankind.

The final Redemption happens after the Jewish people are exiled from the land of Israel and the land of Israel is barren for some two thousand years since from approximately the year 135 CE when the last of the remaining bulk of the Jews were exiled from the land as a result of a Messianic war with Rome that failed.

The final Redemption unfolds in a historical process of stages in this order: 1) the growth of agriculture in the land of Israel and ingathering of the exiled Jewish people back to the land of Israel, 2) the rebuilding of Jewish cities and infrastructure in the land of Israel including the rebuilding of Jewish Jerusalem with a Sanhedrin of 71 elders that is prepared to receive Elijah the prophet or the Messiah, whichever comes first, so as to be able to appoint the Messiah king of Israel, 3) repentance and the return of the Jewish people in Israel to living by the Torah, 4) the Messiah coming to the land of Israel from Edom after three wars of the sons of Ishmael against Israel (in our times these are the 1948, 1967 and 1973 wars), 5) the Messiah son of Josef possibly becoming king first (likely but not definitely) to pave the way for the Messiah son of David, then for sure the Messiah son of David made king, 6) the war of Gog and Magog which marks what the Rambam calls the 'days of the Messiah', 7) the kingship of the Messiah is secured as the world power when the army of Gog and Magog is defeated, 8) the building of the third Temple in Jerusalem, 9) the resurrection of the dead. That is the basic skeleton structure of how the final redemption unfolds historically. The redemption does not happen all at once as some ignoramuses imagine. It is a historical process that takes time and Jewish efforts in all respects. This process has already begun and many big Rabbis say that the Messiah is in Israel today, but as this book shows, the Messiah can not even begin 'to come' unless the Rabbis first make a Sanhedrin to appoint him king.

Although every thing that I will say in the detailed explanations of this book has sources, at this point I will not go into all the detailed sources of the overview so as to make the reading more simply clear and comprehensible. The more detailed explanations later in the book will be more understandable in the context of the bigger picture of which you will already should have a basic understanding. The many detailed sources will be given later in the book and back up every point, assertion, understanding and claim made here in the outline.

Jewish people believe in the Messiah

Some people mistakenly think that only Christianity believes in the Messiah but Judaism doesn't. This is not true. The concept of the Messiah originated with Judaism since before the Creation of the world and was adopted later by Christianity in the first century CE when Christianity (according to Roman/Western/Edomite history) was founded originally as a Messianic Jewish sect that revolted against the Roman occupation of Judea at the time (circa 30 CE) and escalated into war with Rome where the Jewish people, including the Christians, were defeated (70 CE with the destruction of the second Temple) and exiled from the land of Israel. Ironically, Christianity was eventually adopted by Rome as the official religion circa 325 CE under Caesar Constantine in the Mycenaean council that basically invented Christianity as we know it today. At this point Christianity was a far cry from the original Messianic Jewish sect and had even adopted pagan idolatry (May Hashem have Mercy). Religions such as Christianity were man made religions. The Torah is from G-d and is thus the real truth. Jewish people believe in the Messiah according to the Torah's ancient definition, not the Christian's man made religion definition of the Messiah where Christians believe the Messiah is Jesu of Nazareth. Jewish people don't believe that Jesu was or is or could be the Messiah as this book proves conclusively. This book series will help Christians and all people receive the real Messiah and make it a reality in today's world biezrath Hashem.

The Jewish people believe in our Torah's definition of the Messiah which this book series outlines clearly. One of the Rambam's thirteen articles of the Jewish faith is '*I believe with complete faith in the coming of the Messiah and even though he may delay, nevertheless I long for him each day that he will come*'.

The Messiah is called the 'son of the fallen one' in reference to the fallen royal House of David that fell from power circa 500 BCE when the first temple fell along with the kingship of the royal House of David. In the final redemption, the Sanhedrin will reestablish this kingship the Messiah according to Amos 9:11 (Talmud Bavli Sanhedrin 96b) and many other sources cited in the prophets. All Jewish believers await that day when our Righteous Messiah (as defined by the Torah) comes and is re-established as king of Israel and saves the world by bringing back recognition of G-d as the true King of the world, enforces His Torah law worldwide, ingathers the exiled Jews to Israel and builds the Third Temple. Learning these subjects properly as my book shows may enable the Moshiah to come 'mamash' (in reality) in our generation, Without my teachings in my book series, there is as much a chance of Moshiah coming as there is someone learning out the halachot of how to make a kosher mizooza or Tfillin directly from the gemoora without rishonim. This book series may help the real potential Messiah of our generation be identified and appointed king by the Sanhedrin so that he can 'come' for real; the real thing; in our generation as this generation may merit such a thing. This is one reason I write this book series.

First subject: *What is the 'Messiah'*?

The word 'Messiah' comes from the Hebrew word 'Moshiah', which literally means 'anointed one'; as with special anointing oil used to anoint the kings of Israel and the Sacred Temple vessels. King David was anointed by the prophet Samuel (in Hebrew 'Shmuel') circa 1000 BCE and was established as king by Samuel and his Sanhedrin of seventy one elders (Sanhedrin is an Aramaic acronym; 'Sonei hadarath panim biDin'; which means 'hating favoritism in judgment') and thereby securing his paternal descendants as the rightful kings of Israel for all generations (Rambam laws of kings chapter one). Thus, the Moshiah is referred to as the 'son of David', especially in the Talmud. The Davidic line of kings ceased from rulership circa 585 BCE when the ancient kingdom of Judah and the first Temple were destroyed. The 'Moshiah' will be anointed as part of his inauguration as king of Israel as it is Jewish law that kings must be anointed (Rambam laws of kings chapter one section seven, Talmud Bavli Kereisooth 5b). A king must also be established by the Sanhedrin of seventy one elders and a prophet (Rambam laws of kings chapter one section three). It is understood that Elijah will be the prophet who will return before the Messiah comes (Malachi 3:23) and thus may be the prophet who anoints the Moshiah to be king. Thus will be re-established the ancient royal Davidic line of kings when the Moshiah is anointed king. The next step in preparing for the Messiah is that the Rabbis of Israel must make a Sanhedrin. Without a Sanhedrin the Messiah can not even begin 'to come', the meaning of which will be explained later. Rambam, in Laws of Kings chapter one, says that the Moshiah must be a kosher Jew who is a fully paternal descended son of king David, who reveres Heaven and keeps the Torah Mitzvoth (commandments) fully. The Rambam there says that the king does not have to be the wisest because that can be learned.

The Rambam, Laws of Kings chapter 11:4, concisely qualifies who the Messiah is by saying "*And if there stands a king from the House of David meditated in Torah and occupied with Torah commandments as David his father was according to the written and oral transmission of the Torah (the Talmud) and compels all of Israel to walk by it and to strengthen it's minutiae and to fight Hashem's wars, then there is an established status (in Hebrew called 'chezkat haMoshiah') that he is the Messiah. If this is done and he succeeded and was victorious on the nations that are around him and he built the third Temple in its place (the Temple mount in Jerusalem) and he gathered in the pushed out ones of Israel then he is definitely the Messiah*". The Rambam also states here the important point that the Messiah will fight Hashem's wars and infuse into the world the understanding and knowledge of Hashem and thus will re-establish Hashem, the G-d of Israel, as the recognized King in the world. This level of qualification to be the Moshiah can only be attained when the Moshiah is made king by the Sanhedrin and controls the whole system. Before that the Messiah can not even get near that level as explained in my book 'The Messiah According to Judaism' in the chapter titled 'Unrealistic Expectations of the Messiah'.

The Torah gives many other important identifying traits of the Messiah that the Rambam does not cite. Thee points are needed to know in order for the Sanhedrin to identify who the Moshiah is before he is anointed and established as king by the Sanhedrin. This is in the case of whether the Messiah comes hastened before the final end time or at the final possible end time. The Messiah can come at certain opportune times every generation but will for sure come before the final end time. The prophet Isaiah, chapter 11, says about the Messiah: "*The spirit of Hashem will rest upon him, a spirit of wisdom and understanding, a spirit of council and strength, a spirit of knowledge and fear of Hashem. He will be imbued with a spirit of fear for Hashem, and will not need to judge by what his eyes see nor decide by what his ears hear. He will judge the destitute with righteousness and will decide with fairness for the humble of the earth, and He will strike the wicked of the world with the rod of his mouth (for example by rebuke, protest, decrees), and with the spirit breath of his lips (for example prayer, kabala, permissible white witchcraft) he will slay the wicked. Righteousness will be the girdle round his loins and faith will be the girdle round his waist*". The Hasidic master Rav Nachman of Breslov in his book Likootei Moran says that '*Messiah's most powerful weapon (but not his only weapon) is prayer*'.

Talmud Bavli Sanhedrin page 93b says the Messiah is like king David in that he is '*a fine musician, a great warrior, a man of war, understanding of maters, handsome and Hashem is with him*'. Talmud Bavli Succah 52b says that he is an artesian (or craftsman or engineer) so that he can build the third Temple. We can understand from Talmud Bavli Avodah Zara 20b that the Moshiah is humble, morally pure, learns and observes the Torah, is clean from sin, and in his more spiritually developed period of life has Holy Spirit and can also resurrect the dead which he uses to bring back the Messiah son of Ephraim to life in the case that Armilus (AKA 'the anti-christ') slays the Messiah son of Ephraim in the war of Gog and Magog. These are critical identifying traits of the Messiah that can be used to judge who is the potential Messiah of the generation and should be made king so that he can then be fulfilled as the full Messiah and redeem Israel and build the third Temple in Jerusalem. Someone who fulfils thee traits is 'pre-kingship chezkath (established pattern) Moshiah' as the book explains. Rambam's definition of 'chezkath Moshiah' can only be achieved after he is appointed king by the Sanhedrin.

Although apologists against Christianity argue that Isaiah 53 does not apply to the Messiah, the great Torah sage authority Rashi, on Talmud Bavli Sanhedrin 98, brings Isaiah 53:4 that says about the Messiah '*Indeed it was our diseases that he bore and our pains that he endured, whereas we considered him plagued, smitten by G-d and afflicted*'. Midrash Yalkoot Shimoni on Isaiah 53 says that Isaiah 53 applies to the Messiah as well as the people of Israel. Mikraoth Gidoloth says that Isaiah 53 refers to the Jewish people; the people of Israel. The Midrash Yalkoot Shimoni on Isaiah 60 also says that the Messiah endures great suffering for the sins of the people, unlike what the forefathers endured, and is even imprisoned due to and to atone for the sins of the people. This suffering atones for the sins of Adam, the Erev Rav (the mixed multitude), Israel and spiritually cleanses him so he can reach higher degrees of Holiness and service of Hashem in His Holy Torah commandments. Although downtrodden, oppressed, despised and persecuted at the beginning of his life, he eventually succeeds, becomes king of Israel in modern times, helps Israel to succeed and be freed once and for all from the subjugation of the Gentiles, builds the third Temple, and brings the world to recognize that Hashem, the G-d of Israel, is the King of the world, and His Holy Torah law is the law by which all man must live to be blessed for good or face the consequences of Divine retribution. The seven Noahide laws of the Noahide Covenent is the Torah for the Gentiles.

The Messiah can be most succinctly defined as the Torah observant kosher Jew, paternally descended from king David, who brings the whole world to recognize Hashem as G-d and whose Torah laws we must live by. He will compel the world to follow the Torah Laws and will enforce them with his Sanhedrin of 71 elder judges, redeem the Jewish people from exile and the subjugation of the Gentiles, and will build the third Temple in Jerusalem. That is basically who the Messiah son of David really is.

Unlike sources such as the Talmud, Rambam, Zohar and Midrash, the central theme most noted in the prophets about the Messiah is that *he establishes justice worldwide according to the ancient Torah law which is the foundation to true world peace and wholeness with G-d.* Most all of religion overlooks this main point. This is important because justice is a pillar of society upon which society stands in peace and prosperity, and without which society falls in war and destruction. Moshiah comes to bring that justice based peace. If Moshiah comes hastened, then Eisav/Edom/the West will be Moshiah's helper and backer to enforce that. If Moshiah does not come hastened, but only at the final end, then all the corrupt cities under Edom's wicked control of the world will have to be utterly destroyed. Rambam notes that true justice is only that which is in accordance with the Torah. This Torah defined justice is required to free the Jewish people from the sword of war of the Gentiles that HaShem, the G-d of Israel, sends on the Jewish people as a punishment for our own internally generated injustice and the world's evil and injustice as well. It is our own injustice and sin, as well as that of the Gentiles', that directs G-d to guide the Gentiles to subjugate and kill us (Hashem Yirachem).

To redeem the Jewish people from the subjugation of the Gentiles, particularly Edom, who controls the world at the time, the Messiah must establish Torah justice as the foundation to peace, good will, prosperity and equity among people. The Messiah is key in establishing the foundation of True Torah justice, service of G-d, peace and prosperity in the world for all mankind. That is why the theme of justice is so important in the prophets and the Messiah is referred to as 'Our Righteous Messiah' and the 'Sprout of Righteousness' who is a true judge in accordance with the ancient Torah laws. Most of organized religion overlooks this essential point and that is part of the darkness of exile. Good police, judges and government workers understand the need for justice well and dedicate their lives to it as their Holy convocation for the sake of G-d and society. They are helping bring the Messiah on a concrete basis in reality. They live it day to day. It is only with this true Torah justice that true peace can be achieved in the world where the '*They will beat their swords into plowshares and their spears into pruning hooks. Nation will not lift up sword against nation, nor will they learn war anymore.*" (Micah 4:3 and Isaiah 2:4).

Second subject: *What is the 'Redemption'*?

The 'final Redemption' most basically means the salvation of the Jewish people from national and spiritual exile and subjugation from the Gentiles, by being brought back to living by the Holy Torah in the land of Israel, with the Messiah son of David as their mortal king, and Hashem as their G-d, the King of kings and King and Creator of the world, with the third Temple built in Jerusalem and the inner light of Moshiah and Israel felt by all.

Since the redemption occurs in stages, there is partial redemption of the Jewish people at the initial stages, such as the Jewish people being brought back to the land of Israel, and then later complete redemption which will be marked by the Jewish peoples' total freedom from subjugation by the Gentiles and the building of and full worship in the third Temple in Jerusalem with the Messiah son of David as their mortal king. When the Jews feel the inner spiritual light of Moshiah and Israel then and only then will they accept that it is the full redemption.

The first redemptions of the Jewish people were from the exile of Egypt, then Babylon, then Paras, then Greece, and the final Messianic Redemption of Israel will be from the current exile of Edom/Rome (AKA 'the fourth beast' AKA 'the king of the North' AKA 'the evil empire kingship' AKA Rome). It will be in accordance with the laws of nature, although HaShem's Providence will Manifest and may seem miraculous. The final redemption will occur as a developing historical process metamorphosing in stages where the main culminating essential difference is that in the end, Israel won't be subjugated by the Gentiles any longer (Talmud Bavli Brachot 34, Yerushalmi Brachot 4b, Rambam laws of kings).

Wars mark the beginning of the Redemption (Talmud Bavli Megilla 17) along with the rebirth of agriculture in the land of Israel (Talmud Bavli Sanhedrin 97-98) as well as the return Jews to the land (Ezekiel 36) that prepares the infrastructure of the land of Israel, especially Jerusalem (Talmud Bavli Megilla 17) for the Messiah to eventually be king there. Eventually the Messiah will be the accepted king over all of Edom as well which means the entire world population by that time (AKA 'a new world order' but in the Name of Hashem, and not Satan as Armilus (the 'Anti-Christ') will try to achieve establishing the throne of Satan on earth (Midrash Zerubbavel) but 'the Messiah will slay the wicked with the breath of his lips' (Isaiah 11) and the Rabbis received that this refers to Armilus. The spiritual powers of the Messiah are immense so nothing or no one can stand before him. All will serve him as king or perish.

Zohar viEra 32 says that 'There are four stages of war in the redemption period: 1) Ishmaelites will deter the children of Israel from settling the land (these wars may possibly include the Palestinian Arab Ishmaelites' terrorism that started as soon as Jews began to officially settle the land of Israel in the early 1900s as part of Zionism and the three modern Arab-Israeli wars being the1948 war of independence, the 1967 six day war, and the 1973 Yom Kippur war of attrition by which Ishmael attacked the modern Zionist State of Israel established in 1948), 2) sons of Edom (Edom seems to be the West lead by the USA, and *maybe* also aspects of modern Russia) will gather to fight against the sons of Ishmael in order to control their lands (maybe this refers to Afghanistan, Kuwait, Iraq, Arabia, Syria, Lebanon, all Arab countries, etc.) and on the land of Israel but the land of Israel wont fall into their hands, 3) One nation will gather many nations to fight against Edom but they will fall in to the hand of Edom (This is possibly Paras (Iran) and not likely China since Talmud Bavli Yoma 10 tells of the war between Paras and Edom where Edom wins but Paras causes much destruction.), 4) Edom will gather nations against Israel in the war of Gog and Magog and the Holy One, blessed be He, will make a sacrifice of the sons of Edom'.

When the anti-Semites, lead by their mortal leader Gog, attack the Jewish people in the land of Israel in the 'war of Gog and Magog' the criminal anti-Semites 'marked for perdition' will be annihilated, but the good gentiles worthy of life who repent will live. After that, Hashem's Throne and the Messiah's throne will be established and Hashem will be worshiped in the newly built third Temple with a heightened spiritual awareness of Hashem in the world, return of prophesy, the rest of the remaining exiled Jews return to Israel, the light of Israel and Messiah spreading out to all the worlds, no sickness yet still poor so that the wealthy may merit giving charity, and all the nations of the world will recognize Hashem and live by the ancient Noahide laws.

The final Redemption happens in the 'end of days' and according to Rambam laws of kings chapter 12 the war of Gog and Magog marks the beginning of the 'days of the Messiah'. Later in the days of the Messiah resurrection of the dead occurs.

Third subject: *What is the 'war of Gog and Magog'?*

The war of Gog and Magog is the final war in human history; the war that ends all wars. After that there is peace on earth. Ostensibly it is not what some Christians call the Apocalypse and maybe Judaism does not believe in that at all unless someone can find a Torah source. The war of Gog and Magog is Epic, and apocalyptic though, in whose wake the throne of Hashem and his mortal king Messiah are established. In this war the Messiah conquers and inherits the wealth of Edom (AKA 'the fourth beast'). The war of Gog and Magog is basically a massive multi-national military coalition force of millions of anti-Semites who are lead by Gog (an Amalekite human being) to attack Israel with the intent to destroy modern Israel (Heaven forbid), kill all the Jews (Heaven forbid), erase G-d's Name from histories memory (Heaven forbid) and establish the throne of Satan (Heaven forbid) through Armilus (a demonic Golem created by black magic) as king, but the Messiah slays him with 'the breath/spirit of his lips' (as Rabbis learn out from Isaiah 11).

According to the Malbim based on the Midrash, the war is in three attacks over the course of a year. Although a time of trail and tribulation for Israel, the anti-Semites inevitably loose the war in utter defeat and humiliation by the Hand of Hashem through His people Israel lead by Messiah son of David, and possibly along with Messiah Son of Josef in a field general or war minister type of role. If the Messiah Son of Josef dies in this war (as it is written that he could be 'pierced through' Zachariah 12:10 as per Talmud Bavli Succa 52a this refers to Messiah Ben Yosef. This does not refer to the Nazarine but the Messiah son of Josef alone). Everyone after that will recognize that Hashem is G-d and the Messiah from the royal House of David is the uncontested mortal king of the world; no ifs, ands, nor buts. Then the third Temple is built and later resurrection of the dead happens. These are the basics of the war of Gog and Magog. Sources are given in my book 'the war of Gog and Magog'.

"The Messiah According to Judaism"

There are many aspects of the Messiah, his life and his mission in the world. Let's take a look at these different aspects starting from the beginning of his life and moving through his life as it progresses.

We have to remember that the Messiah is considered to be the central person involved with the rectification of mankind since the fall of man when Adam and Eve were exiled from the Garden of Eden which the Torah holds happened over five thousand years ago (the year 2013 is the Hebrew year 5774 which marks 5774 years since Creation of the Garden of Edan and the exile from the Garden of Eden in the same year). In addition to wide ranging political implications of the coming of the Messiah; in that the entire new world order turns back to G-d as King with the people of Israel lead by the royal House of David being the world central government and Sanhedrin court of wise men, with the Temple central in the worship of G-d; there are deep underlying spiritual aspects going on here as well, as in the war between Satan and Man, which the Messiah wins for Man and defeats Satan, whose goal is to defeat mankind and rule on earth over G-d in man's mind.

Since the concept of the Messiah originated from the ancient teachings called the Torah, which was written in the Holy Tongue of ancient Hebrew, through out the book the Hebrew word 'Moshiah' may be used at times for the English word 'Messiah'. This may help people get locked into the reality of what and who the Moshiah really is by saying the proper word for Messiah; 'Moshiah'.

The Messiah that this book focuses on in the Messiah son of David, but there is also another person called the Messiah son of Josef who may come to pave the way for the Messiah son of David to take the throne of kingship.

Concise Relevant Background History of the World Prior to the Messiah

A more thorough background is given in my book the final redemption. In short, the Jewish first temple was destroyed 422 BCE (date according to Seder Olam), was partially rebuilt as the second Temple circa 350 BCE (ibid), and was destroyed circa 70 CE. This time period marked the Jewish peoples being exiled into Edom, known as the 'exile of Edom', which was manifest at the time by the leading and dominant world power Rome. Daniel chapter seven refers to the exile of Edom as the 'wicked beast', commonly referred to as the 'fourth beast', which expresses that the exile of Edom is the fourth exile of the Jewish people. It is also the most harsh, longest and last exile until the Messiah comes.

Edom is the culture of Eisav and is known today as Western culture. My book 'the final redemption and the ten tribes' goes into the traits of Eisav and Edom. One trait that I want to point out here is that the blessing '*the elder (Eisav) shall serve the younger (Jacob)*' (Genesis 25) means that Eisav (and his descendents) serves Jacob (and his descendents) if Jacob lives righteously by the Torah commandments. An example of this includes the USA helping Israel. This also may imply that righteous Eisavians may kill for the Moshiah. Otherwise, on the other side of the blessing, if the Jewish people do not live by the Torah commandments fully, then Eisav (and his descendents) attack and even kill Jacob (and his descendants) (Rashi on Genesis 27:40). An example of this was the crusades, pogroms. holocaust and Western decrees against Israel. The exile of Edom is a spiritual darkness and heresy that spreads out all over the world prior to the coming of the Messiah.

Since the first Temple was destroyed, the House of David was not the fully embodied and empowered kingship of Israel. The Jewish people await the return of the Messiah to re-establish that kingship as the kingship of Israel in modern times.

Since the destruction of the first Temple, there has been a major decline of Jewish and world Civilization. This is marked by the destruction of the Holy Temple in Jerusalem, termination of animal sacrifices, the fall of the royal House of David as the kingship, and the fall of the Sanhedrin as the ruling judicial power in the world. Since the time of the destruction of the first Temple, and even further by the Roman exile circa 135 CE, the Jewish people have been scattered all over the world awaiting their return to the land of Israel, until the final Redemption comes. This process has begun in modern times. Most people in the land of Israel today, even most 'Palestinians', are from the 'lost' ten tribes of Israel as my book on the final redemption conclusively proves. The Redemption is an evolving historical process that happens in stages and is marked by wars. The laws of nature don't change during the Redemption (Rambam laws of kings 12). There are auspicious 'times' in every generation when the final Redemption can occur (Vilna Gaon Even Shleima) but will for sure happen at the 'last end time'. The Messiah son of David doesn't lead the Jewish people back to the Land Israel in the initial stages of redemption but only does so later when he is king.

Six Aspects of the Garden of Eden that will return with the Messiah

'There are six things that were taken from the first Man (Adam) and in the future will return with the Messiah: 1) his glow, 2) his life, 3) his stature, 4) the fruits of the land, 5) fruits of the tree, 6) the lights of his glow' (Midrash BiMidbar Parshat 13).

The Messiah son of Josef: also known as the Messiah son of Ephraim

Most people know about the Messiah son of David, but there is another Messiah called the Messiah son of Josef; also called the Messiah son of Ephraim; who may also appear in the redemption in order to pave the way for the Messiah son of David. If the Messiah son of David comes hastened before the final end time through repentance, then the Messiah son of Josef may not even appear, or be a minister or military leader of the Moshiah son of David as king (Rav Saadia Gaon Emuna viDaoth chapter on redemption). If the Messiah son of David comes at the final end time, the Messiah son of Josef has to pave the way for the Messiah son of David (ibid) and will be king prior to the Messiah son of David.

The Messiah son of Ephraim is descended from the tribe of Ephraim, who is descended from the tribe of Josef.

In the scenario of the Messiah son of David coming in the final end time, the Messiah son of Ephraim will become king prior to the Messiah son of

David being king in order to pave the way as it is written '*I will make them into one nation in the land upon the mountains of Israel, and one king will be king for them all. They will no longer be two nations, and they will no longer be divided into two kingdoms ever again*' (Ezekiel 37:22). The Malbim on Ezekiel 37:22 says that this verse means that the Messiah son of Ephraim becomes king. This is the case if the redemption happens in the final end time, but if it is hastened before the final end time the Messiah son of Josef is not needed to pave the way because the Jews service of G-d is complete enough to merit the king Moshiah son of David hastened before the final end time. Then, after that, two verses later in Ezekiel 37:24, the Moshiah son of David becomes king.

The Malbim on Micah 5 and Ezekiel 37 says the Messiah son of Josef leads the ten tribes back to Israel prior to the coming of the Messiah son of David. By Ruah HaKodesh (the 'About the author' section explains) and my ability to identify tribes I have received that all the main leaders of the Zionists, many religious leaders in Israel and even international music, entertainment and social leaders are from the tribe of Ephraim. This includes the Vilna Gaon (zt'l), Theodore Hertzl (of blessed memory), David Ben Gurion (of blessed memory), Shimon Peres, Yitzchak Rabin (of blessed memory), my namesake General Ariel Sharon (of blessed memory), Tommy and Yair Lapid (of blessed memory), Rambo, Paul McCartney, Albert Einstein, Steve Vai, Peter Frampton, Al Pacino, Barbara Streisand, Bob Dylan, the Kabalist the Baba Sali (zt'l), haRav haGaon Ovadia Yosef (zt'l), General Efi Eitan Shlita, secret leaders of the Mosad, Rav Avroham Stern Shlita, etc.. The list goes on. The Gaon of Vilna in Even Shleima in the chapter on Redemption also says that the ten tribes return before the tribe of Judah returns to the land. This also explains Zechariah chapter 12 verses 2-6 that say that the tribe of Judah comes to attack Jerusalem with the forces of Gog and Magog. This is because the majority of the tribe of Judah is held 'captive' in the exile of Edom until they come to Israel as warriors in the army of Gog and Magog, against their will, as the Malbim explains, and then turn on the anti-Semites in the army of Gog and Magog who are attacking Israel and kill them. My book on the war of Gog and Magog explains this more in depth with the other Torah sources.

Part of the Messiah son of Josef's role in paving the way for the Messiah son of David is killing his enemies as it is written: '*Those who escape from the sword of Messiah son of Josef will fall by the sword of Messiah son of David and those who escape from there will fall into the garbage bin in the war of Gog*' (Rashi on Isaiah 24:18). With all of the Messiah son of David's enemies dead, the Messiah's reign and kingship are thereby fully established over the whole of Edom which formerly controlled the world.

The book Kol haTor discusses the roles and functions of the Messiah son of Ephraim in paving the way for the Messiah son of David. Among these missions include enforcing justice in the land, killing off the Amalekites in Israel, and destroying the abominations of injustice and thievery and slander of Amalek in the society. Rashi on Talmud Bavli Succah 52b also says that the Messiah son Josef is an artisan in order to build the third Temple, which means that he helps build the third Temple since Rambam (laws of kings chapter 11) and Rashi (Talmud Bavli Sanhedrin 20) say that the Messiah son of David builds the third Temple.

In Rav Saadia Gaon's book 'The Book of Beliefs and Opinions' (in Hebrew 'Emunoth viDaoth'), translated by Samuel Rosenblatt), chapter five on Redemption, Rav Saadia Gaon says *'Our forefathers also tell us… there will be the appearance in Upper Galilee of a man from among the descendants of Josef, around whom there will gather individuals from among the Jewish nation. This man will go to Jerusalem after its seizure by the Romans (or whoever is the leading power of Edom at the time; now it's lead by the USA) and stay in it for a certain length of time. Then they will be surprised by a man named Armilus, who will wage war against them and conquer the city and subject its inhabitants to massacre, captivity and disgrace. Included among those who will be slain will be that man from among the descendants of Josef (Zachariah 12:10 'They will look towards Me because of whom they have stabbed')'*. The phrase here '*that man from among the descendants of Josef*' refers to the Messiah son of Josef who is also called the Messiah son of Ephraim. Kol haTor says that Armilus controls the regime of the Erev Rav from Edom. The Erev Rav regime rules over Israel prior to the establishment of the House of David with Messiah as king. The chapter on this in my book on the Messiah explains this in detail with the Torah sources.

'Emunoth viDaoth' continues and says *'Now there will come upon the Jewish nation at that time great misfortunes, the most difficult to endure being the deterioration of their relationship with the governments of the world who will drive them into the wilderness to let them starve and be miserable. As a result of what has happened to them, many of them will desert their Faith, only those purified remaining. To these Elijah the prophet will manifest himself and thus the Redemption will come'*.

'Emunoth viDaoth', chapter six, continues and says that '*if the Jewish people don't repent and the redemption comes at the final time, then the Messiah son of Josef will appear and die as is prophesied in Zehariah12:10* (but the Messiah son of David will then later resurrect the Messiah son of Josef from the dead). *But if the redemption comes hastened before the final time through repentance, then the Messiah son of David will manifest suddenly. If in this case there would be a Messiah son of Josef who would precede the Messiah son of David, then the Messiah son of Josef would serve as the Messiah son of David's herald and as one who puts the nation in proper condition and clears the way. Or the Messiah son of Josef might be compared to one who purges with fire those members of the nation who have committed grave sins, or to one who washes with lye those of its constituents who have been guilty of slight infractions. In the event that the Messiah son of Josef does not come, so that he Messiah son of David makes his arrival to us unheralded... he will bring a retinue of people with him and go to Jerusalem.*'

From here we see that the Messiah son of Ephraim may not necessarily die in the war of Gog and Magog; depending on whether the redemption comes hastened by repentance before the final end time, or at the final end time if we don't repent.

Zachariah 12:*10 says 'I will pour out on the House of David and upon the inhabitants of Jerusalem a spirit of grace and supplications. They will look towards Me because of whom they have stabbed/pierced through. They will mourn over him as one who mourns over an only child and be embittered over him like the embitterment over a (deceased) firstborn*'. Talmud Bavli Succa 52a says that this is referring to the Messiah son of Josef may be killed, without recognizing the possibility that he may not be killed. From this source it is misconstrued by many Torah scholars that the Moshiah Ben Yosef will be killed in the war of Gog and MaGog. This is what is written in Talmud Bavli Succa 52a. But Rav Saadia Gaon in Emuna and Daoth, perek Gioola, says that Moshiah Ben Yosef is not necessarily killed, but may serve a viceroy of the Moshiah or not appear at all if we hasten the redemption.

Rav Saadia haGaon in Emunoth and Daoth also says that the Messiah son of David will resurrect the Messiah son of Josef after Armilus (the anti-Christ) kills him as it is written in Midrash Va-Yosha '*another king will arise, a wicked one and brazen, and he will wage war with Israel for three months (in the war of Gog and Magog as my book on the war of Gog and Magog explains in more detail). His name is Armilos... He will come up to Jerusalem and kill the Messiah of the lineage of Joseph, as Scripture attests 'and those who are pierced will behold him, and they shall mourn for him like one who mourns an only child' (Zech 12:10). After that the Messiah of the lineage of David will come, regarding which Scripture affirms 'and behold with the clouds of heaven one like a mortal man' (Dan 7:13), and it is written afterwards 'he will have authority and royal dignity' (Dan 7:14). He will kill Armilos the wicked, as Scripture attests: 'he will slay the wicked one with the spirit of his lips' (Isaiah 11:4)'.* The Messiah son of David will then resurrect the Messiah son of Josef from the dead (Rav Saadia Gaon Chapter on Redemption Emunoth viDaoth).

The Vilna Gaon (ibid) says that *'The Jewish people have three kinds of spiritual impurity mixed in with them: Ishmaelites, Esavians, and Erev Ravians. The Messiahs, son of David, and son of Josef, will appear and separate the Ishmaelite and Eisavian impurity from the Jewish people. But, this will be insufficient until the Jewish people are cleansed of the Erev Ravians. They are the proud wealthy who cling tightly to Jewry and Jewry learns from their behavior ... and (their bad influence can only be) cleansed off through the hardship of exile. The corrupting generational decline allows the mixed multitude to become ever stronger and the true Torah leaders must decree new restrictions and preventative measures to amend the breaches made by the mixed multitude.... There are five character traits (or types) of Erev-Ravians among the Jews: 1) quarrel mongers and slanderers (in Hebrew slander is called 'lashon hara'), 2) lustful people, 3) hypocritical people who are not what they pretend to be, 4) those who seek honor as a means of fame, 5) those who chase after money. The quarrel mongers (and slanderers) are the worst of all and are called Amalekites. The Messiah son of David cannot come until they are eradicated from this world. All arguments that are not for Hashem's sake originate from these people who rush to lead and to take glory and credit for themselves'*

The Ramchal in Gnizei haRamchal Kinath Hashem Tzivaoth, chapter on Moshiah in the Gate of Rome, says that "the Messiah sits in the gate of Rome garmented in husks of spiritual impurity (in Hebrew called 'klipot') and sits imprisoned in prison with out light and influence (see Yalkoot Shimoni on Isaiah 60), suffering of the sick (Isaiah 53) and this is 'and he gave his grave to the wicked' (Isaiah 53) because Moses had to cleanse Israel of the Erev Rav and Moses is bound with them. But the Messiahs (the Messiah son of David and the Messiah son of Josef) must be at the gate of Rome and this is for them burial.... And they need to be in the klipot (that is Hebrew for 'husks of spiritual impurity') of Eisav and Ishmael that rule over Israel and need to be ruled over by the Messiahs. ... and they sort out (in Hebrew called a 'biroor') the Holy Sparks (in Hebrew called 'Nitsosoth') that Israel needs... and in their suffering the troubles of Israel are lightened'.

It is written that 'There will be jealousy and strife (oppression) between (the tribe of) Ephraim (son of Josef) and (the tribe of) Yehuda until the Messiah comes' (Midrash Tanchuma Section 4). One aspect of the redemption is the reunification of Judah and Ephraim (Ezekiel 37) as my book on the redemption explains in detail.

The Arizal and Gaon of Vilna say that we must pray that Moshiah Ben Yosef be spared death (as it is written that he could be 'pierced through' Zachariah 12:10 as per Talmud Bavli Succa 52a this refers to Messiah Ben Yosef) by the hands of Armilus by praying everyday the Amida's "Kisei David" the *intent devotion* (in Hebrew called 'Kavana') that Ben Yosef be saved and Armilus be destroyed. I like to take this prayer even one step further and to *pray with the Kavana that the Messiah Ben Yosef (and his camp) of our generation, who ever he is, succeeds in all ways and successfully paves the way for the Messiah and establishes and supports the Messiah son of David's thrown in Jerusalem soon in our time.*

The Messiah's birth into the world is opposed by the evil side since Creation

'*Even before the world was created, Hashem created the soul of the Messiah. The forces of evil feared the light of Moshiah for it shone greatly'*... (Midrash Yalkoot Shimoni Isaiah 60 and Yeshayahu 499).

This Midrash goes onto further state that: 'In the future Jerusalem will be a light unto the nations ('light unto the nations' also cited in Isaiah 49:6, 42:6) of the world and they will go by its light...and for the Torah that you have given me is called a source of life which in the future we will be pleased by its light... and what is its light? The light of the Messiah... and G-d stored it for the Messiah and his generation under His Throne of Glory. Satan asked G-d 'For who is this light stored under Your Throne of Glory?' G-d said that is for the future to return you and shame you....When Satan saw the light he was shocked and fell on his face and said 'Surely this is the Messiah who in the future will put me and all my ministers and all the idols in hell....and at that moment the idol worshippers were stunned and asked to G-d 'What is his name and his description? And G-d said 'This is 'Ephraim (in Hebrew the name Ephraim means 'Be Fruitful' and this is the actual intent of the statement of the name. There are different Rabbinic traditions whether this is a reference to the Messiah son of Ephraim or not. In any case, most of this Midrash refers to the Messiah son of David.) our Righteous Messiah (The term our or My 'righteous Messiah' is a term commonly used in the Torah writings to refer to the Messiah son of David, which may or may not imply that this refers specifically and exclusively to the Messiah son of David and *not* Messiah son of Josef. Many of the two Messiah's roles may be shared. This requires further clarification.)... who will light up the eyes of Israel and no Gentile nation will be able to stand before him…. And it was said to him 'These future sins that are stored with you, by which they will put you into an iron yoke and will make you like a calf with darkened eyes and weaken your soul by the yoke, and in their transgressions, in the future your tongue will stick to your cheek, you shall will as such?' And the Messiah said before the Holy One, Blessed be He, Master of the world: 'Lest the same pain will be for years'. The Holy One, Blessed be He, said to him: 'On your life and the life of your head, I have decreed seven years on you, if your soul will be sad I will take them off now. (Ralbag on Mishlei also notes that 'seven' is an expression that means 'many' and not necessarily seven, so 'seven years' would minimally imply three or two years as constituting 'many') He said to the Master of the world: 'In the joy and happiness of my heart I accept this so that not one from Israel will be lost, and not only from my lifetime should be saved, but also those who are stored in the dust, and not only the dead, and not only the living from my lifetime should be saved, but also those who died since the time of the first Man (Adam) until now, and not only these, but also stillborns will be saved in my day, and not only stillborns but also all those who You even thought of creating but weren't created, that is what I want, that's what I accept … that is what I want, that is what I accept'.

'In the seven year period that the Messiah comes they bring boards of iron … on his neck until he is broken from standing and he shouts and cries and raises his voice to the heights. He says to the Master of the world:' How much is my strength? How much is my spirit? How much is my soul? How much are my limbs, am I not just flesh and blood?' At the same time David (the Messiah) cries and says 'My strength is dry like a board'. At the same time the Holy One, blessed be He, says to him: 'Ephraim My righteous Messiah

(Again, the term our or My 'righteous Messiah' is a term commonly used in the Torah writings to refer to the Messiah son of David, *not* Messiah son of Josef, also called Messiah son of Ephraim, as some people may mistakenly confuse the two Messiah's in this Midrash). I have already accepted you since the six days of Creation. From now on your pain shall be My pain' (ibid).

'Hashem asked the Messiah regarding his purpose and mission: 'It is destined that you will suffer greatly. Are you willing to accept this suffering?' Messiah answered, 'If you will agree that in the end of days everyone will live again and even those who were meant to be born will come to life.' When the redemption comes, the forefathers will ask if he has bad feelings toward the Jewish people who sinned and caused him to suffer and don't want them to have a share in the redemption? He will answer that all of his suffering was for their sake so that they can have a share in the redemption'. The above quotes are taken from the Midrash Yalkoot Shimoni Isaiah 60 and Yeshayahu 499.

The great Kabbala master and Torah sage, the Arizal, teaches that there are certain souls which stem from very high spiritual levels, such as Abraham, king David and the Messiah. When these souls are ready to descend to this world, there is great opposition from the evil forces of spiritual impurity in the world; an opposition from Satan in the court of Heaven that must authorize the soul's descent into the world. They argue that "Since these souls are so great, not only will they not succumb to evil, but they will bring others to recognize and serve Hashem!" Hashem's own attribute of judgment acquiesces and concedes, for such souls can overcome the forces of evil, negate free will, and bring about an open revelation of G-dliness. How then can these souls descend? Hashem uses a ruse to trick the forces of evil. He consents to the transmigration of these souls through unsophisticated, even wicked, people. Upon seeing that these great souls are very near the realm of evil, the evil forces of spiritual impurity agree to their descent into the world, thinking that they will prevail over the great soul and cause to it to sin (Hashem forbid) (Ramban's Shaar haGilgooleem #38- Page 19 reference 3 from the book 'Moshiah Who What Why When Where' by Chaim Kramer). Chapter two of the Tanya also quotes the Arizal (remembrance of the righteous is for blessing) on this point and says that these souls may be impeded by shells of spiritual impurity affixed to them through their impure conception.

"The Messiah was born when the Temple was destroyed (on the 9th of Av) and (his soul) was subsequently taken back to the Garden of Eden" (Midrash

Zeira on Eicha, Maharsha on Talmud Bavli Sanhedrin 98a). The Messiah was born out of the Garden of Eden by the agreement of the accuser (Satan) in the heavenly court that he could only enter the world only if there was a sufficient chance that the world and life would destroy him. Since that time, "The Messiah is waiting in the Garden of Eden (by the gate of Rome) for Rome to fall and enter in the Kingdom of Hashem" (The Maharsha and Maharal on Sanhedrin 98).

Talmud Bavli Sanhedrin 97 says that the Messiah is called in Hebrew the bar 'Nafli' which means the 'fallen one' but in Hebrew Nafli also means the 'aborted one' or 'stillborn' This implies that the Messiah may be at risk of being aborted even before birth as David was but when Adam saw this he gave David seventy years of his life to save him. Rav Nahman of Breslov (remembrance of the righteous is for blessing) says that the Messiahs parents wont be so 'Oiy Yoi Yoi', meaning they wont be so great ('Messiah, Who, What, Why, When, Where' by Chaim Kramer). This helps the Messiah to be who he really is by refining him through suffering and forces him to seek a deeper level of understanding and humility in order to cope with the situation of not such great parents who of course he loves, respects and understands any way, because he is the Messiah.

A good heart leads one to do the Torah commandments properly in the way that they are supposed to be done. Service of G-d is all about what's in the heart; evil, good, purity, passions, lusts, love, hate, humility, arrogance, etc.. What we desire to do comes from what's in our hearts. That is why G-d chose king David to be king; because he had a good heart. That is why the Messiah will be so good; because he has a good heart.

Being a potentially aborted baby from parents who are 'not so great' also may imply that he may be a 'mistake' born out of a passionate relations between his parents and his mother will probably not follow the laws of ritual purity (in Hebrew called 'hilchot nida') before relations. This has implications regarding the nature of what type of baby the Messiah will be. The Talmud says that one born out of passionate relations is intelligent. That is good. The Messiah needs to be highly intelligent. The prophets say that one born from a mother in a state of ritual impurity is arrogant, 'high browed'. That is not good since the Messiah needs to be humble. Arrogance and Ego in ones heart are a spiritual killer; it destroys ones service of G-d and eventually leads him to sin and to go to hell. The Kabbala says that one born out of impure relations has spiritual husks of impurity in his heart (in Hebrew called 'klipot'), such as lust for forbidden things, that make his service of Hashem difficult or even impossible (unless G-d intervenes and cleanses them through repentance and suffering for example). This is part of the opposition to the Messiah that the Satan has arranged in Heaven before the Messiah was even born into the world.

These evil spirits of lust and arrogance planted within the Messiah's heart provide severe opposition to the Messiah from becoming the pure hearted humble person who he needs to be in order to live up to the high standards of the Torah that he needs to achieve in order to be the Messiah. The Satan knows this and planned it that way. But, so did G-d, who knows better than the Satan. The Messiah is dealt a loosing hand of cards but will ultimately win the game anyway (with G-d's help). That is part of the miracle and Divine Providence that people who are wise in Torah will come to see. The Messiah will beat the evil in his own heart and will thus lead the others of his generation (including truly kosher orthodox Rabbis of the highest caliber) to do so as well. That is part of the solution for mankind that we need to learn and achieve- spiritual perfection through perfect observance of the Torah.

Ohr HaChaim Bereishis 49:11 says that the Messiah will have the souls of both David and Moses (the soul of David impregnated with the soul of Moshe; through great Torah study; according to the Zohar). This explains how the Messiah will be David the misunderstood warrior musician in some respects but also Moses the law giver in some aspects. Some may view him as an enigma or split personality.

A Torah principle is that there is opposition to good and the greater the good the greater the opposition. Thus we see that the Messiah comes from the Garden of Eden and has extremely difficult beginnings and opposition to even be born reach in this world, even from before his birth, and we can see why.

The Messiah may be Born on the Jewish New Year - Rosh haShana

Many people today say that the Messiah will be born on the ninth of Av. This is a misunderstanding of Midrash Zeira on Eicha and Maharsha on Talmud Bavli Sanhedrin 98a which says that the Messiah *was* born on the ninth of Av during the destruction of the Temple. Since king Hezkiyahoo (AKA king Hezekiah) could have been the Messiah circa 720 BCE, centuries before the Temple was destroyed, it is obvious that the birth date of the ninth of Av was one of the Messiah's reincarnations where he was born on that date during the destruction of the Temple during that reincarnation. It was not the first time he came to the world and not the last. The last time he comes he will be the Moshiah and it is a question when that birth date will be.

Midrash Rabba Shemot Parsha 16 says 'The Messiah will come on the 'first' in the first month'. This means that the Messiah 'comes' in either the Hebrew month Tishrei or Nisan, both being called the first month for different purposes according to the Talmud. The first of Nisan is for counting the years of kings and festivals and the first of Tishrei is for counting new years, shmita years (the seven year cycle where the land 'rests' in the seventh year) and Yovel (the fifty year Jubilee cycle where land returns to the original owners in the fiftieth year), orlah and due dates for giving tithes for produce.

The phrase 'First in the first month' hints that the Messiah 'comes' on the first of the Hebrew month Tishrei or Nisan. The Messiah's 'coming' here could either mean being born, migrating to the land of Israel, becoming king in Israel, or standing on the Temple and declaring that the redemption has arrived (Yalkoot Shimoni on Isaiah 60), or some other event that marks his 'coming' whatever that means. It could mean many things.

Adam, Abraham and Jacob were born on the first of Tishrei which is the Jewish New Year also called in Hebrew 'Rosh haShana'. The matriarchs Sarah and Rachel, and Hana (the mother of the prophet Samuel, who anointed king David to be king) were redeemed from being barren on Rosh HaShana. Josef was freed from twelve years in prison on Rosh HaShana. The Jews in Egypt were released from hard slave labor on Rosh HaShana. Rosh HaShana is a date that signifies major events regarding important people in history. It may be that the birth date of the Messiah will be on Rosh HaShana as well. It would be appropriate since the Moshiah is the reincarnation of king David who was the reincarnation of Adam who was born on Rosh haShana. Rosh Hashana is the Judgment day for the whole world every year, so we can see that he could be born on that day out of favorable Judgment for Mankind. This line of reasoning may or may not apply to the birth date of the Moshiah being Rosh Hashana, though, since other great Jewish Torah leaders were born on other birth dates.

Suspect lineage and raised in Edom

The Messiah has suspect lineage and is raised, but not necessarily born, in Edom; an impure abominate anti-Semitic society of wicked hypocritical atheists ruled by wicked paternal descendants of Eisav. The Messiah's ancestors include Lot who had incest with his own daughters to create the nations of Ammon and Moab, from whom the formerly promiscuous Moabite convert princess Ruth married the aged Boaz who begot Jesse, questionably a Moabite, who begot king David who was thought to be an illegitimate bastard child in his childhood. The Messiah's ancestor Judah had relations with the apparent prostitute Tamar to produce his grand father Perez. King David had a seemingly adulterous affair with Bathsheba.

"I have found My servant David (Psalm 89:21)... *in Sodom* (Midrash Bereshit Rabba 41:4)." Thus the soul of king David, the ancestor of the Messiah, could only descend into the world through a series of questionable relationships. King David was shunned and treated as an outcast in his child hood (i.e. for having questionable Moabite pedigree, mistakenly being thought to be an illegitimate bastard child only to be found out later that this was not true, and having red hair for which people thought he had murder in his blood like Eisav), and was unable to join his father's family and the Jewish community as a kosher Jew.

This is an example of hiding and then raising a Holy spark from a seemingly low place and then elevating it. Rav Nahman of Breslov speaks of 'smuggling in the Holiness' to this lower world. Thus we see that the Messiah's ancestry is rooted in sources of suspicious and questionable behavior and lineage such as Lot's incest of marrying his daughters, the questionable convert Moabite Ruth marrying Boaz in the middle of the night, Yehuda reproducing with Tamar while she was posing as a prostitute, his father Yishai mistakenly thinking that David's mother had adulterous relations which produced his illegitimate bastard child David, and king David marrying Bathsheba under the guise of adultery.

'The stone that the builders despised has become the corner stone' (Psalm 118:22) refers to David son of Jesse who was rejected by his own father and brothers (Targum) and when Samuel the prophet came to anoint one of Jesses' sons king not one of them thought it could be David who was left alone in the field to Shepard the sheep where he would also play his harp and sing (Samuel

I 16). On Micah 5:1 Rashi says that this Psalm *also refers to the Messiah son of David*. "The parents of Messiah Son of David will not be so "Eye yei yei" (not such good parents) (Rav Nachman of Breslov Siah Sarfei Kodesh 1-83)" is also supported by the passage in the section of the Talmud dealing with Messiah "Be careful with the honor of scholars whose parents are ignorant people, for it is written that from them the Torah shall go forth (Talmud Bavli Sanhedrin 96a) which hints (by hekesh-connected passages) that Messiah's parents are ignorant of Torah since Torah goes forth from him. The personal history of the Messiah son of David is one of immense holiness and goodness hidden in cloaks of suspicious and questionable behavior and backgrounds.

This aspect of David is similar to the Messiah who is also rejected for a period of time by his generation, as we shall see later, until he is finally accepted. The process of Messianic redemption is cloaked and hidden in appearances of sin and unlikelihood. Rav Nahman of Breslov calls this 'Smuggling in the Holiness'.

Another aspect of the Messiah's life that makes him highly suspect as 'un-kosher' (unfit) is that he is raised in the unholy, wicked, anti-Semitic, heretical, highly immoral, unethical, hypocritical culture known as Edom-Eisav's culture; now America and the West. In Midrash Rabba Shmoth 1:26 Mivooar it is written that just as Moshe (Moses) who was destined to break the power of Pharaoh was brought up in the Pharaoh's palace, also the king Messiah, who is destined to settle accounts with Edom (currently the USA/the West and Russia) in the future will be raised in Edom and will live with them in their country; the ultimate failure of the empire of Edom will give rise to a new and different kingdom-the Kingdom of the Messiah. We see this 'ultimate failure of the empire of Edom' happening in America and the West today. In America today there are already Americans who are disillusioned by the current two party system and want a righteous fair moral monarch as indicated by the popular song 'Hail to the king'. Qatar is an example of a successful monarchal king with an excellent Queen helping develop the country as well. They have proven that an intelligent beneficent monarchy is better than any democracy is able to be. This is paving the way to Moshiah's monarchal Rulership.

Talmud Bavli Sanhedrin 98b and Yalkoot Shimoni on Isaiah 53 say that Isaiah 53 refers to the Messiah, and Isaiah 53 seems to say that he is born in Edom with out any special known lineage, as Isaiah 53 says "he (the Messiah) grew up before him as a tender plant and as a root out of the dry ground (dry of the waters of Torah meaning Edom)...". In the Torah writings, water is often used as a metaphor for Torah. "Out of the dry ground" means that Messiah comes from a society that is "dry" from Torah, Hashem and His ways; a 'secular' atheist society, such as is characteristic of Edom where the seed of Messiah lays dormant there with its hidden unfulfilled potential waiting to grow until the right time comes along. "Grew up before him as a tender plant" means that he is sensitive and susceptible to damage by this secular society since lack of Torah and Mitzvoth often can damage a Jew in many ways or even destroy him or her. The Talmud teaches an adage that 'a man without Torah is like a fish out of water; as soon as men separate themselves from Torah and commandments they perish' (Talmud Bavli Avoda Zara 3b). This principle also applies to the goyim in that without the seven Noahide commandments the goy dies.

In his work called Iggeres Teman the Rambam says that "(Before the Messiah arises) you will not be able to say that he is the son of so and so and from such and such a family. Rather, a man will arise who was unknown prior to his revealing himself and the signs and wonders that will appear by his hand are proofs of his true genealogy.". Thus, the idea that the Messiah will be an heir in line to a rabbinic dynasty or from a well known recent high caliber lineage (in Hebrew called a 'Yihus') is a commonly held popular myth and contradicts what the Rambam teaches us. Also, according to Talmud Bavli Brachot 34b 'In the place where a penitent stands (a person who returns to the Torah is called in Hebrew a 'Baal Tshuvah') even perfectly righteous (Tzadik Gamur in Hebrew) cannot stand'. Rashi says that this is referring to their place in Gan Eden (Heaven). Rambam (Hilchot Tshuva) says that this means that Baalei Tshuva are on a higher level than the perfectly righteous because they have the added Mitzva (commandment) of repentance and that they have more merit because they have to overcome their evil inclination not to sin whereas a perfectly righteous person does not have this added merit. This implies that the Messiah is likely to be a Baal Tshuvah. In the orthodox Jewish world Baalei Tshuva are usually considered inferior to those born into orthodox families, but in many cases are superior in midoth (character traits) and Torah. Rashi on Micah 5:1 says that Psalm 118:22 'The stone that the builders despised have became the corner stone' refers to *the Messiah son of David.*

Talmud Bavli Sanhedrin 37 brings an expression that says 'the handle of the axe was hewn from the forest that it chops down'. This is also a metaphor for the Messiah's coming from Edom who he eventually destroys its capitol city (Rashi Numbers 24), possibly all its cities according to Ramban if the redemption is pushed off to the final end time (when all the cities of Edom are so corrupt that they can not be redeemed and must all be destroyed), subdues it as a power, and inherits all its vast wealth as king of Israel (Numbers 24) and now Edom (which at that point in history has taken over the entire world) as well. Thus the Messiah becomes mortal king over the entire human race where Edom has paved the way to this new world order.

Midrash Rabba Shmoth Parsha 1:25 mivooar's statement that "the king Messiah in the future will come from Edom and will live with them in their country... and will be raised there" may imply many things about the Messiah's experience growing up in Edom. Edom is the current world power and world power when the Messiah is born. The book later goes more deeply into what is Edom but in short for now we will say that Edom is the world power that throws off the yoke of Torah, makes it's own laws, is corrupt and immoral, has a wicked justice system, is anti-Semitic, and subjugates all the ancient peoples held captive within it- Whites, Africans, Chinese, Jews, Indians, Arabs, etc.. Ostensibly Edom today is the West, USA and maybe Westernized Russia as well. Being born in Edom is also significant because it teaches the Messiah, first hand, the evils and abominate injustices of the world by his own observation and personal experience while living in the evil abominate Edomite culture where injustice is one of Edom's identifying traits and in particular Amalek's trait of the institutionalized perverting justice by routine abuse of the courts as Amnesty international cites in the practice in the USA. This experience teaches the Messiah about the many different ancient peoples who are subjugated within the evil Edomite Empire, and thus prepares him to understand all different kinds of peoples and be sensitive to the intricate details of fair judgment and the necessity for such.

Since 'many ancient peoples live in Edom' (Malbim on Edom) "living with them in their country" implies that the Messiah may live in a multi-cultural metropolitan city like Manhattan. Although living in a multi-cultural metropolitan city and initially being born an assimilated Jew who eventually returns to living by the Torah (in Hebrew called a 'Baal Tshuvah') are not necessarily required in order to have the sensitivities and insights needed for the wise judgment of people, they may though, in fact and reality, be an integral part of naturally helping teach the Messiah, by personal life experience, a sense of people and how to properly size them up, and thus how to properly judge them, which is his central role in the world as king of the world. The Messiah's skills, wisdom and insight of judgment, like anyone else's, are in part a developmental process of learning and development, in addition to the spirit of judgment, wisdom and insight that Hashem gives him (Isaiah 11, Talmud Bavli Sanhedrin 93b). Again, Talmud Bavli Brachot 34b says that 'in the place where Baalei Tshuva (penitents) stand the perfectly righteous can not stand'. Rambam (hilchot Tshuva) says that this means that Baalei Tshuva are on a higher level than the perfectly righteous. Again, this implies that the Messiah is more likely to be a Baal Tshuva than born in to a religious family as most people reason.

The Edomite culture environment in which he grows up gives him an opportunity to live amongst the different ancient Gentile nations subjugated by Edom and witness them first hand, learning about the different peoples. Whereas usually a person who is born into an orthodox Jewish family would usually tend to be insulated and detached from the surrounding Gentile cultures, being an assimilated Jew (then later a Baal Tshuvah) who grows up amongst the Gentiles gives him a deeper and more comprehensive sense, personal knowledge, understanding and insight into the many different peoples and cultures in the world which he will later have to judge and be their benevolent king who works for their benefit and welfare. He will need this knowledge, understanding and insight later in life to judge the nations fairly, fight the enemies of Israel, govern the world well, and help the nations return to Hashem and serve Him alone as G-d and give sacrifices in the Temple. This part of the Messiah's broad life experience makes him fit to be king and know how to deal with the nations, and eventually be king over them.

The Messiah's youth may be like the lion in the movie 'the lion king' where the Messiah as a youth is thrown to the jungle amongst malicious hyenas (anti-Semites and goyisha pseudo Jews whose souls have devolved in to that of goyim and even of the most notorious Amalekite type Erev Rav mixed multitude (Even Shleima perek on Gioola and Zohar Bereishit 25-28) in nature to survive by his own devices with G-d's overseeing Help and Providence leading him of course.

Since a good Jewish king must deeply understand all the various groups and sectors of the Jewish people; religious, secular, anti-religious, rich, poor, educated, uneducated, professional, worker, military, civilian, communist,

Netorei Carta, Hasidic, Litvish, modern orthodox, conservative, reform, Ashkenazi, Sephardic, Yemenite, Moroccan, Russian, American, Israeli, Arab, Gentile, wicked, righteous, pure, impure, kind, unkind, etc., the Messiah, as someone who is destined to be king of the Jewish people must know all the various groups well; first hand. Therefore, a cross cultural exposure that most usually only a Baal Tshuvah has access to, being able to freely cross the bounds of different groups as he explores his own identity, would make a Baal Tshuvah a likely candidate to be the Messiah. He would also be from a group that most Jews would find acceptable. He would be a bridge of understanding and unification between the various Jewish sub-cultures, as well as the Gentiles, for the good of all in his prosperous kingdom happily dedicated to Hashem. His being king would help unify the different groups amongst the Jewish peoples living in Israel.

We see from these Torah passages that the Messiah is born into a Jewish family with parents who are not necessarily so adept in neither Torah nor its observance, likely even ignorant of Torah to the extent of even being secular assimilated Jews. Thus, the Messiah would likely be a secular assimilated Jew in the beginning of his life, or born into a low level religious or semi-traditional Jewish family. He comes from a failing Edomite country, like America, likely from a multi-cultural metropolitan central city of their society (not from the land of Israel) that is sinful, unjust and oppressive as is the nature of Edom. Life is difficult for him. He may likely be poor in the beginning of his life and may not even know what it means to be Jewish in his life's beginning, until he later finds out, one way or another, through G-d's leading Hand.

Genealogy and Tribal Lineage

The Messiah has a kosher Jewish mother and is a paternally descended "son of David" (Rambam "Laws of kings" and Isaiah 11) which means that he is a son of a son of a son etc. descended from King David; a paternal descendant of king David. David is from the tribe of Judah which means that the Messiah is from the tribe of Judah since ones tribe goes according to his father. The tribe of Judah's mascot is a lion. His mother is a daughter of the tribe of Dan (Midrash Genesis Rabba 49:9). The tribe of Dan's mascot is a lion and serpent. Yilkootei Shimoni, Bereshit, section 160, says "A lion cub of Yehuda this is the

Messiah son of David that came out of two tribes, his father from Yehuda and his mother from Dan, and both of them are called 'lion'".

The tribal blessing affects who a person is, what his strengths and talents are, and is carried from father to son, but the maternal families blessing also has influence on him.

The blessings of Judah that the Messiah has are '*Then Jacob called for his sons and said: 'Assemble yourselves and I will tell you what will befall you in the end of days. Gather yourselves and listen, O sons of Jacob, and listen to your father Israel..... Judah, you, your brothers shall acknowledge. Your hand will be at your enemies' nape. Your father's sons will prostrate themselves to you. A lion cub is Judah, from prey, my son, you elevated yourself. He couches, lies down like a lion, and like an awesome lion, who dares rouse him? The scepter shall not depart from Judah nor a scholar from among his descendants until Shiloh (Shiloh is the Messiah-Rashi) and his will be an assembly of nations. He will tie his donkey to the vine, to the vine branch his donkey's foal, he will launder his garments in wine and his robe in the blood of grapes. Red eyed from wine, and white toothed from milk.*" (Genesis 49:1-8) and "*And this to Judah, and he said: Hearken, O Hashem! To Judah's voice, and return him to his people; may his hands fight his grievance and may you be a helper against his enemies.*" (Deuteronomy 33:7).

The blessings of Dan that are on the maternal side of the Messiahs family, and thus also have influence on who he is are "*Dan will avenge his people. The tribes of Israel will be united as one. Dan will be a serpent on the highway, a viper in the path, that bites horses' heels so that its rider falls backwards. For your salvation do I long O Hashem*" (Genesis 49:16) "*Dan is a lion's cub, leaping forth from Bashan.*" (Deuteronomy 33:2).

Although the tribal blessing is carried through the father, the mother's tribe of Dan also has an influence on him. This is important because the Messiah, whose numerical letter value (called 'Gematria') in Hebrew equals that of the Hebrew word for 'snake', or serpent. He must also sometimes, be like a cunning, sublime snake for the good, in addition to being a lion. There is Kabalistic literature that shows that Messiah's being akin to a snake is his power to oppose and nullify the evil angel, the Satan, who is also akin to and once embodied a snake (or serpent) in the Garden of Eden. David is the reincarnation of Adam who was deceived and defeated by the Satan in the form of a snake in the Garden of Eden. The Messiah is the reincarnation of David with the impregnated soul of Moses. It is reasonable that at least one of the Messiahs wives will be the reincarnation of Bat Sheva who was also the reincarnation of Eve from the Garden of Eden.

The Messiah comes from king David who was from the tribe of Judah and David was born in Bethlehem, Israel. The Messiah himself though does not come from Bethlehem as is taught by Christianity and has confused many unlearned people on this issue. The Messiah is raised in Edom (Midrash Parshat Shemot 1:26 mivooar). Today Edom is the West lead by America as the number one power in the world today.

The above blessings show that the Messiah is gifted from Hashem with his powers that come from the tribal blessings of the Tribe of Judah, the tribe of kingship, wars of G-d, prayer and Torah scholarship. These blessings mark the tribal background where from the Messiah derives his powers. He is destined by G-d's blessing to be a righteous king, who fights G-d's wars for Him and Israel, from the tribe of Judah and Dan, like a lion and snake.

From here we see that the Messiah's father is a paternal descendant of king David who is paternally descended from the tribe of Judah, and his mother is a daughter of a man from the tribe of Dan. He bears the traits of these tribes.

Growth of the potential hidden Messiah in every generation

"In every generation there is a hidden person who is potentially the Messiah who will eventually at some point in his lifetime be invested with the spirit of Messiah when the time for redemption comes (Talmud Bavli Sanhedrin 98a Chasam Sofer Responsa Vol. 6 598 Rav Chaim Vital)'. "As with Moses, the Messiah Son of David will not know that he is destined to be the Messiah until the time is ready (Chasam Sofer Responsa Vol. 6 sec 98, R' Chaim Vital)". This tells us that the identity of the potential Messiah of that generation will be hidden from him until a certain period of his life and then as the Rambam says "A man will arise (to be Messiah) who was not known before he revealed himself (Rambam Iggeres Teman Ch. 4)" if the time for redemption comes in his generation (may that time be now).

We see from these Torah passages that the potential Messiah of every generation is a person who in the initial stage of his life does not know that he is the Messiah until it is eventually revealed to him. His becoming the Messiah is a process of self-realization of his hidden potential just as it is with everyone in life. We all have many dormant powers within us that may be developed or lay hidden. For instance, every one has the potential to achieve prophesy, create beings or even the power to resurrect the dead if we focus and dedicate our selves properly (Talmud Bavli Avoda Zara 20, Sefer Yitseera).

Suffering Scapegoat who is Spiritually Refined to rule over the Material World

We know from the Torah that as a rule the spiritual realm rules over the material realm; spirit rules over matter.

Performance of Torah mitzvoth ('mitzvoth' is Hebrew for commandments) and prayer with pure Faith, trust, love, humility, purity, reverence, surrender, and fear for Hashem can literally enable a Jew to rule over the material world and do almost anything he wants. Ethics of the Fathers teaches us that when a Jew nullifies his will to Hashem then the creations bend to that person's will. Even the Lubatcher Rebbe Menachem Mendel Shneerson (Zt'l) taught us the power of positive thinking. Works like Nefesh HaChaim by Rav Chaim of Vilojin (zt'l), Kisvei haArizal, the Tanya, and Zohar, Zohar haHadash, Tinkoonei haZohar, etc. explain the spiritual 'anatomy', 'mechanics' and principles of how this works.

To achieve this lofty spiritual level a Jew must be purified in his character traits (in Hebrew called 'midoth') of faith, trust, love, humility, happiness, moral purity, reverence, surrender, and fear for Hashem. Like any person, the Messiah is not born with all his powers. His powers must be developed and gradually bestowed to him by Hashem in stages 'kima, kima (slowly, slowly)'. The Messiah's spiritual powers must be refined for him to achieve mastery over the world. This development and refinement of his spiritual powers involve laboring in Torah study, Torah observance, self examination, self correction, receiving correction from others, good deeds, correction of the society, castigation, and immense suffering in many different forms to arouse and release many different forms of divine spiritual powers and husks of spiritual impurity dormant within.

Talmud Bavli Avoda Zara 20 describes this process of spiritual elevation through Torah observance that enables a Jew to eventually reach the level of the Holy Spirit and even enact the resurrection of the dead. '*The immense suffering that the Messiah endures refines him spiritually such that he transcends and overpowers the material powers of the world through Holiness*' (The Maharsha on Talmud Bavli Sanhedrin 98). The Ramchal in Gnizei haRamchal Kinath Hashem Tzivaoth also says that the Messiah suffers and undergoes great trials and tribulations so as to refine and elevate him spiritually to that his light can spread out to and illuminate the souls (in Hebrew called Nishamoth) of Israel. There he also says that the suffering of the Moshiah rectifies the sin of Adam's eating from the tree of knowledge of good and evil. This makes sense since the soul of the Moshiah's the soul of David which is also the soul of Adam. There the Ramchal also says that the Moshiah's suffering in the 'gate of Rome' (Talmud Bavli Sanhedrin 98), which means prison, atones for the sin of the golden calf of the Erev Rav.

Rashi on Talmud Bavli Sanhedrin 98 says that Isaiah 53:4 refers to the Messiah. Isaiah 53:4 says "*Indeed it was our diseases that he bore and our pains that he endured, whereas we considered him plagued, smitten by G-d and afflicted.*". The Targum on Isaiah 52:13 says that this refers to the Messiah. Isaiah 52:13-15 talks about the same person as Isaiah 53 and therefore Isaiah 52:13-15 is also speaking about the Messiah. Ramban agrees with this reasoning. Yalkoot Shimoni on Isaiah 53 also points out that that Isaiah 53 also relates to the Messiah. Rashi says in his commentary on Isaiah 53 that Isaiah 53 refers to the righteous Jews in the end of days and in his commentary on Talmud Bavli Sanhedrin 98a he also says that Isaiah 53:4 refers to the Messiah. Both statements are true and don't contradict one another at all. The main points of the passages in Isaiah 53 remain true in both interpretations. As the previous chapter 'The Messiah's birth into the world is opposed by the evil side since Creation' has shown, Yalkoot Shimoni on Isaiah 60 says that before he came into the world the Messiah agreed to offer him self as a suffering scapegoat in order to atone for each and every one of Man's sins and release him from the grips of Satan's power and the evil inclination, so that Man could be free once again from the original sin of the Garden of Eden that brought the evil inclination into Man, and Satan's subsequent power to prosecute man for our sins.

Isaiah 53 tells us that the Messiah is an oppressed suffering scapegoat. This suffering and oppression cleanses and elevates him spiritually to eventually be high enough spiritually to be able to rule over the material aspects of the world through the spiritual. As it is a rule of the Torah that the suffering of the righteous atones for the sins of the generation, the Messiah's suffering also atones for the sins of the generation. This experience of being a victim of unjust judgment also imbibes within him a sincere commitment to judge right from wrong properly, so that he can be fully fair and just, and eventually be the righteous king Messiah and mortal judge of the world. In Hebrew the Messiah is often referred to by the prophets as the 'Tzemach Tzedek'- the 'Sprouting of Righteousness'.

Regarding the Messiah Isaiah 52:13-15 says "(13) *Behold, My servant shall prosper. He shall be exalted and lifted up, and he shall be very high. (14) As many wondered about you 'How marred his appearance is from that of a man (he is initially disregarded by people as the unwanted 'cornerstone' that was 'despised' as per account (*'The stone that the builders despised has become the cornerstone' (Psalms 118:23) refers to the Messiah according to Rashi on Micah 5:1*), and his features from that of people. (15) So shall he cast down many nations. Kings shall shut their mouths because of him, for what had not been told them they saw, and what they had not heard they gazed".* Isaiah 53:1 –12 *"(1) Who would have believed our report, and to whom was the arm of Hashem revealed? (2) For he grew up before him as a tender plant and as a root out of the dry ground (dry of the waters of Torah in Edom), he had neither form nor comeliness, and we saw him that he had no appearance. Now shall we desire him? (3) Despised and rejected as inferior by men, a man accustomed to pain and illness, and as one who hides his face from us, despised and we held him of no account. (4) Indeed it was our diseases that he bore and our pains that he endured (As part of scapegoating, people project what are actually their own faults on to the person who they criticize. Talmud Bavli Kiddushin 70-'kal haposel bimoomo posel' which means people project their own issues on to others.), whereas we considered him plagued, smitten by G-d and afflicted. (5) But he was pained because of our transgressions, crushed because of our iniquities. The chastisement of our welfare was upon him, and with his wound were we healed (it is a Torah rule that the righteous Jews and the Messiah bear the afflictions of the generation as atonement for the sins of the generation). (6) We all went astray like sheep, we have turned, each one on his way, and Hashem accepted his prayers for the iniquity of us all. (7) He was oppressed and he was afflicted, yet he would not open his mouth. Like a lamb to the slaughter he would be brought, and like a ewe that is mute before her shearers, and he would not open his mouth. (8) By imprisonment oppression and false judgment was he taken away, and of his generation who considered? For he was cut off out of the land of the living (Talmud Bavli Avoda Zara 5a says that falling into poverty, childlessness, being blind or a leper is considered as being dead. The Messiah may have any number of* *these afflictions for this period of his life. The Midrash Yalkoot Shimoni on Isaiah 60 also brings, as we shall later see, that the Messiah is even actually imprisoned and possibly tortured by police and prison guards for the atonement of the sins of the people.), for the transgression of the people, for whom the stroke was due. (9) And he gave his grave to the wicked, and to the wealthy with his kinds of death, because he committed no violence, and there was no deceit in his mouth. (10) And Hashem wished to crush him, He made him ill, to see if he would offer his soul as a guilt offering sacrifice (to atone for the sins of the generation), and then he shall see children, he shall prolong his days, and Hashem's purpose shall prosper in his hand. (11) From the toil of his soul he would see, he would be satisfied. By his knowledge did my servant justify the righteous One to the many and did bear their iniquities. (12) Therefore, I will alot him a portion in public, and with the strong he shall divide spoil, because he poured out his soul to death and with transgressors he was counted, and he bore the sin of many and interceded for the transgressors."*

Thus we see that for an initial period of his life the Messiah will be a poor, suffering, oppressed scapegoat, imprisoned by false judgment, and counted among the diseased and transgressors. After he will become successful, wealthy and prosper.

Another principle that is operating here is the principle of opposition to good in the world. The more good something is then the more opposition to it there is. That is why there is so much opposition and libelous slander against the Messiah; because he is the ultimate good and purpose for creation in the world. Therefore even Epic wars are fought in his wake and emergence in to the world, in his name and against his name.

This experience of being an oppressed, libeled, scapegoat and victim of oppression, and the miscarriage of justice committed by a corrupt system, makes the Messiah very sensitive, motivated and adept to righteously administer Torah justice in the land of Israel and the world, which is one of the main functions of a king, along with fighting the wars, and making sure every thing in society is going well. The suffering also spiritually purifies him and atones for the sins of the generation.

Due to his own personal experiences of the affects and consequences of the proper or improper administration of justice on society, the Messiah is highly qualified and motivated to see to it that justice will be properly administered when he is king. The part of the Messiah's experience with the administration of justice also makes him fit to be king.

Statements in the Talmud corroborate with Isaiah 52:14-53:8. "What is his distinguishing feature? He sits among the poor and afflicted with disease (Talmud Bavli Sanhedrin 98a)". The Maharal says that "He sits among the poor and diseased" means that "the natural world is hostile to him". The Maharsha on Talmud Bavli Sanhedrin 98b and 93b says that "The Messiah will undergo terrible suffering" and that the "Messiah will be loaded with Mitzvoth and suffering through which he bears Israel's sins. Like great exertions of a millstone to produce flour, so too great exertions of Moshiah to produce benefit for Israel and Redemption."."He grew up before him as a tender plant and as a root out of the dry ground…(Isaiah 53)" means that the Messiah will sprout up, starting to be noticed suddenly by some, but not all, and will grow gradually, like a tender plant grows, in stages, day by day, as a process of gradual growth. This statement implies that the Messiah is likely a Baal Tshuva (a Jew born into an assimilated family and then later accepts the Yoke of Torah Mitzvoth on himself). Thus we see that just as "the Redemption unfolds as a process a little at a time, slowly slowly (kima kima), just like the awakening of the dawn from darkness (Jerusalem Talmud Brachot 1:1)", so too will the personal life of the Messiah unfold as a process a little at a time. That is how people grow. The "Messiah Son of David is 'Righteous, performing many meritorious deeds, thus constantly elevating himself, bringing him to achieve level of Yihidah (the highest level of the Jewish soul), … he will realize who he is and what his mission will be. Heaven will endow him with power to fulfill his task.' Thus he is similar to Moshe the first redeemer" (Arizal. Arbah Meot Shekel Kesef, page 241 Zohar II 7b-8b).

Yalkoot Shimoni on Isaiah chapter 60, section 499, supports that the Messiah will suffer immensely for Israel's sins and will even be imprisoned as Isaiah 53:8 says. There, it is written: "*They said to Him;" Praise Him that it is stored with You their future sins when they will put you in a yoke of iron and will make you as a baby calf, who was dimmed in his eyes and it will cleanse your spirit in the yoke and in their sins of these who in the future your tongue will stick your cheeks as your will was as such. …The week (a 'week' here refers to seven years which according to the Ralbag on Mishlei can mean not literally seven years but many years) before the son of David (son of David refers to the Messiah) comes they bring iron pillars and they put them on his neck until he buckles and he screams and cries and raises his voice on high and says 'Master of the world How much is my power? How much is my spirit? And How much is my soul? And How much are my limbs? Am I not of flesh and blood? At the same time that David (this shows that the Messiah is the soul of king David as the Zohar says) cries and says that 'my powers are dry like clay'. At that same time the Holy One blessed be He says to him: 'Ephraim (in Hebrew the name Ephraim means 'Be Fruitful' and this may be the actual intent of the statement) My righteous Messiah (The term our or My 'righteous Messiah' is a term commonly used in the Torah writings to refer to the Messiah son of David, not Messiah son of Josef, also called Messiah son of Ephraim, as some people mistakenly confuse the two Messiah's in this Midrash), already accepted on you from the six days of creation, now will be your troubles as My troubles.'*

Yalkoot Shimoni on Isaiah chapter 60 continues: '*Our Rabbis learned that the future, the fathers of the world will stand in (the Hebrew month of) Nisan and they will say to him: "Ephraim our righteous Messiah, for even though we are your fathers, you are better than us in that you have suffered the sins of our children, and you went through hard and bad measures that the first and last fathers did not go through, you were a mockery and scorn by the nations for (the cause of) Israel, and you sat in darkness and fog and your eyes did not see light and your skin was stuck on your bones and your body was dry like wood and your eyes were dark from fasting and your strength was dry like clay and all of these were because of the sins of our sons (and daughters too). You wished that our sons (and daughters too) would enjoy the good that the Holy One, blessed be He, influenced for Israel, lest for the trouble that you were most troubled by them, and were imprisoned in prison, such that your mind isn't settled regarding them (this being mentally disturbed may make the Messiah be perceived by some as being mentally ill). He will say to them: 'Fathers of the world, all that I did I did not do for any other reason other than for you, and for your children, that they will enjoy from the good that the Holy One, blessed be He, that influenced Israel, they the fathers of the world say to him "Ephraim our righteous Messiah, rest your mind that your mind should be rested… I will have mercy on him at the time he leaves prison. Not one kingdom, nor two kingdoms come on him, but one hundred and forty kingdoms surround him and the Holy One, blessed be He, says to him: 'Ephraim My righteous Messiah, Don't be afraid of them, rather by the spirit of your lips make them die, as it is said: 'By the spirit of his lips he will make the wicked die (Isaiah 11).' Rise and shine because your light has come. At the time that the Holy One, blessed be He, says to Zion 'Go up to Zion', she says to him : 'Master of the world, Stand at the head and I will follow.' He said to them 'You said well, as it is written: 'Now I will rise, Hashem said'.*

Part of the suffering that the Messiah endures may be what the Talmud defines as suffering that a man has by not having a wife. This part of the Messiah's suffering in life ends in Isaiah 53 verse 10 when he is granted children which also implies at least one wife but in the case of the Messiah he has many or at least seven wives as the section of this book quoted from Yalkoot Shimoni on Isaiah chapter 60 on the seven hupas (marriage canopies) of the Messiah's seven wives points out. The Ralbag on Mishlei says that seven can also mean 'many'.

We learn from Talmud Bavli Megilla that one of David's traits was 'katnoot' which means making himself small. That may be one of the reasons why so many people stepped on him and disrespected him throughout his life, other than jealousy and opposition to Tzadikeem. Being the soul of David, the Messiah may also have this trait of katnoot and be stepped on for this too.

We see from these Torah passages that the Messiah is at some point in his life a poor, oppressed, suffering scapegoat, falsely condemned and imprisoned by the corrupt, sinful Edomite (Western) and morally corrupt society in which he lives and he is counted among the transgressors even though he is guiltless and committed no crime. The world is hostile toward him but he gives himself over as a scapegoat in order to free them. He comes from a society that has the potential to deter and damage him but he eventually rises from this challenge only to be stronger, wealthy and to take on the whole world using his powers of Holiness and prayer, not just mere wealth, which he will be given by righteous individuals to empower him and enthrone as king, possibly by an even questionable source, but that is clean of gezel (gezel is iniquitous gain that is forbidden by Jewish law, not US laws that are against the Torah, to accept as donations or possibly even charity), or police confiscated monies thereof, so as to keep a question of doubt over his credibility so that people will be tested and have free choice. This godfather or other rich party may in this case have literally bought a stairway to Heaven and it is understood that one needs merit to give to the Messiah and it be accepted and used to build the people of Israel and support Torah Mitzvoth and re-establish the royal House of David in modern times. The Messiah in any case at some period of his life will undergo terrible suffering. His suffering and Mitzvoth (Torah commandments) spiritually refine him until his spirituality eventually rules the material, and by which, takes on the whole world for the sake of Hashem and Israel.

Messiah's Process of Spiritual Growth

"*The Messiah's ability to unerringly sense the truth derives from the purification from material impediments he has achieved through Mitzvoth and suffering.*" (Maharal Netzach Yisrael Ch. 32). Kabalisticaly the Messiah Son of David "*rectifies the world through judgment and compassion of Keter*" and "*brings the sweet smell of Hashem into world by Tochacha (Rebuke) with Love*". "*He will strike the wicked of the world with the rod of his mouth, and with the spirit of his lips he will slay the wicked*" (Isaiah 11).

'Keter' is a kabalistic term meaning 'crown' which means kingship over the spiritual worlds which rule over the material worlds- basically ruling over all worlds. The book Nefesh HaChaim by Rav Chaim of Vilojin, explains the powers within Man and how these powers within man, of spiritual realms, can over ride the material realms. In practical terms, it means that one can make reality happen with his thoughts, like in the movie called 'the Matrix' that kiruv Rabbis like those of Aish haTorah discuss, which is a parable about the Messiah in Edom where people who meet the protagonist 'Neo', the long awaited savior, are waiting for 'the one' in order to 'bring them back to Zion'. The Smiths (US Federal agents also known as 'Feds') are the under cover secret police agents of Edom who oppose and attack Neo and his flock (the Jews). They fight back. As shown in this book, Neo also portrays the Messiah in that he is also a 'man of war' and is 'handsome' as the Messiah is described in Talmud Bavli Sanhedrin 93.

A Matrix is a mathematical representation of numbers that are arranged in columns and rows often used in Linear Algebra. In this movie a Matrix represents the code of discreet figures, numbers in this case, by which the world was Created by G-d and is Run today as wee speak. According to the Torah the discreet figures through which the world was created and G-d emanates in 'reality' are Hebrew letters. The first Matrix of numbers that appears in the beginning of the movie starts with the number sequence '555', which in Hebrew, the number five has the same letters as the word Moshiah, which means Messiah. The occurrence of three fives in a row means an 'established pattern' in Jewish law (in Hebrew called a 'chazaka'), meaning in the Rambam's codes of law for kings, chapter 11, 'established status of being the Messiah (in Hebrew called 'chezkat Moshiah'). This is a Remez in the world of Sod to the Moshiah and is Hashem's way of preparing people in society for the coming of the Messiah in terms that they can understand. The movie demonstrates the principle of Keter and rise of the Messiah from Edom to a mortal kingly dominion over the world.

His becoming the Messiah is a process of growth and self-realization of his hidden powers, which Hashem endows him with, as he develops and elevates them through Torah study, performance of Torah commandments (in Hebrew called 'Mitzvoth'), and meritorious deeds. He likely starts life as a secular assimilated Jew from ignorant parents in the corrupt Western society of Edom, not an orthodox Jew from a pious family in the land of Israel as some people unfortunately imagine. If not born religious, he eventually becomes a repentant Jew who returns to Hashem and Torah observance (in Hebrew called a 'Baal Tshuva'). The Messiah's life is one of developmental transformations of inner spiritual metamorphosis. It is a journey of inner spiritual growth and fulfillment leading to his ultimate destiny that we all must embrace as part of our own personal destinies. The Messiah takes the risk and lives the dream which eventually comes true as it does with all successful people.

A Righteous king's Application of true Mortal Justice: Mercy for the law abiding citizens and no mercy for the criminals, murderers and wicked

We learn from king David what a righteous king truly is. Rav Nahman of Breslov summarizes it best in his Masterpiece of Torah wisdom work called Likootei Moran that learns out all four levels of Torah; Pardes-Pshat, Remez, Drash, Sod; in addition to commentary on how it applies to our times. There he says that a righteous king; in addition to being kind, morally pure, fearful of Heaven (and therefore sinless), compassionate, loving, caring and pointing out the good of all his law abiding citizens; he is merciful to the law abiding people when they commit a crime. Mercy means 'forgiving a person when he has committed and is guilty of a crime'. But when a criminal, wicked person or murderer commits a crime, then the righteous king is not merciful to him and punishes him with the full stringent letter of the law. This is in part based on the principle that it is forbidden to have mercy on people who don't care about checking the Torah to see what is the right thing to do and doing it (Talmud Bavli Sanhedrin 92 and Brachot 33). People who don't have understanding as with children and the mentally incompetent to stand trial should also be treated mercifully according to the Torah in most cases.

Does this mean that all criminals and even murderers are wicked? No. Some are not wicked, even some basically righteous, and would be treated mercifully, as with some murderers who are justified in killing people or did not have understanding of what they were doing was wrong. A thief who steals because he is poor and needs to eat or feed his family might also be treated with mercy, as a opposed to a rich person who steals not because he needs the money but because of greed. An offender of the Torah law may be treated with mercy in some cases where don't understand their wrong or do it accidentally (i.e. in Hebrew called 'Shogeg', 'Shote', 'Tinok sheNishba') or can't control them selves (i.e. Anus). There are fine distinctions in judgment that the Messiah will know from the Torah that he has learned and the Holy Spirit and prophesy and Divine Presence of G-d that guide him in judgment (Isaiah 11).

The Importance of Justice to the World and Mankind

'*The world rests upon True Torah Justice, Truth, Torah study, Temple Service, Peace and Kind Deeds*' (Ethics of the Fathers chapter 1). '*Perversion of justice, delay of justice and teaching the Torah law not in accordance with the Torah bring the sword (war, violence) to the world*' (Ethics of the Fathers chapter 5). '*Failure to uphold capitol punishments for death penalty sins brings disease (cancer, AIDS, e Boli, viruses, dangerous bacteria) to the world*' (Ethics of the Fathers chapter 5). '*Failure to tithe charity brings famine to the world*' (Ethics of the Fathers chapter 5). '*If you see a generation that many troubles come on them, go and check the judges of Israel, because all Divine retribution that comes to the world comes for no other reason than the (bad) judges of Israel*' (Talmud Bavli Shabbat 139a). '*Reviewing the considerations of Torah judgments is equal to learning Torah*' (Talmud Bavli Brachot Chapter 1). '*And Moses stood from morning until evening judging the people. When was his Torah learned? Think of it this way: 'Every Judge who judges true judgments that are true even one moment, G-d views him as if he is a partner to the Holy One, blessed be He, in Creation of the world*' (Talmud Bavli Shabbat 10a).

From the above passages we can see how important true Torah justice is to the world and how deadly it is to fail to uphold it. Most of the calamities of war and disease prophesied for mankind in the end of days (Zechariah 13:8 commentators say that two thirds of man will die from war and disease) may be able to be avoided if only we were to uphold Torah law as we are supposed to. This is why we need the Messiah; to righteously judge us, Israel and the entire world, so that we can live and succeed.

Isaiah 1:*26-27 'And I will restore your judges as at first and your counselors as in the beginning. Afterwards you shall be called City of Righteousness, Faithful City. Zion shall be redeemed through justice (redemption shall come through practicing justice) and her penitents through righteousness'.* Some say, based on Rambam, that in addition to being an obligation at all times, that this also means that the Sanhedrin must be re-established in order to hasten the coming of the Messiah. See the chapter 'Sanhedrin may be needed to bring the Messiah Hastened before the final time'.

Unlike the Talmud, Rambam, Zohar and Midrash, the central theme most noted in the prophets about the Messiah is that *he establishes justice according to the ancient Torah laws which are the foundation to true world peace and Salvation on Earth.* This justice is required to free the Jewish people from the sword of war of the Gentiles that HaShem, the G-d of Israel, sends on the Jewish people as a punishment for our injustice as well as that of the Goyim (Ethics of the Fathers chapter 5, Talmud Bavli Shabbath 139 & 10). It is mostly or at least in part our own injustice as Jews that allows the Gentiles to mistreat and subjugate us in addition to their own wickedness (apologies to the good Gentiles who are over powered by the not good ones). As an emissary and Prophet of Hashem, the Messiah solves that problem of injustice in society. That is why the theme of justice is so important in the prophets and the Messiah is referred to as 'Our Righteous Messiah' and the 'Sprout of Righteousness' who will be mankind's true chief judge in accordance with the ancient Torah laws. It is only upon this true Torah justice that true world peace can be achieved in the world where the "*They will beat their swords into plowshares and their spears into pruning hooks. Nation will not lift up sword against nation, nor will they learn war anymore.*" (Micah 4:3 and Isaiah 2:4).

The main aspect of the Messiah that the prophets reveal over and over again, in many sources, is his being a true judge who establishes true justice in the world. This problem of failing to uphold true Torah justice has plagued the Jewish people and world society all throughout history. It has been a source of demise for mankind that the Messiah comes to fix. Until then there will be no peace. The Temple can only be built in times of peace which happens after the last war, the war of Gog and Magog if that has to happen.

Talmud Bavli Shabbat 139 says that troubles and Divine Retributions fall on the people of Israel due to the misjudgments of Torah law by the bad judges of Israel and this pushes away G-d's Presence. Along with the abhorrent abominations of man having immoral relations with man and idolatry, *injustice* is one of the only three sins in the Torah that is castigated most harshly than other sins and is referred to as an 'abomination' and 'abhorrence'. Injustice and repentance are two things that touch the Heavenly throne.

The Torah commands people to uphold Torah laws of justice and holds us responsible for not doing so, and by failing to rebuke wrongdoers and bring testimony to the court of law to prosecute criminals. Peoples' failing to forewarn wrongdoers is also considered wicked by the Torah (Talmud Bavli Shavuot 39b). In the destruction of the first Temple the righteous (Tzadikeem) were marked for death by the Heavenly court, along with the wicked, for failing to protest against the wrongs that were going on at the time (Talmud Bavli Shabbat 54-5). The Codes of Jewish Law (the Tur and Shulhan Aruch Hoshen Mishpat chapter two) say that societies' success and health and peace depends on the proper enforcement of Torah law. Otherwise things may go into chaos and Mutually Assured Destruction (MAD) by weapons of mass destruction like those of America and possibly Iran if she gets them (Heaven Forbid).

G-d takes justice seriously. We are required by G-d Almighty to enforce justice as the Torah defines it; not according to the modern values and beliefs, nepotism, economic interests, racism, nor political arrangements. G-d Judges us people on how well we enforce Torah law in this world. He destroyed the world once already in the great flood of Noah's times for general wickedness but it was the injustice of robbery (amongst other sins such as adultery, inter breeding of different species of animals and man having immoral relations with man) that tipped the scales of Justice in the Heavenly Court and decreed the flood holocaust in those days as we learn from the Torah. The 2010 Hurricane Sandy epicentered in New York City and ranging down in diameter of destruction from Boston to Washington DC in the USA implies 'Shen dai' which in Hebrew means 'enough of gaining un warranted benefit from other peoples' damages'; as I witnessed was rampant in all levels of the society and the establishment in the New York Metro are and East coast when I lived there in the 1990s until 2010, so I have insight into the situation and the arguably possible or even likely Torah reasons why G-do would do such a thing. I am saying this for musar (moral) reasons so that people can learn that G-d is alive and Sees everything we do, judges it, and reacts to it with Divine Retribution if we sin and don't repent, or with Blessings when we merit them. I hope people repent in accordance with the Torah. The book 'Gates of Repentance' (Shaarei Tshuvah') explains how to repent according to the Torah.

At this stage in society, we have come to be uncomfortably habituated, as the song 'uncomfortably numb' so to speak goes, to the routine injustice in world society that is supported by the corrupt regimes of Edom and the non righteous Gentiles under which we are subjugated (as is also reported by Amnesty International human rights and injustice watch dog organization based in England); all the while being brainwashed to accept the 'democracy' and to 'believe' that it is the best system that there is, at least better than that of tyrants like Hitler's fascism or Stalin's communism that killed so many without fair trials. What a choice we have?!? We are trapped. What's the solution? The Righteous Messiah is the world Leader who Enforces Torah Law and thus establishes True Peace in the world. The Messiah is the solution.

The Corrupt World is in Dire Need of the Messiah to Enforce Justice

"Behold, the hand of Hashem is not to short to save, neither is His ear to heavy to hear. (2) But your iniquities were separating between you and between your G-d, and our sins have caused (Him) to hide (His) face from you that you do not hear (Ezekiel 36:22,32 discusses the desecration of Hashem's name that Jews commit before coming to Israel in the redemption period and was atoned for and repaired by what seems to be referring to the holocaust - see Deuteronomy 29:31 for hint to the holocaust)....(4) No one calls in justice (Ibn Ezra, Radak- No one calls his friend to rebuke him with sincerity. Jonathan-No one prays sincerely), and no one is judged faithfully (Radak- For the judge perverts his judgment). Trusting in vanity and speaking lies, conceiving injustice and begetting wickedness. ... (20) And a redeemer (Ibn Ezra - The Messiah.) shall come to Zion, and to those who repent of transgression in Jacob, says Hashem." – (Isaiah 59).

Rav Saadia Gaon in his book "Emuna and Daath" in the chapter on redemption states that many people will come to associate with the Messiah. Those who are able to heed his advice and succeed in it will live, but those who fail to head his advice will be marked for perdition. It's their free choice to decide on what to do; right or wrong. *"And a redeemer (Ibn Ezra says that this is the Messiah) shall come to Zion, and to those who repent of transgression in Jacob, says Hashem*" (Isaiah 59:*20*) indicates that the Messiah will redeem the worst sinners if they repent. Radak on the previous and following verses says that all of Israel will repent fully at that time after seeing the miracles of Hashem in the land of Israel.

As a righteous leader of justice who truly cares about the well being of the people, the Messiah will be available to help sinners with criminal pasts (even the most heinous of crime such as idolatry, heresy, murder, sodomy, rape, molestation, thievery, injustice) who want to repent truly and sincerely, to show them the way how to return to Hashem and gain personal redemption, atonement, and forgiveness for their sins.

Mankind and the Messiah Must Enforce True Torah Justice or *Face G-d's Wrath*

"*Hear the word of Hashem, O House of David* (the Messiah's establishment), *said Hashem, administer justice diligently and save the robbed from the hand of the oppressor, lest My anger rage forth like a fire, it will burn, but there will be no one to extinguish it, do to the wickedness of your deeds*" (Jeremiah 21:11).

For a little musar (moral) to our times I will say that mankind and the Messiah of the House of David must enforce true Torah justice or face G-d's wrath. 'Wrath' includes such Divine Retributions that we are experiencing now such as Tornadoes, Hurricanes, Sunamee, floods, AIDS, economic disaster, rampant crime, the Oklahoma City and World Trade Center bombings, poverty, famine, war, terror, limited tactical nuclear war, all out nuclear war where the Prophets indicate that Israel remains as the sole survivor in that scenario. As Hashem gives us messages in life (see 'Derech Hashem') and works 'measure for measure' (in Hebrew called 'Mida kineged mida'), the terror group Hamas is a punishment for our sins of Hamas which in Hebrew means gezel, treachery, false testimony. In Hebrew 'Nazi' means to revile Hashem and is used in that context in scriptures. Talmud Bavli Brachot chapter one says that when tragedy or travails befalls us we must investigate our deeds to see what we did wrong that made Hashem bring this on us and to repent, instead of blaming the agent of Hashem who is punishing us, as we are all too often accustomed to do. This is a little musar (Moral) here.

Unlike the Talmud, Rambam, Zohar and Midrash, the central theme most noted in the prophets about the Messiah is that *he establishes justice according to the ancient Torah which is the foundation to true world peace.* Ethics of the fathers chapter five says that the perversion or delay of justice brings the sword to the world. This means that wars, destruction and violence are caused by delay and perversion of justice.

Upholding of the Torah laws of justice with a kosher Beith Din is required to free the Jewish people and the Gentiles from the sword of war that HaShem, the G-d of Israel, sends on us a punishment for our perversion and delay of justice as per Ethics of the Fathers. Torah education, including education of the Noahide Covenant for Gentiles, including learning to be truthful and to be honest in business is key now for all of us and our children so they can have a brighter future. YouTube has videos on the subjects of teaching honesty and truthfulness to children. Its better that they learn this now than being executed later as criminals (Heaven Forbid).

If someone wishes to learn about Torah justice then he may do so by learning the ArtScroll Tractate called 'Sanhedrin' with foot notes. Take you time and be patient. Like an encyclopedia, the Babylonian Talmud has some 2700 pages and by learning one page a day he may complete it in seven years. This is what many Jews do. Then you may come to learn the wisdom of king Solomon and the king Moshiah. Only Jews are allowed to learn Torah. The Gentiles should come to us for advise. There are Noahide groups as well as daily Talmud lessons on the Internet. If you want to get a taste of how to judge, and I recommend this article to any professional judge not sitting on the bench, check out my article in the appendix of this book called "How to Judge".

As a musar warning to our generation I will say here that the sword of Iran may now be able to be averted if we accept and enforce Torah justice now in the target countries such as Israel ('the little Satan' according to Iran), Spain, Saudi Arabia, the United States ('the Great Satan' according to Iran), the West and the world. Otherwise we will get what we deserve. It is our own injustice (and sins in general as well) that allows the Gentiles like America, Germany, Iran and Palestinians to subjugate us Jews. Our own evil inclination is our own worst enemy; more than Iran, the US government and Satan combined. The Messiah solves that problem. That is why the theme of justice is so important in the prophets and the Messiah is referred to as 'Our Righteous Messiah' and the 'Sprout of Righteousness' who is a true judge in accordance with the ancient Torah laws. It is only upon this true Torah justice that true peace can be achieved in the world where the 'nations beat their swords into plowshares' (Micah 4:3, Isaiah 2:4). If we repent with Tshuva Shleima including upholding justice according to Torah then the wars can be prevented.

The Messiah will Emerge as the True Human Judge who Enforces Torah Justice

"Behold, days are coming, the word of Hashem, *when I will establish a righteous sprout from David, a king will reign and prosper and he will administer justice and righteousness in the land. In his days, Judah will be saved and Israel will dwell securely. This is the name people will call him; "Hashem is our righteousness"* (Jeremiah 23:5).

"*In those days (the "end of days"-the time of the Redemption), at that time, I will cause a sprout of righteousness to sprout forth from David, and he will administer justice and righteousness in the land. In those days Judah will be saved and Jerusalem will dwell in security, and this is what people will call: Hashem is our Righteous One*" (Jeremiah 33:15). This means that the MESSIAH WILL SPROUT UP, growing like a stalk out of the ground from where he was hidden as is written in Isaiah 53:*2 "Formerly he grew like a sapling or like a root from arid ground. He had neither form nor grandeur. We saw him but with out such visage that we could desire him"*.

'A staff (Torah true authority leader) will emerge from the stump of Jesse (king David's father) and a shoot will sprout from his roots (a descendant of Jesse). The spirit of Hashem will rest upon him, a spirit of wisdom and understanding, a spirit of council and strength, a spirit of knowledge and fear of Hashem. He will be imbued with a spirit of fear for Hashem, and will not need to judge by what his eyes see nor decide by what his ears hear. He will judge the destitute with righteousness and will decide with fairness for the humble of the earth, and He will strike the wicked of the world with the rod of his mouth (Rebuke and Protest), and with the spirit of his lips he will slay the wicked (Rav Nachman of Breslov says Messiah's

most powerful weapon is prayer). Righteousness will be the girdle round his loins and faith will be the girdle round his waist' (Isaiah 11:1-5).

Through justice the king supports the world (Rashi on Proverbs 29 on Talmud Bavli Shabbat 10).

The Messiah will provide fair restitution to the poor, humble and destitute and not allow the justice system to be abused by the powerful, haughty and wealthy to commit the abomination of miscarriage justice as is done today in the Gentile courts that plague the entire world until the Messiah becomes king and rectifies the justice system by bringing it back to proper Torah judgment.

The Messiah's G-d Given Holy Spirit and Prophesy used in Judgments

The Messiah Son of David "*sniffs and judges.*" (Talmud Bavli Sanhedrin 93b). The word in Hebrew for sniff (Rai-ah) is connected to the word for spirit (Ru-ah). This is a metaphor which refers to the spirits *of wisdom and understanding, a spirit of council and strength, a spirit of knowledge and fear of Hashem* (Isaiah 11:1-5) used in judgment that every true judge of his level really can have which Hashem gives him that enables him to decipher between truth and fiction when judging between people and nations.

"*And for a spirit of justice (Rashi-Hashem guides the judges' mental process in judgment) to him who sits in the judgment (Radak-king Hezekiah. Jonathan- The Messiah son of David whose true judgment and justice gives victory to Israel in war so that they return back home safely), and for might for those who bring back the war to the gate (Rashi-the war of upholding the halacha of Torah. Ibn Ezra-The Sanhedrin)*" (Isaiah 28:6). Megilla 15b and Sanhedrin 111b give rabbinical interpretation.

Messiah Will Administer True Justice Fairly and Won't Hurt Innocent People

"*Behold My servant, who I shall uphold, My chosen one (Ibn Ezra-the righteous of Israel, Isaiah. Rashi, Rav Saadia Gaon, Kara- Cyrus. Radak-The Messiah) whom My soul desired, I have placed My spirit upon him so he can bring justice to the Nations. (2) He will not shout, nor raise his voice nor make his voice heard in the street. (3) He will not break (even) a bruised reed, nor extinguish even a thickering flax (Rashi-the king will not rob nor break the poor and weak. 'He will not break (even) a bruised reed, nor extinguish even a thickering flax'* means that he will not make judicial errors in his judgments that cause damage to innocent people in even the slightest way, thus victimizing people by the unaccountable power of the erroneous court, as is often the case with most justice systems in history, as well as today including the courts of Edom USA who Amnesty International has admonished critically for its routine abuse of its own citizens rights as well as abroad.*), but he will administer justice in truth. He will not slacken nor tire until he sets justice in the land and the islands will long for his teaching." (*Isaiah 42:1*).*

"*The Messiah... will be the advocate of true justice. ... he will exonerate those who rectify themselves and will destroy the totally wicked.*"(Page 284, Reference 3 'Messiah, Who, What, Why, When, Where' by Rabbi Chaim Kramer Shlita).

The Messiah Will Judge the Nations Which Will Bring World Peace

"*He (the Messiah- Ibn Ezra) will judge between many peoples, and will settle the arguments of mighty nations from far away. They will beat their swords into plowshares and their spears into pruning hooks. Nation will not lift up sword against nation, nor will they learn war anymore.*" (Micah 4:3). The more commonly known Isaiah 2:4 repeats the statement '*They will beat their swords into plowshares and their spears into pruning hooks. Nation will not lift up sword against nation, nor will they learn war anymore*'.

The sword (war and violence) is brought to the world for perversion and delay of justice, and improper teaching of the Torah law (Ethics of the Fathers chapter 5:10-11). By this we see that establishing righteous Torah justice averts war and violence and is the prerequisite required basis for peace. This is part of the manor in which the Messiah establishes peace on earth, by establishing a solid foundation of social justice in accordance with Torah law. People and nations usually go to war because they feel they have been treated unjustly or want to rob land, resources or something of value from the other, and need to fight for their rights in war. When these disputes and misunderstandings are settled in court then they will not need to go to war and there will be peace. The Messiah will enforce this policy as king: No more war; just arbitration in court.

"He will strike the wicked of the world with the rod of his mouth (Rebuke and Protest), and with the spirit of his lips he will slay the wicked. Righteousness will be the girdle round his loins and faith will be the girdle round his waist." (Isaiah 11). Rav Nachman of Breslov says Messiah's most powerful weapon is prayer; but not his only weapon by any means as he is also literally 'a man of war' (Talmud Bavli Sanhedrin 93b).

The Messiah exposes, illuminates and elaborates on the practices, dangers, and unwanted social consequences of wickedness and injustice in society; sometimes harshly condemning them and rebuking them; thus leading others to destroy and uproot the wicked as well. Sometimes he slays the wicked himself with prayer.

"The Messiah... will be the advocate of true justice... he will exonerate those who rectify themselves and will destroy the totally wicked. ... The building of the Holy Temple (where the Sanhedrin judges and king Messiah sit to administer juice), and the building of Knowledge of Hashem (Daath-which connects wisdom, insight, giving kindness and brave action.) is the building of Judgment (in the world). Messiah will bring this Knowledge of Hashem (Daath) into the world.... Every person's ability to decide upon the necessary steps to take in life with be cultivated through this Knowledge (Daath) of Hashem. ... Thus, the great Knowledge of Hashem (Daath) to be revealed is a high degree of intellect which guides one on the proper way of life- with compassion towards others (of course). This is why the revelation of Knowledge of Hashem (Daath) leads to greater understanding between people, as can be plainly seen, because Knowledge of Hashem (Daath) is compassion." (Page 284. Reference 3 Rabbi Chaim Kramer Shlita, author of the book 'Messiah, Who, What, Why, When, Where').

The Messiah will destroy Amalek's Unjust World System of Dishonesty in Business

"(The Messiah rectifies the world), but rectification occurs only when people conduct themselves honorably and honestly in business. ... Amalek (an evil race-see chapter on Amalek), symbolizing avarice, has always been an unprincipled enemy of holiness. He tried to "gather" whatever holiness he could by lying, cheating, stealing, and so on. Those of other nations who break their lust for wealth will merit the revelation of the Malchuth (kingship) of holiness. This will be at the time of the ingathering of the exiles, for the sparks of holiness will be gathered and rectified, opening the way for the Messiah to come. Amalek, on the other hand, is completely evil. The only good that he might possibly contain is that infinitesimal spark of G-dliness that sustains him. When the Messiah comes, that spark will depart, and nothing will be left of Amalek. This is the meaning of the Torah's injunction to leave no trace of Amalek (Deuteronomy 25:17-19). When the Messiah comes, every iota of good must be elevated, and nothing will remain of Amalek the evil race that must be destroyed in order to makes G-d's Name Whole and save the world). We can understand this point better if we recall that he Torah calls Amalek "the head of the nations" (Numbers 24:20. … indicating that Amalek's goal is honor and the wealth that accompanies it, to be first and at the head of whatever is taking place. That is, the evil forces represented by Amalek correspond to haughtiness and false leadership, which as we have seen (chapters 14-15) are a major impediment to the Messiah and messianic ideals (Likutei Halachoth, Orla 5:16). In addition, we find that "Hashem's battle with Amalek lasts from generation to generation (Exodus 17:16)." (Reference 3, Pages 265-266 Rabbi Chaim Kramer Shlita, author of the book 'Messiah, Who, What, Why, When, Where')".

The Righteous Davidic dynasty will return to Israel

"Behold, the days are coming, the word of Hashem, when I will fulfill the favorable matter that I spoke concerning the House of Israel and the House of Judah. In those days (the "end of days"-the time of the Redemption), *at that time, I will cause a sprout of righteousness to sprout forth from David, and he will administer justice and righteousness in the land. In those days Judah will be saved and Jerusalem will dwell in security and this is what people will call: Hashem is our Righteous One*" (Jeremiah 33:14-15).

The Messiah will be king

'My servant David will be king over them and there will be one Sheppard for all of them. They will follow My ordinances and keep My decrees and fulfill them' (Ezekiel 37:24). The Messiah is established as the Jewish king of Israel during the redemption period at some point (Radak, Mitsoodath David, Malbim on Ezekiel 37:24-25). *'I will establish over them a single shepherd and he will tend*

*them, My servant David (the Messiah)' (*Ezekiel 34:23). "*They will serve Hashem their G-d and David their king, who I will establish over them*' (Jeremiah 30). "*I will make an eternal Covenant with you, the enduring kindness (promised to) (king) David. Behold, I have appointed him as a witness over regimes, a prince and a commander to the regimes. Behold, you will summon a nation you had not known, and a nation that had not known you will run to you, for the sake for Hashem your G-d, for the Holy One of Israel, Who has glorified you.*" (Isaiah 55).

My books 'the final redemption and the Ten Tribes' and 'the war of Gog and Magog' discuss more about the events that come before and after the Messiah's becoming king.

The Messiah Will Inspire Worldwide Social Rectification

"*The Messiah inspires the fear and reverence for Hashem in the society (breathes the fear of Hashem to people). People close to the Messiah are influenced by him, and they, in turn, influence others; like a social catalyst, effecting social change.*" As a student of Rabbi Chaim Kramer Shlita, author of the book 'Messiah, Who, What, Why, When, Where', this is the authors understanding of a personal quote heard directly from a conversation with Rabbi Chaim Kramer Shlita.

The Messiah is Given to Judge the Persians

'*Rabbi Shimon son of Pazi said that at the time that the Holy One, blessed be He, raises up the Messiah to the Heavens and He gives him from the glow of His honor before the nations of the world and before the wicked Persians. They say to him:* "Multiply (*Ephraim*) *our righteous one and judge those and do to them what your souls desires*' (Yalkoot Shimoni on Isaiah 60). The Persians are Paras. Maybe the Messiah will have to judge Paras since Paras will want to '*put the sword to the world*' (Yalkoot Shimoni on Isaiah 60) which will have to be judged to what extent it is a crime according to the Torah laws.

Until 1935 Iran was called Paras. The etymological similarity between the words 'Paras' and 'Prussia' may also indicate that Paras may be Prussia as well. Maybe not coincidentally, Prussia also lost its identity in 1935 when it was absorbed by Germany. Prussia was and may still be a far more competent and professional military power than Iran, who depends heavily on Russia for development and even depended on the USA and even Israel for protection during the Iran Iraq war. The ancient nation of Paras son of Yafeth (AKA

Japheth) may be spread out throughout the world like the Jews are but still concentrated at some key centers such as Iran, Turkey (Talmud Bavli Yoma 10) and Prussia possibly. They may be also among Western Caucasians as well, not just Middle Eastern Iranians. The Talmud lists one of their character traits as Givoora which made it difficult for the Romans to conquer. Rashi on Talmud Bavli Sanhedrin 97 says that before Moshiah comes there will be Parsim in the land. Today Iran (Paras) has implanted its military arms of Hamas in Gaza (Gaza is the land of Israel), Hezbollah in Lebanon (also the land of Israel) and plans on setting up a third front of Parsim, or at least their agents, in Yehuda and Shomron (AKA 'the West Bank'). This means that Israel is surrounded by Parsim and that Parsim are in the land of Israel as Rashi says. Although Yalkoot Shimoni on Isaiah 60 says that the people of Israel will fear the Parsim, the Messiah does not fear the Parsim and knows very well what he can do to them which is basically anything that he wants in his judgments of them.

This judgment of Paras most likely comes after the war of Gog and Magog when the Messiah is in full power and can do what he wants to do with them as his judgment sees fit.

The Messiah and Elijah the Prophet will Beat anti-Semitic Criminals with Clubs

"'Lift up your eyes around you and see.' At the same time the Holy One, blessed be He, brings Elijah and the Messiah and a bottle of oil in their hands and clubs in their hands and gather all of Israel before them and the Divine presence before them and prophets after them and Torah at their right and angels of service at their left and they bring them to the valley of Yeheshpat and gather all the Gentiles there, as it is said 'And I will gather all the Goyim'" (Yalkoot Shimoni Section 500).

The Gentiles who are to be beaten here are not innocent Gentiles but criminals and possibly anti-Semites who have survived the war of Gog and Magog but still need correction through capitol punishment of some form, ostensibly through beating with clubs. That is why they are being beaten, for their crimes as a punishment as part of their judgment and rectification. The fact that they are beaten by the Messiah and Elija means that they have merit since haShem only chastises the ones he loves. Other wise He would have killed them out right in the war of Gog and Magog.

The Messiah is the son of G-d

'The kings of the earth take their stand and the prices conspire secretly against Hashem and His anointed... I Myself have anointed My king over Zion, My Holy Mountain.... 'You are My son who I have begotten this day. Ask Me and I will make nations your inheritance and the ends of the earth your possession. You will smash them with an iron rod. You will shatter them like a potter's vessel' (Psalm 2).

Rashi says that 'My son' in Psalm two refers to the chosen leader of Israel from the royal House of David who will save His people Israel. This obviously refers to the Messiah son of David. Rabbi Emanuel Gentilcore Shlita pointed out that in some editions of Mikraoth Gidoloth, Mitzoodat says that this refers to the Messiah and some editions leave that statement out. This may be either an example of Jewish censorship intended to defer Christianity's claim of Jesu being the son of G-d or Christian manipulations of the text. I really don't know. That is a job for further investigation. It does not matter to me at this point. The printers of Mikraoth Gidoloth might want to get their books straight on this issue though. It's interesting how Hashem brings us the truth, despite people's trying to hide it at times. In any case, Rashi means the Messiah here.

This concept of 'son of G-d' has been used to rationalize and deceive people into idol worship of Jesu of Nazareth. As Rabbi Emanuel Gentilcore Shlita points out, "'son of G-d' does not mean 'a baby G-d son of G-d'". It is a perversion of the meaning of the scripture and is abused by Christianity. This idolatrous concept of 'a baby G-d son of G-d' has been reviled the Torah and Noahide Covenant to the point where we were not able to accept the concept of 'son of G-d' being the Messiah due to its abuse for idol worship by Christianity. By Jewish law we are not allowed to get any benefit from idol worship at all so many of the Rabbis may have rejected or hidden the concept altogether in order to protect society from idol worship of a human being.

The Rabbis teach us that Adam, the first Man, who it could be said was the son of G-d since his father was G-d, saw through his immense prophesy of all the history of mankind that there was to be born a great boy, king David, who was to die at birth for some reason. Adam decided to bequeath to this great boy/man 70 years of his life so that he could live his life and be who he is meant to be. This may (or may not) imply that king David was the reincarnation of Adam but it is usually understood that king David is the reincarnation of

Adam as I understand it. 'The Messiah is the reincarnation of king David' (Zohar). This means that the Messiah is the reincarnation of Adam, the first Man. Thus it is appropriate that the Messiah be called 'son of G-d, because the Messiah is the reincarnation of Adam, whose Father is G-d since Adam did not have any parents; just G-d as his father. Adam in Hebrew has the same letters of the first letter of the names Adam, David, Messiah. Adam's soul mate Eve was reincarnated into Bathsheba who was king David's main soul mate. Eve and Bat Sheva were musical and King David's and Bat Sheva's son, king Solomon, knew over one thousand songs as excellence in music and song writing, as well as war and judgments, is part of the tradition of the House of David.

In any case Psalm two shows clearly that the Messiah son of David is referred to as G-d's son '*My son who I have begotten this day*'. It is a title that the Christians learned from psalm two, the Jews have since then lost its relevance to the Messiah son of David, and so I just thought that I'd return our true Jewish Messiah's title to his rightful place as *the real son of G-d, the REAL KOSHER MESSIAH.*

The Messiah is of the Ancient G-d, not the modern emanation of G-d

'*I was watching in the night visions and behold: With the clouds of Heaven as a son of a man he came (Rashi-the king Messiah), he came to the One of Ancient days and they brought him before Him. He was given dominion, honor and kingship, so that all peoples, nations and languages would serve him. His dominion would be an everlasting dominion that would never pass and his kingship would never be destroyed*' (Daniel 7:13).

Since the Messiah is of the Ancient G-d, of Adam in the Garden of Eden, his relationship with G-d is not through the modern understanding of G-d but through the ancient understandings which is actually a deeper understanding of how the world really works, through the name 'KaVaya' that Adam called G-d in the garden of Eden (source: 'Apples of the Orchard'- a Kabalistic work) and not YKVK as is Hashem now known. Thus the Messiah may not be understood by any other than the wisest of true Holy Tzadikeem Rabbis in his generation.

Messiah will Bring back the ancient Torah and tribal lineages

The Moshiah identifies the true Cohaneem, Levieem and tribal identities by Ruah HaKodesh, but does not reveal who is a kosher Jew, a mamzer or slave, as Rambam's halacha on laws of kings 12:3 says 'in the days of the Messiah, when all of his kingdom rests and the all of Israel sits with him, their genealogical pedigree will be determined through his Ruah HaKodesh… and will identify who is from the tribe of Levi... and who is a Cohen… and who is from which tribe… but will not identify who is a kosher Jew or who is a mamzer or slave….'

The "*Messiah Son of David brings back the Torah of the ancients* (Torah Atik)" (Rav Nachman of Breslov Likutei Moharan I, 60:1). The Messiah Son of David determines tribal linkages and pedigrees of Levi and Cohaneem (Malachi 3:3, Talmud Bavli Kiddushin 70b, Zohar III-170a).

The Zohar says the Messiah is the reincarnated soul of king David with the impregnated soul of Moses. Therefore we can see why the Messiah will be '*a sage wiser than Solomon and a prophet whose greatness approaches that of Moses. The Messiah king will teach the way of G-d to the world*' (Rambam Hilchot Tshuva 9:2).

The Messiah may learn of the ancient Torah and tribal lineages through prophesy as a Chacham (Talmud Bavli Baba Batra 12a) and Biur (reasoned clarification), as opposed to 'drash' (Talmudic exegesis) which has been the Rabbinic tradition of learning Torah since Ezra the prophet (Rav Avraham Kook-remembrance of the righteous is for blessing).

Since the Messiah is of the Ancient Torah of Moses that is learned from 'Biur' (reasoned clarification) and not 'Drash' (exegetical law derivation from the Talmud) as the modern Rabbis learn Torah, many modern Rabbis may not understand the Messiah since his source and method of learning Torah is different at times than theirs. This is not to say the Messiah will not also learn Torah through drash of the Talmud, for this is the modern accepted basis of halacha which he too must accept as the halacha, but it his learning through Biur and knowledge through Nivooah and Ruah HaKodesh that may baffle many and make his wisdom hidden and not understood. The Messiah's Torah will also come from his prophesy and Holy Spirit through which the ancient Torah will also return through him and Elijah the prophet when he returns.

This is how the Messiah may learn the Torah of the ancients (Torah Atik) and determine tribal linkages and pedigrees of Levi and Cohaneem.

Messiah will Conquer the World

'A star has issued from Jacob, and a scepter bearer has risen from Israel, and he shall pierce the nobles of Moab, and undermine the children of Seth (shall undermine and defeat Gentile subjugation of the Jews). Edom (USA, Russia, Europe, the West; who will be in control of the whole world prior to the rise of the Messiah) shall be his conquest, and Seir shall be he conquest of his enemies, and Israel will attain success. One from Jacob shall rule and destroy the remnant of the city (an important city, the capitol of Edom, its Rome, according to Rashi. Ramban says 'every city'.).' (Numbers 24:19).

The Talmud and thus Rashi refer to Rome as being the capitol of Edom. Maybe that's because Rome was the capitol of Edom circa the Talmud redaction which was circa 500 AD. The question is what is the capitol of Edom today? Washington DC? Rome? All the major Western cities? The Zohar speaks about at least one of Edom's capitol cities being destroyed by a 'flash of light'. Maybe this refers to a nuclear explosion destroying the capitol of Edom. Maybe it is spiritual light alone that leaves no physical destruction yet 'breaks their vessels' because in the spiritual world too much light, like in that of the Moshiah, is interpreted as 'din' (judgment) that breaks spiritual 'vessels'. The vessels cant withstand the light of Israel, Torah and the Moshiah, so they break. The Zohar also says that in the end of days the tribe of Reuven, known for being capricious, will attack the world which may be part of the cities of Edom being attacked and thus Messiah's conquering the world by military force.

Rav Nahman of Breslov says that prayer is the Messiah's strongest weapon and that he can conquer the world without even firing a shot (Likootei Moran). This usually misquoted by Breslov Hasidim when they say that Moshiah's 'only weapon' is prayer and that he conquers the world with out firing a shot. As 'a man of war' (Talmud Bavli Sanhedrin 93b) the Moshiah can also uses military force as well as directing others to do so as the king. At the same time he can kill people without weapons since he can 'slay the wicked by the spirit of his lips' (Isaiah 11). He has many tools in his tool box to wage war, which are at his disposal as his choice sees fit.

Although the Messiah can conquer the world '*without even firing a shot*' it seems that he will '*destroy the remnant of the city*' (Numbers 24:19) with methods of war as part of the war of Gog and Magog where Edom attacks Israel and Edom is defeated by G-d and Israel. By defeating Edom the Messiah conquers the world since Edom was the world power up to that point, and by defeating Edom then the Messiah becomes the new world leader. The Ramban says that all of Edom's cities are destroyed, which by reason is the case if the redemption is pushed off to the final end time, when all the cities of Edom are so corrupt that they can not be redeemed and must all be destroyed. This may be what the Zohar is talking about when it says that in the end of days the tribe of Reuven will attack the world.

If the redemption is hastened before the final end time by Tshuvah Shleima and kindness, to arouse G-d's Kindness to redeem us, then maybe no cities have to be destroyed.

The Messiah's Many Wives

"*When the Messiah is released from prison... the Holy One, Blessed be He, makes for the Messiah seven marriage canopies of precious stones and rubies... and from every marriage canopy flows four rivers of wine and milk and honey and pure aphirsimone ... and He says to him Rise and Shine because your light has come...*" (Yalkoot Shimoni on Isaiah 60).

The Ralbag on Mishlei says that seven can also mean 'many'. The codes of Jewish law (the Shulhan Aruch) say that a man may marry as man wives as he likes as long as they agree and that it is advisable to marry four wives. We don't do this in our time due to monogamy having become the accepted custom since the Middle Ages as opposed to the ancient practice of polygamy as Jacob and David practiced for instance. A king is limited to eighteen wives by Jewish law. I heard of one kabalistic source that says a man has seven soul mates with one main one that he needs to marry in order to be complete and fulfill his purpose in this world. I also heard a Gemora that says a man has a higher and lower soul mate. It seems that the kabalistic understanding is relevant here and these seven wives, or many wives based on the Ralbag, many of whom will likely be reincarnations of the matriarchs and other big Jewish female souls, particularly Bat Sheva, help the Messiah be who he really is, accomplish his mission as a good help mate does and must be for Hashem and the people of Israel as well as for the Moshiah.

There are people today who have kosher rabbinic heterim to marry more than one wife with their wives consent of course since this is also required by halacha.

It is popularly believed in the Yeshiva world today that the custom to have only one wife was due to Rav Yona ('Meir haGola') of Gerona's halcahic (legal) ruling to prohibit men from marrying more than one woman due to jealousy between his two wives. This ruling has now ended and now we just keep the custom (minhag). Rabbi Rav Emden says that the real reason Jews only marry one wife is that Christianity forced the Jews to practice monogamy out of fears of being considered immoral if we had many wives as we should naturally do so. The Talmudic encyclopedia says that the Rama and other rishonim say that a minhag (custom) is uprooted when there is a 'Dvar Geroua Bo' (a not good thing associated with it). Is not preventing a man to marry all his wives, which leaves him incomplete, many woman barren, and many children unborn to the world a 'Dvar Gerona Bo'? Unfortunately, many women in Israel and the Diaspora today never marry due to this tradition of a man's marrying only one wife. Thus many Jewish women go childless in life where they could have had many children for the man they love, and many men remain unjustly frustrated with only one wife where they are really supposed to have many wives. Therefore, it can easily be argued that he custom of monogamy, as opposed to polygamy, is destructive and must be uprooted. The custom is evil and must be purged from us Jews where most men naturally want and need many wives. The wives also may benefit from the comradery of co-wives.

Rectifying this law to permit a man to have many wives will also help bring the Messiah since '*The Messiah does not come until all the bodies are gone from the chamber of the souls* (a place in Heaven where souls are stored)' (Talmud Bavli Yivamoth 63b). This means that having more children helps bring the Messiah.

The Messiah and his righteous wives will be happy to have him marry his many wives, be fruitful and multiply, and break that misguided and tainted pagan tradition of the exile and bring back the way of the ancient Torah to Israel, thus freeing many men and woman who want to be free to marry many wives to one man and thus fulfill their purpose here on earth. Any mature, giving, righteous woman of valor in Israel will be happy to permit her husband to have many wives and be best of friends with them all.

There is a general principle in the world that there is opposition to good. The greater the good the greater the opposition. A man's wife is his home and success. David and Moshiah need their wives to succeed. David haMelech (king David) had great difficulty marrying his wives. There was much opposition king David's marrying since a man's wife makes him a man and a king's wife is the root of the kingship. Obviously Satan does not want these marriages to occur (Hashem Yirachem-may Hashem have mercy) as part of opposing the kingship of Israel. Also, being the reincarnation of David, the Messiah will also have a hard time in this area like other areas of his life. The Messiah will only be fully empowered when he marries his many wives. The society must help him do this.

To illustrate kings David's difficulties in marrying here are some examples. King Saul offered David his first wife, Merav, as a plot to try to kill him and she ended up marrying someone else. David married he sister Michal who later scorned him in public where he returned sharp tongued words and she died barren as a punishment for disrespecting the king. When David met his wife Avigail she was married to the wicked man named Noevoel who refused to release her, he belittled David, later died, and David ended up marrying Avigail anyway. When David slew Goliath with the five stones in the sling he was unable to lift Goliaths heavy sword and behead him, so his servant Uri the Hivi did it for him and David, in appreciation said that Uri should have any woman in Israel for this great act. Hashem then said: "Oh yeh? Any woman? How about your wife Bat Sheva', and then Hashem gave Bat Sheva to Uri to be his wife. Later, David took her back when she was divorced from Uri (on account of his being in the midst of serving in battle for Israel at the time), and David just could not wait until a more opportune time. When Uri rebelled against David, then David did the most unusual thing for his behavior of usually being totally merciful with Jews even when they deserved death as in for rebelling, he then had Uri killed for being a rebel in order to hide his affair with his (David's) wife Bat Sheva. Two of David's wives were actually even kidnapped by Amalekites (may their memory be erased) and he had to hunt down and kill the Amalekites (may their memory be erased) to rescue his wives (Samuel I chapter 30:5). King David's wives loved him so much that after he died they all then died of broken hearts.

David had a real hard time getting married and so will the Messiah. Just think about it: Would you want your daughter to marry a man who was in prison like the Messiah was? Heard 'voices of G-d' like the Messiah does? A musician like the Messiah will be? Would you believe someone who is claiming to be the Messiah or rightful king of Israel because he wants his bride to be and in laws to understand who he really is and to explain for his dire situation and accept him? Look at the practical reality of the situation as it would play out in reality today. Who would understand the Moshiah to accept him for who he is? It could be a comedy or a tragedy, or a love story gone bad or a multiple love story gone good and they all live happily ever after like snow white and the seven dwarves, or in this case, the Messiah white and the seven white wives. We Jews hope the later scenario.

We know that the Moshiah brings back the ancient Torah, and polygamy is part of that ancient Torah. Let's look at the issue of polygamy a little differently than most women usually view it. As to the wives concern that if a man has many wives then he won't love her as much I will point out that it may actually be exactly the opposite. It could actually be that the more wives that a woman lets her husband have, then the more he may love her. He may love her even more for letting him have more wives and may even hate her and leave her for trying to prevent him from marrying his other wives. Maybe women have to stop being so selfish, insecure and childish and let the man have his many wives as is his G-d given right by the Torah.

The Messiah's lack of Peace of Mind

'*It was for the worst suffering that you (the Messiah) suffered and that you were tied in the house of prison confinement that you don't have peace of mind because of them … that you were tied up in the house of prison confinement where every day they would grind their teeth at you and would hint with their eyes*' (Midrash Yalkoot Shimoni on Isaiah 60). The statement here '*don't have peace of mind because of them*' shows that the Messiah has a really difficult time coping with the persecution that he endured. It is hard for him to just forget about his being persecuted and move on. As being one of the most powerful minds in the world, and the effect the mind of a man like him has on reality (the book 'Nefesh HaChaim' says that our thoughts affect reality and bring down forces from Heaven to the world), every time he thinks about his tormentors not only does he suffer but Heavenly accusations against his persecutors may attack them. The only way to stop this is for the Messiah to be fully appeased with wealth as compensation which is what Jewish law requires. Other wise his anger turns into G-d's wrath against his oppressors; those supposed to appease him. His lack of peace of mind may seem like mental illness to some, especially some psychiatrists who tend to 'diagnose' every one as mentally ill since they are mentally ill and projecting their issues onto others and they have an economic interest to gather customers for their 'service'.

'*You don't have peace of mind because of them*' is a reality that the Messiah has to live with, like Josef had to live with his twelve year imprisonment that resulted from his brothers throwing him into a pit to try to kill him, then later he forgave them, but they were still cognizant of the fact that it would be possible that he would want to take just revenge due to the horrible crime that they committed against him, that almost killed him and lead to twelve years in prison for him. The righteous Messiah and 'Josef the righteous one' are very similar in this respect. They are both very righteous men who are both highly victimized and both had emotional problems as a result, even though it is these sins that the Messiah has agreed to atone for by his suffering due to our sins.

It is no wonder that the Messiah '*lacks peace of mind because of them*'. Look at what he went through; imprisonment and cruel disparagement for the sins of others. He is only human like every body else. But in that he is a man of war who can 'slay the wicked by the spirit of his lips' (Isaiah 11), but never takes revenge on his oppressors, he is Divine in that he forgives the wicked people who oppressed him, even his brothers, who committed such grievous crimes against him that made him suffer so much that he '*lacks peace of mind because of them*'. As Midrash Yalkoot Shimoni on Isaiah 60 points out, that is why he is greater in some aspect than the fathers Abraham Yitzchak and Jacob, that 'he suffered so much due to their children, and he too is counted among the fathers'.

The Messiah is rejected at first like king David was

'*The stone that the builders despised has become the cornerstone*' (Psalms 118:23) refers to David son of Jesse who was rejected by his own father and brothers, and when Samuel the prophet came to anoint one of Jesses' sons king, not one of them thought it could be David, who was a left alone in the field to Sheppard the sheep where he would also play his harp and sing (Samuel I 16).

He really seemed like the most unfit candidate for king. On Micah 5:1 Rashi says that '*this Psalm also refers to the Messiah son of David'*.

What is the main identifying trait of the Moshiah?

'*What is the main identifying trait of the Moshiah? He sits with the poor and afflicted' and he is also considered afflicted* and while sitting at the gate with the other wounded he removes only one bandage of his at a time so as to be ready to move into action when needed (Talmud Bavli Sanhedrin 98). He intercedes on peoples' behalf, councils them to return to HaShem, and comforts them in their disease and afflictions.

In today's terms this could mean that the Messiah may live in a poor city of Israel, but even when he becomes wealthy he will sit with the poor and afflicted in order to help them.

The Messiah is Imprisoned

As Midrash Yalkoot Shimoni on Isaiah 60 says, quoted in the beginning of the book, the Messiah offers himself to suffer on behalf of mankind and the Jewish people, to free them from subjugation of the evil side and enable the full redemption to happen. Midrash Yalkoot Shimoni Isaiah 60 and Yeshayahu 499 say 'And it was said to him 'These future sins that are stored with you, by which they will put you into an iron yoke and will make you like a calf with darkened eyes and weaken your soul by the yoke, and in their transgressions, in the future your tongue will stick to your cheek, you shall will as such?' And the Messiah said before the Holy One, Blessed be He, Master of the world: 'Lest the same pain will be for years'. The Holy One, Blessed be He, said to him: 'On your life and the life of your head, I have decreed seven years on you, if your soul will be sad I will take them off now. (Ralbag on Mishlei also notes that 'seven' is an expression that means 'many' and not necessarily seven, so 'seven years' would minimally imply three or two years as constituting 'many') He said to the Master of the world: 'In the joy and happiness of my heart I accept this so that not one from Israel will be lost, and not only from my lifetime should be saved, but also those who are stored in the dust, and not only the dead, and not only the living from my lifetime should be saved, but also those who died since the time of the first Man (Adam) until now, and not only these, but also stillborns will be saved in my day, and not only stillborns but also all those who You even thought of creating but weren't created, that is what I want, that's what I accept … that is what I want, that is what I accept'.

Midrash Yalkoot Shimoni on Isaiah 60 goes on to say: "Even though we are your fathers (this includes the patriarchs Abraham, Isaac and Jacob) you are better than us in that you suffered the transgressions of our children, and you went through harsh and wicked measures which the first and last ones of us did not endure, and you were a mockery and a scorn amongst the Gentiles (including when the Moshiah lived in Edom from where ha came) for the sake of Israel, and you sat in darkness and even your eyes did not see light and your skin clung to your bones and your body was dry as clay and all this because of the transgressions of our children, it was your will and grace so that from this favor the Holy One Blessed be He would influence good to our children. It was for the worst suffering that you suffered and that *you were tied in the house of prison confinement that you don't have peace of mind because of them* … that you *were tied up in the house of prison confinement* where every day they would grind their teeth at you and would hint with their eyes". This Midrash, as well as Yalkoot Shimoni on Isaiah 53, also supported by Ramban, also Rashi on Talmud Bavli Sanhedrin 98, supports that Isaiah 53, which also talks about imprisonment (Isaiah 53:8), pertains to the Messiah son of David. Rashi on Talmud Bavli Sanhedrin 98 says that Isaiah 53:4 "*he is desecrated by our crimes and he bears the burden for our sickness*" refers to the Messiah. Isaiah goes on to say '*By imprisonment oppression and false judgment was he taken away, and of his generation who considered? For he was cut off out of the land of the living, for the transgression of the people, for whom the stroke was due*' (Isaiah 53:8).

Yalkoot Shimoni on Isaiah 60 also talks about seven years of suffering decreed on the Messiah which *may* mean many years or seven years of suffering that might fall in the seven year period before the Messiah comes (cited in Talmud Bavli Sanhedrin 98). Ralbag on Mishlei also notes that 'seven', as in seven years of suffering, also is an expression that means 'many' and not necessarily 'seven', so 'seven years' of suffering can mean 'many' years of suffering. 'Many' implies a minimum of three years.

Yalkoot Shimoni on Isaiah 60 also says that when the Messiah gets released from prison 'Not one kingdom, nor two kingdoms come on him, but one hundred and forty kingdoms surround him' which may mean that the Messiah will be released from prison at the start of the war of Gog and Magog. His release from prison may happen well before the war of Gog and Magog though and when he is released from prison he is simply surrounded by the one hundred forty kingdoms with no war yet. His full kingship over the entire world is only fully established after the war of Gog and Magog when the enemies of Israel are defeated and his throne thus secured as the world power, not just over Israel.

It is interesting to note that also Avraham (Abraham) was imprisoned for ten years by Nimrod, Josef was imprisoned for twelve years and Moses was imprisoned for ten years.

The wicked of the Gentiles, particularly Amalek (may their memories be erased), the wicked of the Jews and mixed multitude regime (Quasi/pseudo Jews) in power when the Messiah arrives to Israel who commit these crimes against the Messiah are eventually punished for the crimes they commit against him, other than those who repent and compensate him. This suffering and imprisonment only pertains to a real Messiah of any particular generation, not false or failed ones like Bar Cochba (circa 135 AD), Shabetai Tzvi (1600s), and others. The Baal haTanya of Lubavitch (remembrance of the righteous is a blessing), for example, was a real potential righteous Messiah of his generation (1700s) who was imprisoned for the sins of the people. The Malbim (1800s) was also imprisoned by the reform Jews in Germany for speaking out against their heretical movement and wickedness. It must be noted that unlike many false Messiahs, Isaiah 53 says that the real Messiah is imprisoned for no crime of his own; only as a scape goat to atone for and offered up to compensate for the sins of the people. This means that a real Messiah must be sinless, which means that he fully abides by all of the Torah laws with no sin for which he did not repent. He could be a Baal Tshuva (a repentant Jew). Any one who would have an unrepented sin, or disparage the Torah or Rabbis, would therefore not be real Messiah. False Messiahs are most usually identified in that they have a sin. The real Messiah will be falsely accused by his opposition of sins and crimes that he really didn't do. That is how he is framed and imprisoned for no crime of his own as Isaiah 53:8 says.

I would like to note here that someone who fully repented from even the worst sins of his past, even 'abominations', as is the case with a Baal Tshuva (a repentant Jew), could be the Messiah. This is because 'repentance from love' for G-d (in Hebrew called 'Tshuva meiAhava') fully erases any and all sins and even turns them into merits (Reish LaKish in Talmud Bavli Rosh haShana 29). Even though many are familiar with the Zohar that says that 'there is no rectification for spilling semen in vein', and any have fallen into hopelessness from this statement, I would like to say a little known Torah principle that people need to know. Chapter four of Igeret haTshuva from the Likootei Amarim Tanya says that only 'lower repentance' does not rectify the sin of spilling semen in vein, but 'higher repentance' does rectify it. Religious people need to know this to avoid being overwhelmed by guilt and feelings of hopelessness for spilling semen in vein by which many are afflicted. Igeret haTshuva here also means that the Messiah could have been involved in any of the worst sins in his past, even 'abominations', but by 'higher repentance' from love for G-d, he erases them all, turns them in to merits, and goes on to the highest levels of being fully righteous, Holy, and even a 'chariot' who is totally nullified to the will of Hashem, as the Messiah will eventually be when he is most fully developed spiritually.

Isaiah 53 gives more details about the Messiah: '(1) *Who would have believed our report, and to whom was the arm of Hashem revealed? (2) Formerly he grew like a sapling or like a root from arid ground. He had neither form nor grandeur. We saw him but with out such visage that we could desire him. (3) Despised and rejected as inferior by men, a man accustomed to pain and illness, and as one who hides his face from us, despised and we held him of no account* ('The stone that the builders despised has become the cornerstone' (Psalms 118:23) refers to the Messiah according to Rashi on Micah 5:1) *(4) Indeed it was our diseases that he bore and our pains that he endured (5) But he was pained because of our transgressions, crushed because of our iniquities (8) By imprisonment oppression and false judgment was he taken away, and of his generation who considered? For he was cut off out of the land of the living (Talmud Bavli Avoda Zara 5a says that falling into poverty, childlessness, being blind or a leper is considered as being dead), for the transgression of the people, for whom the stroke was due. (10) And Hashem wished to crush him, He made him ill, to see if he would offer his soul as a guilt offering sacrifice, and then he shall see children, he shall prolong his days, and HaShem's purpose shall prosper in his hand. (11) From the toil of his soul he would see, he would be satisfied. By his knowledge did my servant justify the righteous One to the many and did bear their iniquities. (12) Therefore, I will a lot him a portion in public, and with the strong he shall divide spoil, because he poured out his soul to death and with transgressors he was counted, and he bore the sin of many and interceded for the transgressors*'.

'*The immense suffering that the Messiah endures refines him spiritually such that he transcends and overpowers the material powers of the world through Holiness*' (The Maharsha on Talmud Bavli Sanhedrin 98).

Thus, we see that the suffering and imprisonment of the Messiah is part of what he must endure to help him become on the highest of spiritual level that he needs to be. It is part of the plan since creation.

Messiah sits in the Gate of Rome

Let's take a look at the meaning of statement 'the soul of the Messiah sitting in the gate of Rome'.

Talmud Bavli Sanhedrin 98 says "*Rabbi Yehoshua Ben Levi asked Elijah (the prophet)* when *is the Messiah coming? He said Go ask him yourself. Where is he sitting? At the opening of the city. And what are his distinguishing features? He is sitting among the poor suffering of sickness*". The Gaon of Vilna on Sanhedrin 98 says that '*the opening of the city*' means 'the gate of Rome'.

'*The students of Rabbi Yosi Ben Kisma asked: When does the (Messiah) son of David come? And he said … when the gate (of Rome) falls, and it will be built and it will fall and it will be built and will fall and they aren't able to rebuild it until when the son of David comes.* The simple meaning is that "*The soul of the Messiah is waiting in the Garden of Eden (by the gate of Rome) for Rome to fall and enter in the Kingdom of Hashem*" (The Maharsha and Maharal on Sanhedrin 98).

Rashi on Talmud Bavli Sanhedrin 98 says that the '*opening of the city*' is the part of the Garden of Eden which is counterpart to the world and specifically the soul of the Messiah sits in the part of the Garden of Eden that is counterpart to the city where he is bound; i.e. Rome, or the head city of Edom at the time. Rashi also says he is also '*counted amongst the diseased*' as is written in Isaiah 53 and '*he is desecrated by our crimes*' (Isaiah 53) and 'our sickness he bore' (Isaiah 53).

The Ramchal in Gnizei haRamchal Kinath Hashem Tzivaoth, chapter on Moshiah in the Gate of Rome, says that "the Messiah sits in the gate of Rome garmented in husks of spiritual impurity (in Hebrew called 'klipot') and sits imprisoned in prison with out light and influence (see Yalkoot Shimoni on Isaiah 60), suffering of the sick (Isaiah 53) and this is 'and he gave his grave to the wicked' (Isaiah 53) because Moses had to cleanse Israel of the Erev Rav and Moses is bound with them. But the Messiahs (the Messiah son of David and the Messiah son of Josef) must be at the gate of Rome and this is for them burial…. And they need to be in the klipot (that is Hebrew for 'husks of spiritual impurity') of Eisav and Ishmael that rule over Israel and need to be ruled over by the Messiahs. … and they sort out (in Hebrew called a 'biroor') the Holy Sparks (in Hebrew called 'Nitsosoth') that Israel needs… and in their suffering the troubles of Israel are lightened'.

Rav haTzadik Dov Kook Shlita of Tiberius says is quoted to have said that "there are many people in mental hospitals who say that they are the Moshiah. And one of them is.". This means that according to Rav Kook Shlita the Messiah's imprisonment is in a mental hospital. Can you think of a better way to make a man suffer, destroy his life, and disrepute his good name and reputation, than by putting him in a mental hospital? The 'side effects' of psychiatric drugs that prisoners in mental hospitals are forced to take against their will include depression, mania, psychosis and suicide. Many prisoners in mental hospitals say that the psychiatric drugs are like chemical torture and commit suicide. The inmates often refer to mental hospitals as 'concentration camps' and the psychiatrists as 'Nazis' and demons. Would you like to spend time imprisoned in a mental hospital? Would you marry your daughter to such a man? Hire him? Make him a Rabbi in Yeshiva? Make him king? Take him seriously? Believe his claims? Believe his Torah? Respect him? Respect his word? Spread his good name? Be careful about judging people who were in mental hospital who say they were the Moshiah, because "one of them is". If he has the other midoth (traits) of Moshiah that are given in this book then be really careful, because you might just be libeling and pushing off the Moshiah. This is exactly what Satan, Amalek (may their memory be erased), the Erev Rav, enemies of Israel and your own personal yester hara (evil inclination) want you to do and you are playing into their trap. But no more; since you have read this and are now wiser not to do so.

Murder Attempts on the life of the Messiah are Part of his Fate

The Messiah, as a paternal descendant of king David who is kosher, tahor (pure), and fit to be the Davidic king, thus bears the blessings of the Covenant of the House of David, which includes that "the sword shall never cease from your House forever" (II Samuel 12:10). This means that there will be an established pattern of murder attempts on the life of the Messiah, from all of which he will be saved. Even without this blessing one could reason that any person aspiring to kingship and attempting to establish true justice in the world would have opposition that would include murder attempts from criminals attempting to evade prosecution as well as political rivals for the throne. Just this reality alone of the Messiah being an uncompromised crime fighter and establisher of Torah true justice will attract many repeated murder attempts on his life from criminals, including those in power and the establishment, who try to evade prosecution. They may get him in prison at first, but they will eventually get punished though, in this world or the next. One needs merits to get punished in this world instead of the next world because the next world's punishments are far worse; Gehinnom (hell).

In today's terms, this would include murder attempts ranging from local street criminals to individuals in organized crime from the corrupt government establishments who fight against him in order to oppose his ascent to the throne. This includes corrupt government officials, bad police, bad 'judges', criminals inside and outside of prison, Amalek (may their memories be erased), the wicked of the Jews and those of the mixed multitude regime (Quasi/pseudo Jews) in power when the Messiah arrives to Israel. There are also many people in the government and even orgianized crime Mafia who have a vested interest in supporting the Messiahs rule as king in order to prevent the society holding their assets from being destroyed. They will realize that they need him to be king for many personal reasons, like to raise their children in a healthy society and to protect their children from dangers, and see the great benefit to society and themselves where he will be as king. Their children need him for a brighter future which he will be happy to provide. In spite of the opposition, there will be many people who guard him and watch his back since they need him for their society to succeed.

The Messiah is Man of War

'*The Messiah is a man of war*' (Talmud Bavli Sanhedrin 93b). This is literal just a king David was a man of war and the Messiah is his reincarnation (Zohar). Some people misunderstand the meaning of this passage and say that it is not literal but is only a metaphor that means that the Messiah (and king David) fight wars in learning Torah. This is not true. It is true that the Messiah and king David fight wars of Torah, which we already know with out this passage here coming to tell us this, but the passage is coming to tell us something new that we wouldn't know if it was not given here, namely, that the Messiah is a man of military war in the most real sense possible. He knows war in many its aspects and serves best as a military planner.

'A star has issued from Jacob, and a scepter bearer has risen from Israel, and he shall pierce the nobles of Moab, and undermine the children of Seth (shall undermine and defeat Gentile control and manipulation of the Jews). Edom (USA, Russia, Europe; who will be in control of the whole world prior to the rise of the Messiah)) shall be his conquest, and Seir shall be he conquest of his enemies, and Israel will attain success. One from Jacob shall rule and destroy the remnant of the city (an important city, the capitol of Edom, its Rome, according to Rashi. Ramban says 'every city').' (Numbers 24:19). Rashi and other commentators say that these verses refer to the Messiah son of David. Thus here we also see he is a man if war in the literal sense and uses war to conquer Edom and destroy its capitol city.

Rav Nahman of Breslov says that 'prayer is the Messiah's strongest weapon' and that 'he can conquer the world without even firing a shot' (Likootei Moran). Don't be confused because this is almost always misquoted by Breslov Hasidim when they say that Moshiah's *'only'* weapon is prayer and that 'he conquers the world with out firing a shot'. The Messiah is literally 'a man of war' (Talmud Bavli Sanhedrin 93b) who can also uses military force and has others under his command to do so for him so also in that sense he does not have to fire a shot because others do it for him. It may also be possible to conquer the world by spiritual force as per the verse 'not by force, not by power, but by the spirit of Hashem' will he conquer the world. At the same time he can kill people without weapons since he can 'slay the wicked by the spirit of his lips' (Isaiah 11). He has many tools in his tool box which are at his disposal as his choice sees fit.

Although the Messiah can conquer the world '*without even firing a shot*' it seems that he will '*destroy the remnant of the city*' (Numbers) where Rashi says that he destroys the capitol city of Edom (Rome) (Ramban says every city) with methods of war as part of the war of Gog and Magog where Edom attacks Israel and Edom is defeated by G-d and Israel as is written '*Hashem will destroy Edom through his people Israel*' (Ezekiel 25:14). The Ramban says that all of Edom's cities are destroyed, which by reason is the case if the redemption is pushed off to the final end time, when all the cities of Edom are so corrupt that they can not be redeemed and must all be destroyed. This may be what the Zohar is talking about when it says that in the end of days the tribe of Reuven will attack the world. If the redemption is hastened before the final end time by Tshuvah Shleima and kindness, to arouse G-d's Kindness to redeem us, then maybe no cities have to be destroyed.

By defeating Edom, whether hastened peacefully or by war in the final end time, the Messiah conquers the world since Edom was the world power up to that point, and by defeating Edom then the Messiah becomes the new world leader. Thus, the Messiah becomes the king of the world and Israel the new number one world super power through military conquest. Some say that if the Jews and Gentiles repent then the war of Gog and Magog won't have to happen and in that scenario 'he can conquer the world without even firing a shot'.

'At the time of war one must prepare weapons as is the practice of the day and the Holy One, blessed be He, will do that which He wills to do. It is forbidden to depend on a miracle' (Rav Nahman of Breslov Sefer haMidoth Perek Miriva 101). The Messiah knows this Jewish law of war well and practices it, even though he can use his supernatural powers of 'Holiness over the material aspect of nature' and 'slaying the wicked with the spirit of his lips' to fight wars.

The Messiah is a military leader of Israel and will likely lead or contribute significantly to the Jewish and Israeli military systems used in the war of Gog and Magog as well as the other self defense wars of Israel against Ishmael and Paras (Iran). In addition to standard military means, he also uses 'the spirits of his lips' and Torah Holiness to slay the enemies of Israel, such as the demonic war Golem Armilus, a leader of the anti-Semites in the war of Gog and Magog (Isaiah 11 and Yalkoot Shimoni on Isaiah 60) who attempts to establish the throne of Satan (see Midrash in the appendix).

The Messiah is a Musician

'The Messiah is also a musician' (Talmud Bavli Sanhedrin 93b). This is literal just a king David was a musician and the Messiah is his reincarnation (Zohar). Some people misunderstand the meaning of this passage and say that it is not literal but is only a metaphor that means that the Messiah (and king David) 'plays music' in learning Torah. This is not true. Like David who has the same blessing he will be one of the great musicians of his time.

'Rav said: The world was created only for David' (Talmud Bavli Sanhedrin 98b). Rashi says that the world was 'created in the merit of David who was destined to offer many many songs and praises to G-d'. 'Rav Yohanan said: (that the world was created only) for the Messiah' (Talmud Bavli Sanhedrin 98b). Yad Rama says that his 'greatness is supreme'.

More subtle a point than being a man of war, but more obvious if you really understand who king David was, and the power and importance of music and song to Jewish society and world society, and that the Messiah is the reincarnation of king David, is the point that the Messiah is a fine musician like king David was. Like David, who wrote and sung most of the Psalms, he is also likely a great songwriter and singer.

Remember that when king Saul sought a musician to sooth his 'evil spirit' he was brought the young king David to play for him. Obviously this meant that David was one of the best musicians in the land, fit to play for the king. Also, king David was known as the 'pleasing songwriter of Israel' (usually translated 'sweet singer of Israel'- Samuel II 23) who wrote, sung and played most of the Psalms; songs with music and lyrics, and they were the 'hits' of his day. This attests to king David's musical greatness.

The Zohar teaches us that the Messiah is the reincarnated soul of king David with the impregnated soul of Moses. The Messiah will similarly be this level of musician and likely songwriter and possibly singer as well. He may be as great a musician and songwriter as king David was and may help bring back the level of music of king David to modern times, in modern music styles to which the people relate, as king David did. The Messiah will also play the modern version of the harp, the popular string instrument of the day, which today is guitar. The guitar is today's harp. It is written that 'David played music with his hand as he did every day' (Shmuel 18:10). This shows that David was a serious musician who practiced every day. The Messiah will also practice every day, and play it well, very well indeed. If he is made famous his influence on the world through his music will be immense.

Everybody knows the power of music and song. Rabbi Nahman of Breslov says that music can damage a person's soul if it is performed by a sinful person, or be beneficial to a person's soul if the music is played by a moral and ethical person clean of sin. He says that the heretics (apikorseem) of the world can *only* be brought back to Hashem through the playing a musical instrument and singing of a very great righteous Jew (Likootei Moran chapter 3 by Breslov

Research Institute and 'Advice' by Rav haGadol Avraham Greenbaum Shlita chapter on Melody).

Rabbi Perets Ohrbach Shlita of Jerusalem said that 'the Zohar says that the redemption can come through music'. This is supported by Psalm 57:8-9 where king David said 'I will sing I will make music. Awake my soul awake. (with my) Harp and violin I shall awaken the dawn (meaning redemption)'.

The Messiah may have the ability to bring the redemption through music. I am not sure if he has to be famous or not to make this happen. There may be some other spiritual significance to his music that only requires him to play for G-d, and G-d alone. Maybe his music is just for the people who believe in G-d and the redemption is meant exclusively for them as a private party by invitation only; only for the friends of G-d.

Some Torah on the Laws of Music

Everybody knows the power of music. It can make you feel happy, sad, angry, passive, in a rush, relaxed, holy to Hashem, depraved, passionate, depressed, or otherwise. Rashi in Sotah 49b says that the tambourine stimulates excessive joy. People use mood music to get them in the mood for love and armies use music to get their troops in the mood for war. The great and Holy king David and his great great grandson Moshiah ben David are great musicians, singers and songwriters.

The Levieem (Jewish people from the tribe of Levi) who are the ministers to the priests (in Hebrew called 'Cohaneem') in the Beit HaMikdash spent great time, cost and effort composing, practicing and performing musical and choral works in order to get people into the mood of Holiness needed to connect to Hashem and worship Him in His Holy Temple. They had the best talent. I know this because I have witnessed that today Jewish musicians who are Levieem are still among the best when trained and equipped properly. You can see one of them on YouTube called Michael Avraham HaLevi with his song 'Free at Last'. The Sanhedrin heard this music as they sat near the Temple where they learned Torah and made critical Torah judgments for Israel all day long. People who worship the 'other side' also have their music that gets them into the mood. Music is a power that is described by the Torah as the 'Quill of the Heart'; that which sets the background setting to our mood which in turn affects our behavior, and how well we live by and perform Mitzvoth and learn

Torah, or otherwise. There is great investigation and divergence of opinions in the Jewish community regarding what is Jewish music.

The Mishna Brura in chapter 260 brings down that during the times of the Hoorban Beit HaMikdash (destruction of the Temple) it is forbidden to listen to music that makes one happy, nor to listen to music with alcoholic beverages on the table, other than at a simha (a Bar Mitzvah, wedding, sioom or other Mitzva festivity) occasion. The following passages are the sources for some of these laws: Talmud Bavli Sota 48a says that '*From the time the Sanhedrin ceased to function song was abolished (prohibited) from wine feasts*'. Talmud Bavli Gitten 7a says that '*How do we know that music (including song) is prohibited? (as it is written) 'With music they shall not drink wine*'". Rashi says that this refers to music at parties. Tosfos says that it refers to other forms of indulgent music such as music during waking or going to sleep. Artscroll note 24 on Sota 48a3 says that 'The Gemora Talmud Bavli Gitten 7a refers to playing musical instruments or singing. This applies only when there are lyrics that glorify beauty or express love between friends. Singing lyrics that praise G-d or commemorate His kindness are permissible. It is permissible to sing such songs at Mitzva parties or weddings (Rif, Rambam, Hilchot Taaniot 5:14, Meiri, Beer Sheva)'.

The Gidoleem (the biggest Rabbis) agree with this as psak halacha limaase (the Torah law as it stands for practical application) of forbidding listening to music during the times of destruction of the Temple. There are heterim (permissions) for music if some one is 'nervous' or depressed (a growing problem in our times- Handel's water music was written for the king of England and his depression problem) and with out it he cant serve Hashem, for kiruv (bringing people closer to Hashem), getting someone in the mood to serve Hashem or stop sinning, or for pikuah nefesh (saving someone's life) in taking someone out of depression (which I have encountered with my music with mental patients in hospitals). My friend, Michael Avraham HaLevi, who is a Levi, is the best singer songwriter guitarist I have ever heard and his music and song defiantly connects me to Hashem. I can see why the Levieem played and sung in the Beit HaMikdash (Temple)-it connects people to Hashem and helps bring people closer to Holiness. That is my observation.

Rav Nahman of Breslov in Likootei Mohoran chapter three and in Likootei Yiotz chapter on Mangina says that (paraphrased) 'music comes from either a bad bird or a good bird. If someone listens to the music or performance of an artist who is motivated by money or fame then his music or song is damaging to the listener spiritually. Someone is only allowed to listen to the music and performance of someone who is hagoon (meaning free of transgression, defined in the Mishna Brura on Or Chaim chapter 53 on shaliah tziboor (prayer leader). This means that a shaliah tziboor must be at least a bainoni (intermediate level person as opposed to righteous or wicked) by the Tanyas' definition of bainoni). If someone listens to the music of a Tzadik then he can be spiritually elevated closer to Hashem. Only a great Tzadik has the power to bring back the apikorseem (heretics) to Hashem through music and music may be the only way to do that'. Listening to the music of the impure is equivalent to one connecting his soul to a conduit of impurity (has viShalom-Heaven Forbid) and listening to the music of the pure of transgression helps make one pure and connects him to G-d.

The Tanach (the Bible in the original Hebrew) says that the prophets used to play music in order to get them into prophetic states. Music prepares a person to be a vessel to receive prophesy. This makes sense since Rav Nahman of Breslov says that both music and prophesy come through the spiritual channels of Hod and Netzach. The music arouses the channels to receive prophesy. Its not a coincidence that David haMelech was a fine musician, maybe one of the best in the land of Israel then, since king Saul specifically called for him to get rid of his 'evil spirit'. David was the righteous musician playing music to get rid of Saul's evil spirits that were plaguing him. The right music at the right time hits the spot like no drug can. Again, the king of England hired Handel to write music to cure him of his depression too, just as king Saul did.

Greece and many recent governments knew the power and influence of music on people and therefore regulated the music that they allowed to play in their society. The Russian government recognized the power and influence of music over people, and thus, until recently, had laws (that they actually enforced) prohibiting certain types of music, such as Jazz and Rock. I know of musicians who went to prison in Russia for playing rock music and jazz. Many types of American rock music, especially heavy metal, are said by some to make people aggressive and foster immorally and depression. There are mixed opinions on this matter and one Rabbi who is a great musician who I know said that music has a mixture of good and evil.

Another interesting point in Jewish law regarding to music is derived from the following source. Likootei Maharal (cited by Magen Avraham to Orach

Chaim 560:10) rules that '*it is forbidden to appropriate scriptural verses for ones own songs*'. '*Scriptural verses*' means the five books of Moses. When this happens the 'Torah dons a sackcloth' and says to G-d: 'Your children have treated me like a lute on which scoffers play'.(Talmud Bavli Sanhedrin 101a). The Mishna Brura Orach Chaim 560:3 further clarifies this point. This seems to be the halacha (Torah law) at this point until further clarification.

Furthermore, Talmud Bavli Sanhedrin 101a says '*One who recites a verse from Song of Songs and makes it into a type of melody, and one who recites a scriptural verse in a banquet hall at an inappropriate time (Rashi says this mean for the amusement of his guests over a cup of wine. Maharsha says this means a dinner that is not for a religious reason), brings evil to the world for it is like covering the Torah with a sackcloth that stands before the Holy One, blessed be He, and says: 'Master of the universe! Your children have treated me like a lute upon which scoffers play*'.

The Gidoleem and most Baalei Tshuva who have grown up with popular Western music don't like what people call today 'Jewish music'. When I am asked 'what is Jewish music?' the only two answers that I can think of that I like are: 1) The Holy ancient trop (taamim) melodies of the scripture and 2) 'music that brings people closer to G-d' as said by the famous Jewish singer songwriter Abby Rotenberg from Kew Gardens, NY. Whether a certain type, artist, band or performance of music brings you closer to G-d is a matter of your own personal reaction to that music. I don't think its objective so it's hard to generalize what brings people closer to G-d. For some people, certain heavy metal brings them closer and for others it sounds evil. Some people like the guitar to bring them closer and one person I know says that the guitar arouses immorality.

The 'Signs and Wonders' of the Messiah

"*The Messiah will have 'signs and wonders'*" (Rambam in Igeress Teman). The Rambam also says that "*The Messiah does not have to do 'signs and wonders' and make miracles in the world*" (Rambam laws of kings chapter 12). How do we reconcile these two apparently contradictory statements?

In chapter twelve of laws of kings the Rambam says that Hashem's direct Divine Providence over the world during the time of Moshiah will be in accordance with the laws of nature. The last stage of the redemption period which brings the resurrection of the dead (Zohar I 139a) may or may not be considered a 'miracle' in accordance with the laws of nature or not in accordance with the laws of nature depending on how you define 'miracle'. Therefore, according to the Rambam, the 'signs and wonders' to which the Rambam refers and *will indicate* who might be the Messiah, but *not prove* who is the Messiah, are not supernatural miracles, are in accordance with the laws of nature, and constitute acts and deeds that show that Hashem is with Him. The Rambam also comes to tell us that although there will be signs and wonders associated with the Messiah, that performing miracles does not prove that one is the Messiah, since this could be the feat of a mere magician, scientist or illusionist.

We must differentiate the distinction in our minds that the redemption will demonstrate Hashem's direct Divine providence over the world, but does not necessarily require nor imply that supernatural miracles not in accordance with the laws of nature will occur, and certainly does not require the Messiah to perform such supernatural miracles in the initial stages of the redemption before or after he becomes king of Israel.

The "Names" of the Messiah

"*Before the world was created the name of the Messiah was created* (Talmud Bavli Nedarim 39b)".

Midrash Zeira on Eicha says that the name of the Messiah that was born on the ninth of Av during the destruction of the Temple was Menahem. This shows that this was the Messiah's name in that generation. 'Sefer Zerubabel' also says that the name of the Messiah, predicted for the year 1060, was 'Menahem ben Amiel'. Talmud Bavli Pesachim Chapter one says his name is Menahem. Yalkoot Shimoni on Isaiah 60 says his name is Ephraim. Talmud Bavli Sanhedrin 98b says that his name is either Shiloh, Yinon, Haninah, Menahem son of Hezkia, or Hivarah leper of the House of Rebbe. So what is his name?

The Talmud Bavli Sanhedrin 98b discusses the names of the Messiah. This is an interesting discussion in the Talmud because even in modern times some people like to think that they themselves or their Rabbi who has one of the names of the Messiah, particularly the name Menahem, is the Messiah, and they look for scriptural sources to justify their belief.

The Talmud Bavli Sanhedrin 98b asks "*What is the name (of the Messiah Son of David)? The school of Rabbi Sheila says that Shiloh is his name as it is written 'Until Shiloh comes'.* This is from Genesis 49:10 meaning 'final peace' as referring to the Messiah, but also meaning, from other contexts, a gift to him; meaning that the Messiah will receive gifts from people later in his life from people who want to appease him. *The school of Rabbi Yannai says that his name will be Yinon as it is written 'may his name be forever before the sun as Yinon'.* 'Yinon' here means authority, majesty, from psalm 72 which talks about the king Solomon establishing justice in the land, protecting the rights of the poor. Verse 72:17 talks about foreign peoples giving homage to him and his name will be always considered 'Yinon' and all the peoples will bless themselves in his name in praise of him". *The school of Rabbi Haninah says that if it is Haninah as it is written 'where I will not give you Haninah'* This is taken from Jeremiah 16:13 which speaks about the Jewish people being cast into a foreign land where the idols they worship there will not give them 'Haninah'. 'Haninah' here means grace or mercy. Mercy means not meeting out punishment even when it is deserved; implying that the Messiah will have mercy on some people, in the sense that he won't always meet out punishment, even when it is deserved. *The school of Rabbi Menahem says that Menahem son of Hezkia is his name as it is written 'because it is far from me Menahem to restore my soul' (*This is taken from Lamentations 1:16 which talks about crying many tears without 'Menahem' to restore the soul. 'Menahem' means comfort; meaning that the Messiah will comfort some people, or, that he will be in situations in life, as per Isaiah 53, where there will be no comfort to restore his soul.*). The Rabbis say that Hivarah, leper of the House of Rebbe, is his name, as it is written 'he bore our illnesses and our pains, he carried them, but we counted him as plagued and smitten by G-d and oppressed'* (referring to Isaiah 53:4, which as the remainder of Isaiah 53 says, that the Messiah will suffer immensely as an oppressed scapegoat greatly disregarded and despised by society, yet suffering for their sins and atoning for them, as part of his own personal test of faith in Hashem)".

Talmud Bavli Sanhedrin 98b continues: "*Rav Nahman said: If the Messiah is among the living he is like me as it is said 'and their prince shall be one of their own and their ruler shall emerge from their midst' (Jeremiah 30:21). Rav said: 'If the Messiah is among the living, he is like our Holy Rabbi Yehuda (the president of the Sanhedrin circa 250 AD). If he is among the dead, he is like Daniel (the prophet chapter 10:11 is called) the greatly beloved. Rav Yehuda said in the name of Rav: 'The Holy One, blessed be He, in the future will raise for the Jewish people another David' as it is said 'They will serve Hashem their G-d and David their king, whom I will raise up for them' (Jeremiah 30:9).... And it is said 'My servant David will be a prince over them for ever' (Ezekiel 37:25).*" The Zohar resolves this by saying that the Messiah is the reincarnation of king David himself.

According to the Maharsha and Maharal, Netzach Yisrael, chapter 41, "*the many names of the Messiah means that each of these attributes will be found in the Messiah and the character (*and root soul*) of Messiah encompasses the virtues of every human being. Hence, one who studies Messiah will naturally be drawn to seeing his own personality. For this reason, when the sages attempted to determine the Messiahs name, they concluded that it was the same as their own. There is no dispute whatsoever between these sages. Each one is simply stressing the aspect of the Messiah personality with which he is most familiar.*" From logic, we would have to deduce that this discussion in the Talmud of what is the name of the Messiah is really a parable to show some of the multi-dimensional attributes of Messiah son of David. It doesn't mean necessarily that these will be one of his names, other wise the Talmud would contradict itself, and the Talmud never does that on the deeper level of understanding with all specifics of the case brought to the upper level from the hidden. As Moses had many names, the Messiah may have many names, possibly in different situations of his life; i.e. Yinon (majesty, authority) when he is king and Hivarah, leper of the House of Rebbe, when he is suffering as an oppressed imprisoned scapegoat. Moses had many names. Being from Edom, especially if he was born an assimilated Jew, the Messiah may likely have an Edomite name as well as a Hebrew name. As a musician he may have a stage name. As a man of war he may have a nick name as they often have in the military.

He may have many names for the many purposes that he serves. The particular name may reflect the need of the generation and his relationship to it.

Obviously, when he is a child in the highly heretical, anti-Semitic Edom, he will have far less majesty and authority than when he is a king in Israel, although he may have some degree of these even while still a child in Edom, depending on how well people there merit to get to know him on a personal day to day basis and are able to see his hidden greatness cloaked in humility and disregard of the false rules of modern society. When people are mocking him and deriding him in prison he will not have much majesty at that time.

In conclusion, we don't know what the name of the Messiah will be. It is a hidden secret until the time of redemption comes and is then revealed.

The Messiah can make mistakes

Mose hit the rock instated of talking to it. Avraham questioned Hashem's promise to give him the land of Israel. David did not sin with Bat Sheva but was viwed as a mistale for aman on hos level.

King Hezekiah was almost the Messiah in his time. Talmud Bavli Sanhedrin 12b shows that the sages of his generation believed that king Hezekiah erred in intercalculating an extra month into the Jewish year in order to allow for Jews to offer Passover sacrifices while still in a state of spiritual impurity. The Talmud teaches us that this error was *not* the reason why he was not the Messiah, but because he *failed to sing praise to Hashem* when Hashem defeated Sanchereb's siege of Jerusalem and miraculously killed 180,000 of their soldiers by a plague while king Hezekiah lay in bed trusting that HaShem will defeat them. Talmud Bavli Brachot 10 also shows three things that king Hezekiah did that he sages did not agree with, thus thinking he was mistaken. This shows that the Messiah is not perfect and can make mistakes, even in Torah, according to the sages, who we hold are always right. How can that be if Rambam says that he will be wiser than king Solomon, the wisest man in the history of the world? Did not Kings 10-11 say that Hashem thought that what king Solomon did was an abomination? Is that not a mistake? Did not Moses strike the rock instead of speaking to it? Is that not a mistake? Did not king Saul fail to heed Hashem and kill all the Amalekites? All throughout the Torah even the greatest leaders made mistakes. Why should the Messiah be any different?

This tells us that even the wisest man can make mistakes and that not all the wise Rabbis of the generation will necessarily acquiesce to the Moshiah and view his actions on every issue as being totally correct. Remember that since there is no Sanhedrin before the Messiah comes that the true halacha cannot be known (Rav Yosef Kara-the Shulhan Aruch book of halacha) so therefore who can judge what is correct in some cases.

There are different definitions of what is 'wise' and people don't always view the truly most wise as wise. For example some may mistake impressive speakers with articulate vocabularies and smooth talkers as wise but slow talkers as not wise. Ethics of the Fathers asks: 'Who is wise? He who learns from others.'. This means that the Messiah may also be the wisest because he will learn from everyone. This may make him appear not wise to some people if they see him asking questions to people to learn their wisdom, but in truth the humble Messiah will be among the wisest Rabbis but cloaked in humility so that only those wise enough to appreciate him will be able to see his wisdom. As it often is, many of a wise man's simple deep truths may be regarded as the foolishness of an imbecile. The Zohar says that during the redemption people will be confused, won't see that it is the redemption, and that only the truly wise will circle themselves around the Messiah.

The Messiah can make mistakes and also be viewed to make mistakes when he has not.

The Messiah will have some kind of a speech impairment or difficulty speaking

Similar to Moses who had a speech impairment or some kind of difficulty in speaking and needed his brother Aaron to speak for him (Exodus Shmoth 4:10) the Messiah will also have some kind of a speech impairment or difficulty speaking (in Hebrew called "arel sfatayeem" meaning 'uncircumcised of lips') (The Arizal).

The Messiah comes from Edom which is the West and most likely America. Many foreigners and most Americans who emigrated to Israel have difficulty speaking Hebrew and I question if this could be considered to be the Messiah's speech impairment; the accent of a foreigner, especially an American foreigner, who has the heaviest accent and often can not be understood by native born Israelis. Maybe it is some kind of other form of speech impairment or difficulty speaking. The term "Arel sfatayeem" means uncircumcised of lips which literally means a speech impediment regarding the lips which would include any vowel or consonant aided in expression by the lips. It could be a heavy 'mem' for instance. Maybe "Arel sfatayeem" means a general speech deficiency not just wit the lips but for instance with impure vowels known as diphthongs or lack thereof as may be the proper way of speech. In any case it is not possible to judge what is the proper language of Hebrew today since the speech has been lost in the exile and the traditions which we have today may be far from the real original Hebrew spoken in the Garden of Eden. If he is from America maybe he also is speech impaired in English. British people who many view as the true kingship of Edom may certainly view him as such even in English.

It is difficult to understand how the Messiah will be a world leader and king of Israel with a speech impairment since most leaders gain and maintain their popular support by their powers of speech. This is yet another wonder of the Messiah. Maybe the wise Rabbis around him will interface for him to the public to disseminate his wisdom.

Arizal says the Messiah will first be revealed in Tsfat

The Arizal is known as the biggest or one of the biggest Kabbalists in Jewish history. He made his name in Tsfat (also spelled Safed) some five hundred years ago and since then Tsfat has been known as the city of Kabbala (largely based on a mystical book called 'the Zohar' and other writings).

'*For Hashem selected Zion. He desired it for His dwelling place*' (Psalms 132:13). From this passage the Arizal saw in the Hebrew word for 'desired' that the Atbash Gematria for 'desired' spells 'Tsfat' which he understood means that the Messiah will be first revealed in Tsfat. I learned this pasuk while living in Tsfat from 2006 to 2009 where I recorded my CD "Rise and Shine" in a cave there.

Tsfat's Masonic lodge where I was invited to attend meetings is interestingly called 'the Zohar lounge'.

The Messiah Builds the Third Temple; it doesn't 'float down from the sky'

Rambam in Laws of kings chapter 12 says that 'In the days of the Messiah the natural order of the world doesn't change. There will be nothing new in the creation and the world will act in its normal natural order'. This tells us that miracles that go against the laws of nature don't occur during the Redemption.

A common misconception is that the third Temple 'floats down from the sky'. This is learned from Rashi on Talmud Bavli Succa 41, which he learns from the Midrash. This understanding contradicts Rashi on Talmud Bavli Succa 52b that says that "The Messiah must be a craftsman since he will build the Temple". Rashi doesn't contradict himself so we must resolve the apparent contradiction in our understanding of Rashi. Rambam also holds that the

Temple will be built by the Messiah (laws of kings chapter 11:4). Therefore it seems the Temple is built and does not float down from the sky. How do we explain the understanding of Rashi on Succa 41?

To resolve this apparent contradiction in our understanding of Rashi and the Talmud, Aruch La Ner suggests that the Messiah will build the physical body of the Temple, but its spiritual counterpart will descend from heaven and inhabit it, just as the soul enters the body. This means that the Messiah will understand architecture and engineering, at least on a managerial level as king, if not as an engineer himself, to be able to build the Temple at the quality level that will be required.

We also learn that although it is a commandment for all Jews in every generation to build the Third Temple (Rambam, laws of the Temple), and that a generation that doesn't build the Temple is like a generation that destroys the Temple (Talmud), and there are Jews who would like to do this today, the Third Temple can only really be built by the Messiah as Rashi (Talmud Bavli Sanhedrin 20) and Rambam (laws of kings chapter one) both agree that the king from the royal House of David (the Messiah in this case) has to come back into power in order in order to build the Temple. They both say (Talmud Bavli Sanhedrin 20, laws of kings chapter one) that upon coming into the land (the Rabbis say that this is when the majority of Jews are in the land), first we do the Mitzvah of appointing a king (Deuteronomy 17:14), then the Mitzvah of eradicating Amalek (Deuteronomy 25:19- may their memories be erased), then the king Messiah build the Temple. Furthermore, "the 'Urim and Toomim' of the High Priest's breast plate wont return until the Messiah comes" (Rashi on Talmud Bavli Kiddushin 69b, Rashbam on Talmud Bavli Baba Batra 133b) so we need the Moshiah for a fully operational Temple.

The Temple cleanses the spiritual impurity from the world that is blocking people from achieving their full blessing and potential in life and having a direct clear connection to G-d. The sacrifices in the Temple atone for our sins and bring great blessing and forgiveness for our sins from G-d. The Rabbis say that if the Jewish people and Gentiles knew the great blessing that the Temple brings, they would see to it that the Temple would be built today.

The Temple is built by the Messiah. It doesn't 'float down from the sky'.

The Rambam's 'halcahic' definition of the Messiah

"And if their stands a king from the House of David, meditated in Torah and occupied with Mitzvahs as David his father was according to the written and oral Torah (the Talmud), and compels all of Israel to walk by it and to strengthen it's minutiae, and to fight Hashem's wars, then it is an established pattern (in Hebrew called 'chezkat haMoshiah') *that he is the Messiah. If this done, and he succeeded and was victorious on the nations that are around him (the war of Gog and Magog), and he built the Temple in it's place, and he gathered in the pushed out ones* (Hebrew: Needhei) *of Israel, then he is definitely* (Hebrew: 'Vadai Moshiah') *the Messiah*". This is the common source among orthodox Jews that define their impression of what the Messiah is, largely disseminated in the merit of the Lubavitch Rebbe (memory of the righteous is for blessing), as per Rambam Mishne Torah, Judges, Laws of kings and their wars, Chapter 11:4. This is accepted as the Jewish law (Halacha) that defines most succinctly who is the Messiah. The details in this book that cover aspects of the Messiah that Rambam does not cover gives a more comprehensive and detailed halacha than the Rambam had done. The book also details the important issue of how to identify the Messiah before he becomes king; which the Rambam did not do. This is in the next chapter titles "Pre-Kingship Character Traits that identify the Messiah before he becomes king".

Rambam chapters laws of kings 11-12 says that the main difference between our times and the days of the Messiah is that the Jewish people won't be subjugated by the Gentiles anymore (this Rambam is based on Talmud Bavli Brachot 34b).

Note that Rambam's laws of kings and their wars, chapters 11 and 12, which discuss the Messiah, does not even *specifically* mention the issue of Messiah's establishing true justice and righteousness in the world, which is the central theme of the Messiah in the Prophets. The theme of enforcing justice though is included in the Rambam's statement *'compels all of Israel to walk by it (the Torah) and to strengthen it's minutiae, and to fight Hashem's wars'*. Rambam's commentary on the Messiah includes a discussion of Rabbi Akiva's support of the potential Messiah Bar Cochba (circa 135 AD). There he holds that if a person dies (dying includes being killed since being killed is also a form of death), then he cannot be the Messiah. This is *part* of the reason why Jeshu of Nazareth (see chapter on Christianity for more details) and the Rebbe of Lubavitch were not the Messiah, are not the Messiah, and will never be the Messiah. I hope this book corrects people in thinking that a dead man can be the Messiah and brings people to the real potential Messiah of the generation, who ever he is or may potentially be. Many ignorant and delusional people claim that certain people, who don't live by the Torah, living and dead, including themselves, are the Messiah. This book proves they are not, and shows who could potentially be the Messiah; who real most likely or potential Messiahs of the generation. This is one reason this book is needed to be learned by everyone. We are getting closer to receiving him and need to know how to identify him.

Pre-Kingship Traits that identify the Messiah before he becomes king

Rambam says in Hilchot Melcahim 11:4 that the son of David is established as having an 'established pattern' ('Chezkat haMoshiah') of being the Moshiah if he compels *all of Israel* to live by the Torah, and that he is '*definitely the Moshiah' if he gathers in the exiles and builds the Temple*. Both Rambam (Hilchot Melachim ch. one) and Rashi (Talmud Bavli Sanhedrin 20) agree that only a king from the House of David will build the third Temple, which means that the Moshiah must be appointed king before he builds the Temple. If we follow the chronological order of events of the redemption process verse by verse in Ezekiel, Ezekiel verse 37:24 says that Moshiah Ben David will become king at that point in the Redemption process before he builds the Temple (Ezekiel 40). A Sanhedrin and a prophet must appoint the Moshiah king (Rambam laws of kings 1:3). As the chapter 'Unrealistic Expectations of the Moshiah' explains, the Moshiah can only achieve an 'established pattern' of being the Moshiah by compelling the Jewish people to live by the Torah or gather the exiles and build the Temple to be 'defiantly the Messiah' if he is first made king of Israel by the Sanhedrin and a prophet. This prophet need not necessarily be Elijah the prophet as the chapters on Elijah the prophet explain. As reason shows, the Messiah must first be made king in order to compel the Jewish people to love by Torah because in order to compel the Jewish people to live by the Torah he must have total control of the media, music industry, educations system, economy and judicial system first in Israel and also eventually the world. In today's terms this means that the leader of Edom, the USA, and eventually the

West, must back the Moshiah in fulfillment of the blessing 'the older Eisav will serve the younger Israel' (Genesis 25). May this be part of the hastened Moshiah in our time; Eisav USA serving the Moshiah who will save them and be their benevolent and righteous king that they always wanted to govern them for their own good. As two American senators came out in 2014 and said: "America is going down the tubes. Only the Jewish Messiah can save us", this shows that even leaders of Edom want the Moshiah since they recognize that America will fall unless the Moshiah saves them.

For this reality to manifest, a question arises. How do we identify who the real Moshiah of the generation really is in order to appoint him king before he establishes himself as an 'established pattern' of being the Moshiah and later '*definitely the Moshiah' by* building the Temple? There are at least two ways to identify the Moshiah. How is this person going to be identified as the Messiah before he becomes king if he has not yet built the Temple? According to the Rambam this is the only way to know for sure that he is the Messiah. One way is through logic. Another way is through Ruah HaKodesh and eventually prophesy.

The Talmud Bavli Baba Batra 12 says that since the destruction of the first Temple, prophesy was taken away from the prophets (who were not wise-Rashi) and was given to wise (prophets), odd balls (the definition of 'odd ball' is an unresolved discussion in Talmud Bavli Megilla 3b) and children. Hevroota on Talmud Bavli Baba Batra 12a, citing the Ramban and Chasam Sofer, says that this form of prophesy is prophesy through Ruah HaKodesh (Holy Spirit) to know the truth through the vessel of wisdom in our mind; not full blown prophesy of 'Hazon vi mareh' (pictures and visions) and 'hida' (riddle) that the Bible prophets such as Isaiah, Ezekiel and Jeremiah had. This is an interesting statement since we know from the Arizal and Rav Nahman of Breslov that prophesy comes through the sfeeroth of hod and netzach and ruah HaKodesh comes through malchoot. Ramban here also says that prophesy can be given to the pious who are not sagaciously wise, as in the case of prophesy being given as an agency like Yona the prophet. Around the same time that the Sanhedrin of the Knesset Gidola took away the evil inclination for idol worship (Talmud Bavli Yoma 69b), the last prophets, Haggai, Zechariah and Malachi, all died in a single month in 313 BCE (Rabbi Arie Kaplan's book called the 'handbook of Jewish thought' chapter on Inspiration). That is when prophesy is said to have ended. In Igereth Teman, page 174, the Rambam says that prophesy returns before the Moshiah. Some say that this prophesy has returned to Israel by 2005. I believe this. This prophesy that returns is full blown prophesy of 'Hazon vi mareh' (picture and vision). Although there is prophesy today, one is only obligated to believe and listen to a person with prophesy on the condition that he has proven himself to the Sanhedrin (Rabbi Arie Kaplan's book called the 'handbook of Jewish thought' chapter on Inspiration) and only at that point can be called 'a prophet'. 'A Prophet' is obligated to report his prophesies to the Sanhedrin, be recorded by a scribe, and the people must listen to him or they will be punished by G-d, the One who gave him the messages he received (ibid). Ruah HaKodesh (Holy Spirit) is another way that the Messiah can be identified. There are people with Ruah HaKodesh in our times. I know this. For a thorough coverage of the history and principles of prophesy and Ruah HaKodesh from ancient times to our times see Rabbi Arie Kaplan's book called the 'handbook of Jewish thought'.

For those of us who don't yet have prophesy or Ruah haKodesh, let's take the logical approach. Maybe we will know by both logic and prophesy supporting one another by the Rabbis of the generation. If a Sanhedrin is made prior to the Moshiah (as is implied by Talmud Bavli Eruvin 43b), then the Sanhedrin and a prophet, maybe Elijah the prophet, will have the wisdom or prophesy to help identify the Moshiah.

How do we identify the Moshiah as the Moshiah before he becomes king or builds the Temple? First of all, if someone comes along and compels the Jewish people to live by the Torah that is enough of an established pattern of being the Messiah to anoint him king. That has not ever happened other than by king Hezkiahoo. If someone doesn't compel the Jewish people to live by the Torah, then we can look at the identifying traits of the Messiah to make him king.

Since it is unlikely that a Jew will be able to compel the Jewish people, *including the youth*, to live by the Torah; even if he were the wealthiest and most powerful man in the world, president of the US, Chief Rabbi, head of the education system and all media programming; then the way to identify the Messiah is to look at his identifying traits to see if he is really the Messiah. This book gives these identifying traits that are needed to know in order to identify who the Messiah of the generation really is. This is the main purpose of this book. These identifying traits qualify him to be the Moshiah before he becomes king or builds the Temple. Any person with these traits identified in this book with all valid Torah sources could be the potential Messiah of the generation, and any person who does not have these traits is most likely not the Messiah of the generation, unless he develops these traits later. That is how the Messiah can be identified before he is anointed king and builds the Temple. Just to recap these traits include being a man of war, a musician, handsome, accomplished, understanding of matters, Hashem is with him, from Edom, imprisoned as a scapegoat, and artesian to build the Temple to list the main traits. There are few people in any generation who fulfill these traits so identifying who is the Messiah won't be difficult once you have found someone with these traits. The requirement of being a son of David can only be known through prophesy or a reliable paternal lineage to a Rabbi such as the Baal haTanya who can be relied upon that he is being truthful that he claimed to be son of David, and thus any son of a son of his is also a son of David. By these criterions, we narrow the list of possibilities to only a very limited number of possibilities in any generation.

People may be making a *mistake* in thinking that the Messiah must be as 'wise as Solomon' and 'great a prophet as Moses', as Rambam (Hilchot Tshuva 9:2) describes the Messiah, before he is made king. But on the other hand, maybe this is a good criterion to judge who can be the Messiah.

Since a king must be established by the Sanhedrin of seventy elders and a prophet (Rambam laws of kings chapter one section three), and Bavli Eruvin 43b says that there is a Sanhedrin before Elijah the prophet arrives, we see that there must be a Sanhedrin to receive the Moshiah as well as Elijah so as to give a reliable and authoritative judgment that these people are who they really are. As of today there is no *real* Sanhedrin today to do this, since the Gidoleem have not given their consent and the current New Sanhedrin has not received the Moshiah's consent or Elijah's smeecha much less recognized the potential Messiah of the generation as the head or at least the king of Israel. See more about this in the chapters on Sanhedrin.

List of Identifying Personal Traits of the Moshiah son of David

The Messiah has many traits which can help one identify who he is even before he is made king. It can be useful to know these traits so that he can be identified as being the most likely person in the generation who could be the potential Messiah and can made king before people know for sure that he is the Messiah which according to Rambam is only when he compels the Jewish people to live by the Torah and builds the third Temple. The traits of the Messiah that the Torah gives is an unlikely combination of traits which are extremely rare, if not impossible, to find in any one person. Most people in our generation don't know even one person with even half of these traits. Therefore, finding him is easy if one looks for his traits in one person.

1) The Moshiah is a Jew raised in Edom (i.e. modern Rome which can be identified as the most dominant power in the world at the time. i.e. now the West and in particular the USA) (Midrash Parshat Shemot 1:26 mivooar). The Moshiah comes from Edom to the land of Israel after three major wars of the sons of Ishmael against Israel (Yalkoot Shimoni Isaiah chapter 21). These wars seem to be the 1948 war of independence, the 1967 sic day war and the 1973 Yom Kippur war. This would mean that he comes after 1973. Israel's famous Kabalist Rav Yitzchak Kadoori (the remembrance of the righteous is a blessing) said that the Moshiah had already come to Jerusalem (from Edom) by the year 2001 (quoted in Yidiot Ahronoth). If this is true, then this means that the Jewish peoples' Torah, good deeds, misirath nefesh (self sacrifice) and Tshuvah (repentance) are succeeding to redeem Israel and the hidden potential Moshiah of the generation has come to Israel and needs to be identified and make king.
2) Similar to Moses who had a speech impairment or some kind of difficulty in speaking and needed his brother Aaron to speak for him (Exodus Shmoth 4:10), the Messiah also will have some kind of a speech impairment or difficulty speaking (in Hebrew called "arel sfatayeem") (The Arizal). Maybe this is a heavy accent in Hebrew since he comes from Edom.
3) The Moshiah is handsome (Talmud Bavli Sanhedrin 93b). The literal meaning holds true as it did for king David as we learn from Samuel 16:18. Some people like to distort the meaning of this as merely being a Mashal (Metaphor) to his Torah learning but they are mistaken. The literal meaning holds true. Be careful of not being mislead by them. This is one of the points of Talmud that is learned incorrectly in our generation. In addition to the literal meaning, Radak says that this means that he is handsome and has great character traits. The Ralbag

says that he is handsome so that he is more fitting to come into the chambers of the king.

4) The Moshiah is a musician (Talmud Bavli Sanhedrin 93b). Again, the literal meaning holds true as it did for king David as we learn from Samuel 16:18. See the section on the Messiah being a musician for more details. Some people like to distort the meaning of this as merely being a Mashal (Metaphor) to his Torah learning but they are mistaken. The literal meaning holds true. Be careful of not being mislead by them. This is one of the points of Talmud that is learned incorrectly in our generation. In addition to the literal meaning, the Malbim says that this means that he knows the wisdom of music completely.

   Since David was a top musician and also had this blessing it means that the Messiah is also a top musician of his time (not just an amateur level) as was David, fit to play for the king as he did for king Saul to sooth his soul from an evil spirit.

5) The Moshiah is a man of war (Talmud Bavli Sanhedrin 93b). Again, the literal meaning holds true as it did for king David as we learn from Samuel 16:18. See the section on the Messiah being a man of war for more details. Some people like to distort the meaning of this as merely being a Mashal (Metaphor) to his Torah learning but they are mistaken. The literal meaning holds true. Be careful of not being mislead by them. This is one of the points of Talmud that is learned incorrectly in our generation. Since king David also had this blessing it means that the Messiah is a top military talent of some sort as was king David. Radak says that this means that he knows matters of war and he is practiced in them. Malbim says that this means that he knows stratagems of war and occupies himself with them. Ralbag says that he is one who knows how to invent stratagems to defeat his enemies. He is some how connected to the military of the Jewish people, in some way, either as a soldier, leader, planner, intelligence, scientist, etc.. As a king he is probably a planner. He could also be involved with the military parts of Edom that serve Israel, since he comes from Edom. As king he will need to be a man of war in order to help lead Israel to victory over her enemies; especially against Ishmael ('the Arabs'), Paras (Iran) and in the war of Gog and Magog. The Torah law and

understanding of a Jew's obligation and practice to go to war is best expressed by being a 'kam taase' when learning Torah and no one else can do it (Shulhan Aruch hilchot Talmud Torah) and by the statement: *'At the time of war one must prepare weapons as is the practice of the day and the Holy One, blessed be He, will do that which He wills to do. It is forbidden to depend on a miracle'* (Rav Nahman of Breslov, Sefer haMidoth Perek Miriva 101). The Messiah follows this Torah law as he follows all Torah law. It is also written that Hezkiyahoo won the wars due to the Torah study so Messiah will have decide who studies Torah and who goes to war.

6) The Moshiah is a man of understanding (Talmud Bavli Sanhedrin 93b). Again, the literal meaning holds true as it did for king David as we learn from Samuel 16:18.
   Radak says that this means as in all maters of advice. Ralbag says that this means that he is a man who makes his words perfect in judgment and understanding. Malbim says that this means that he is an educated advisor.
7) Hashem is with the Messiah (Talmud Bavli Sanhedrin 93b). Like king David, as difficult as his life is, with all the barriers and problems that were caused him, Hashem still is with him to get him through these difficulties. Mitsoodath David and Radak say that this means that like David he is successful in all his ways. This is the case even though he is an oppressed scapegoat who is imprisoned for no crime of his own. See chapter on the imprisonment of the Messiah and the gate of Rome. Malbim says that this means that he is reverent of G-d and flees evil unlike most musicians where in his case he doesn't chase lusts for woman and is befitting to stand in the chamber of the king. Ralbag says that this means that he is successful in all his ways and can drive the evil spirit from you (i.e. as he did with king Saul by his playing Harp) with his vitality.
8) The Messiah is a 'gibor hai-il' which I translate to mean a 'strong soldier' or 'mighty warrior' (Talmud Bavli Sanhedrin 93b). Again, the literal meaning holds true as it did for king David as we learn from Samuel 16:18 where he slew Goliath and the many other wars he fought in as a soldier, captain and later soldier king. On Talmud Bavli Nedarim 38 the Ran says that 'gibor' means physical strength

whereas Rambam says it means subduing his evil inclination. Both meanings are true regarding the Moshiah but in this case it seems to implied the physical strength aspect. Radak says that this means that he has a strong heart in all things as his strength was made known in the incident where he beat the lion and the bear in a fight. Malbim says that this means that he is not like most of the poet songwriters who are filled by the power of imagination. Ralbag says that this means that he is brave and aggressive. Mitsoodath David says that this means that he is befitting to stand in the chamber of the king

9) The Moshiah has the spirits of wisdom, advise, insight, understanding, Holy Spirit and prophesy (Isaiah 11, Talmud Bavli Sanhedrin 93b). '*The spirit of the Messiah is the ray of hope to which we can cling, the sweet smelling fragrance of joy and expectation that everything will turn out for the best'.* (Reference 3, Page 24 'Moshiah Who What Why When Where' by Rabbi Chaim Kramer Shlita). As a true leader, the Messiah's behavioral example and words give hope and joy to others. People who think 'we don't have prophesy today' may view the Messiah as being not truthful, crazy or just simply delusional in the beginning part of his life when he has prophesy but before it is clear that he is the Messiah.
10) The Moshiah is humble, morally pure, observes the Torah commandments and is clean from sin (a logical outcome of the Sanhedrin 93b and Talmud Bavli Avodah Zara 20b). Since the Messiah follows Jewish law to the fullest degree, he is most likely what is called Haredi (ultra-orthodox). Being fit to be king and necessarily caring about the whole Jewish nation, he is also most likely nationalistic. This means that he is likely an 'ultra-orthodox' nationalistic Haredi Jew or national religious Haredi (in Hebrew called 'Hardal').
11) The Messiah is an artesian, craftsman or engineer in order to build the third Temple (Rashi on Talmud Bavli Succa 52b).
12) '*The Messiah is hard with the idol worshippers and soft with the people of Israel'* (Rashi and Radak on Zechariah 9:1). 'Idol worshippers' here refers to Gentiles who worship idols because no Jews today really worship idols.
13) The Messiah is righteous and pursues fair justice for all, regardless of wealth or social stature or politics, and establishes righteous judgment

(Isaiah 11). The Messiah Son of David is "*Righteous, performing many meritorious deeds, thus constantly elevating himself, bringing him to achieve level of Yihidah, he will realize who he is and what his mission will be. Heaven will endow him with power to fulfill his task.*" Thus he is similar to Moshe the first redeemer (Arizal Arbah Meot Shekel Kesef, page 241 Zohar II 7b-8b (Ref 3 page 241 Rabbi Chaim Kramer Shlita, author of the book "Messiah, Who, What, Why, When, Where").

14) The Messiah will '*strike the world with the rod of his mouth*' and will '*slay the wicked by the breath/spirit of his lips*' (Isaiah 11).
    This refers to the power of rebuke by a Tzadik. There is a Torah principle that G-d upholds the words of a Tzadik (a Righteous Jew), and thus G-d upholds the Messiah's statements that he speaks (in Hebrew 'Tzadik gozer, Hashem mikaaim'). The Messiah rebukes wicked people and they have to obey the Messiah or G-d will punish them, and that *he can literally kill wicked people with breath/spirit of his lips.*
    Rav Nahman of Breslov says that 'prayer is the Messiah's greatest (but not only) weapon'. This is obvious if he can kill people with prayer, but in addition he is also a man of war (Talmud Bavli Sanhedrin 93). As any man of war, he chooses the appropriate tool of death at the appropriate time for the appropriate enemy or criminal who is deserving of death by Torah law. Rav Nahman of Breslov also explains that it is more merciful to execute a wicked person by physical means rather than through prayer because through physical means (such as by Torah death penalty) the person receives atonement for his sin for which he is being executed, whereas by prayer the wicked person does not receive atonement and must suffer more in the next world since his sin was not atoned for in this world.

15) The Messiah is a righteous man who is imprisoned for the sins of the people (Yalkoot Shimoni on Isaiah 60 and Rashi on Talmud Bavli Sanhedrin 98 and Yalkoot Shimoni bringing that Isaiah 53 pertains to the Messiah, Ramchal Gnizei Tzvaaoth). Rav haTzadik Dov Kook Shlita said "There are many people in mental hospitals who say that they are the Moshiah. And one of them is the Moshiah". According to Rav Kook Shlita the imprisonment of the Messiah is in a mental hospital.

16) The Messiah lacks of Peace of Mind for what they did to them. 'It was for the worst suffering that you (the Messiah) suffered and that you were tied in the house of prison confinement that you don't have peace of mind because of them ... that you were tied up in the house of prison confinement where every day they would grind their teeth at you and would hint with their eyes' (Midrash Yalkoot Shimoni on Isaiah 60). The statement here 'don't have peace of mind because of them' shows that the Messiah has a really difficult time coping with the persecution that he endured. It is hard for him to just forget about his being persecuted and move on. His lack of peace of mind may seem like mental illness to some, especially some psychiatrists who tend to 'diagnose' every one as mentally ill since they are mentally ill and projecting their issues onto others and they have an economic interest to gather customers for their 'service'. *You don't have peace of mind because of them'* is a reality that the Messiah has to live with, like Josef had to live with his twelve year imprisonment that resulted from his brothers throwing him into a pit to try to kill him, then later he forgave them, but they were still cognizant of the fact that it would be possible that he would want to take just revenge due to the horrible crime that they committed against him, that almost killed him and lead to twelve years in prison for him. The righteous Messiah and 'Josef the righteous one' are very similar in this respect. They are both very righteous men who are both highly victimized and both had emotional problems as a result, even though it is these sins that the Messiah has agreed to atone for by his suffering due to our sins.
17) Talmud Bavli Sanhedrin 93 says that he has Holy Spirit. Talmud Bavli Avoda Zara 20 explains that humility, as well as other levels of Torah observance, is needed to reach the level of Holy Spirit and therefore humility is key for this. Arrogance immediately disqualifies one from being the Messiah. Midrash Raba on Biholetheicha says that like the Jewish Sanhedrin elders in Egypt, who refused to beat the Jewish people when the elders were employed taskmasters, one who is moser nefesh (risks his life) for clal Yisrael (the people of Israel) also merits Ruah HaKodesh like the elders did.
18) He fights Hashem's wars (Rambam laws of kings 11) which can have many expressions in many ways. As the many sources in this book give,

it for sure will involve fighting for justice, peace and making war with those who oppose G-d and his Torah or people Israel. It can involve tikoon Olam (fixing the world) regarding the environment, animal rights according to the Torah, human rights, children's rights, fighting for any Torah cause, serving in the Israeli military, establishing Torah in the world, supporting Torah Mitzvoth, teaching Torah, etc..

19) The Messiah has Ruah HaKodesh and can identify tribes of Israel (Talmud Bavli 93b, Rambam laws of kings 12).

20) The Talmud often refers to the Messiah son of David simply as the 'son of David'. This is because the Messiah son of David is a direct paternal descendant of king David. This means that he is the son of a son of a son of a son of a son, etc. going all the way back to king David. Only someone with Ruah HaKodesh can know such a thing. Someone paternally descended back to a known son of David such as the Baal haTanya or Maharal of Prague can also be relied on because it can be understood that the Baal haTanya and Maharal of Prague has Ruach HaKodesh so as to verify that they are sons of David. Rashi said that he was a son of David but only had daughters so one can not prove being a 'son of David' if he is descended from Rashi.
    I was not able to find any reliable sources that identify the traits of the Messiah son of Ephraim other than Talmud Bavli Succah 52b that says that he is an artesian so as to build the third Temple. The book 'Kol haTor' (written by a student of the Vilna Gaon and whose authenticity in representing the Torah wisdom of the Gaon accurately is not accepted by some Torah scholars, as per Rav Gideon Friedman Shlita, such as Rabbi Israel Eliyahoo Weintraub (zt'l) in his book 'hatkifa bisaarath Eliyahoo' and Rav Moshe Sternbuach Shlita in his work 'Tshuvoth viHagaoth') may not to be reliable in terms of being reliably the words of the Vilna Gaon (whose many words are totally reliable), but may says things that are true anyway. Therefore, we can only know who he is through Ruah HaKodesh.

21) The Messiah suffers massive opposition, rejection, vilification, persecutions, libeling, attempted murders, poverty, framed imprisonment, etc. as the Torah sources given in my book show. '*What is the main identifying trait of the Moshiah? He sits with the poor and afflicted' and he is also considered afflicted* and while sitting at the gate

of Rome with the other wounded he removes only one bandage of his at a time so as to be ready to move into action when needed (Talmud Bavli Sanhedrin 98).

22) As the chapter in my book titles 'Unrealistic Expectations of the Messiah' shows, the Messiah can not fulfill Rambam's traits of being 'as wise as Solomon' and 'greater a prophet than Moses' until he is king and sits and learns Torah with the Sanhedrin and acts with power as king for many years. Therefore, these above listed traits are the pre-kingship traits of the Messiah son of David.
23) The chapter in my book The Messiah According to Judaism titled 'Suspect Lineage and raised in Edom' shows that the Moshiah is most likely a Baal Tshuva who is a high soul brought down into the world in a low place. This is based on Talmud Bavli Brachot 34b 'In the place where a penitent stands (a person who returns to the Torah is called in Hebrew a 'Baal Tshuvah') even perfectly righteous (Tzadik Gamur in Hebrew) cannot stand' and other sources as well.

The above listed traits are how the Sanhedrin or any person with intelligence can identify the Moshiah of the generation.

The Golden Crown of the House of David and the Messiah

Rashi on Talmud Bavli Sanhedrin 21b says that the crown of king David has a rod in it that makes the crown only fit those kings who have a groove in their heads. This is how we know who is fitting to be king or not. There is also a story or two about the underground tomb of king David on Mount Zion, Jerusalem, that stores this crown and his sword. There is also a story that demons protect the underground tomb and they killed someone who went down there.

Elijah the prophet and the Messiah

Under grave danger from fighting Hashem's wars in Israel during the reign of the wicked king Ahab in the ninth century BCE, Elijah the prophet was relieved from his mission as prophet and went up to Heaven with his body as it is written in second kings 2:11 "Suddenly a chariot of fire and horses of fire appeared and separated the two of them, and Elijah went up to heaven in a whirlwind."

The Torah teaches us that Elijah the prophet will return to the world at some point during the times of the Messianic redemption as it is written "*Behold I will send Elijah the prophet before the coming of the great and dreadful day*" (Malachi 3:23). Most people regard this source to infer that the Messiah is preceded by Elijah the prophet. The Chasam Sofer holds that the great and dreadful day is the war of Gog and Magog which the Rambam (laws of kings chapters 11 and 12) cites is the beginning of 'the days of the Messiah'. Rambam Laws of kings 12:2 rules inconclusively whether Elijah will come before or after the Messiah. Different sources say that Elijah the prophet can come at different times in relation to the time of the coming of the Messiah depending on the circumstances. Within the orthodox Jewish community there are stories of Elijah coming on secret missions to help people and having visitations to various people in the Jewish community dressed as an Arab, a goy, a policeman, Rabbi, etc..

The Messiah either comes 'like a poor man riding on a donkey' at the final end time if the generation is guilty, or hastened before the final end time like the 'clouds of Heaven' if the generation is worthy (Talmud Bavli Sanhedrin 98). This is usually interpreted to mean that the Messiah will come in the appointed final end time if the Jewish people don't repent (and are not kind), or he can come hastened 'hastened' before the final time if the Jewish people repent fully (and are kind; which pushes away the heavenly judgment that pushes away the redemption). The Gaon of Vilna says that it is according to Hashem's Divine Kindness for His Names' sake that the redemption is decreed in Heaven. We can arouse Divine Kindness by being kind and living by the Torah in repentance. We must always pray for Mercy.

Although Malachi 3:23 states the more popularized ideal that Elijah will precede the Messiah to herald his coming, according to the book 'When Moshiah Comes' by Rabbi Yehuda Chayoon, the Pleisi in Beit HaSafek chapter 110, says that Elijah will precede the Messiah to announce his arrival only if redemption happens 'in its appointed final end time' (Yeshayahu 60:22), and if not, where the coming of the Messiah is in the category of 'I will hasten it (before its appointed final end time)' (ibid), then Elijah need not come prior to the Messiah to announce his arrival. In this case of being hastened, the Jewish people will simply have the merit to receive the Messiah and make him king and return to the full Torah lifestyle. This implies that the smeecha is reinstated as per Rambam Mishna Torah Hilchot Sanhedrin 4:11 by the agreement of the Rabbis of the generation (A comprehensive detailed explanation of the laws of Sanhedrin and reinstating smeecha is given in Arie Kaplan's 'handbook of Jewish thought' and more supporting information is given in 'Jerusalem Eye of the Universe'). Rav haGadol haTzadik viHasid Avraham Stern Shlita says that this means 'the majority' of the (relevant kosher orthodox) Rabbis.

In Milchamot Hashem, chapter 24, the Ramban says that Elijah will come before the coming of the Messiah. Ramban says that all of Edom's cities are all destroyed, which could mean all of the cities of the world if Edom controls the whole world at the time. This is because they are so wicked that they can not be redeemed, which by reason is the case if the redemption is pushed off to the final end time. Therefore, by logical reason, we see that the Ramban is referring to the case of the final end time redemption; not hastened. If the redemption is hastened before the final end time by Tshuvah Shleima and kindness, to arouse G-d's Kindness to redeem us, then maybe no cities have to be destroyed. I hope this is the case. For this we must be kind and repent fully. The book 'Gates of Repentance' explains how to repent fully.

In Mishna Torah, Hilchot Melachim 12:2, Rambam rules inconclusively, based on the different views of the sages, that it is not sure whether Elijah will precede the Moshiah or not (laws of kings 12:2). As Rav Yehuda Chayoon Shlita points out in his book 'When Moshiah Comes', Tosfos Yom Tov and Maharal Chaviv hold that Moshiah and Elijah come together. Again, the Pleisi, in Beit HaSafek chapter 110, says that Elijah will precede the Messiah to announce his arrival only if the redemption happens in its appointed final end time', and Elijah need not come prior to the Messiah to announce his arrival if the redemption is hastened. In this case of being hastened, the Jewish people will simply have the merit to receive the Divine Kindness of being redeemed. In Igereth Teman, page 174, the Rambam says that prophesy returns before the Moshiah. This is full blown prophesy of 'Hazon vi mareh' (picture and vision) since we know that prophesy through Ruah HaKodesh (Holy Spirit) to know the truth exists all though the exile (as per Hevroota citing Ramban and Chasam Sofer on Talmud Bavli Baba Batra 12a). Thus, another prophet, other than Elijah, may be the prophet, with the Sanhedrin, who is needed to appoint the Moshiah king as per laws of kings chapter 1:3. In the orthodox Jewish community there are many credible stories of Elijah the prophet coming to the world to carry out different missions at various times so in any case Elijah is in the world regardless of his heralding the Messiah's arrival. For a thorough coverage of the history and principles of prophesy and Ruah HaKodesh from ancient times to our times see Rabbi Arie Kaplan's book called the 'handbook of Jewish thought'.

In any case, the Moshiah and Elijah are both aware of each other, but Elijah, being in Heaven, is far more aware of the Messiah because he can see more from Heaven where Elijah resides, and can even see the Messiah after the Messiah has been sent to live on earth, even before he is revealed to people, even to the Sanhedrin who must proceed Elijah and the Moshiah in order to recognize, authoritatively certify that is in fact them, and to establish the Moshiah king of Israel.

The purpose, roles and functions of Elijah the prophet

People often confuse the purpose, roles and functions of the Messiah son of David, the Messiah son of Yosef (AKA son of Ephraim) and Elijah the prophet.

If the Messiah son of David comes hastened, then the Messiah son of Josef may not even appear, or be a minister (possibly or even likely the Prime Minister) of the Moshiah son of David as king (Rav Saadia Gaon Emuna viDaoth chapter on redemption). If the Messiah son of David comes at the final time, the Messiah son of Josef has to pave the way for the Messiah son of David (ibid). See the chapter of this book on the Messiah son of Josef for details of his function and mission.

We need to learn the purpose, roles and functions of Elijah the prophet so as to distinguish between his role and that of the two Messiahs.

As Rabbi Yehuda Chayoon Shlita brings down in his book 'When Moshiah Comes', different sources attribute different purposes, roles and functions to Elijah the prophet. Among these are: he will inspire the Jews to repentance (Mikroth Gidoloth Malchi 3:23), effect world peace between Jews and Gentiles (Ravad Eduyoth 8:7), restore the ancient jar of manna, bring the purifying water and anointing oil and Aaron's staff (Mechilta Shemot 16:33), resurrect the dead (Metzudos David on Melachi 3:23), clarify doubtful halachos (Bechoros 24a, 35b, Eduyos 8:7, Shekalim 2:5, Pesacheem 13a and 34a, Chagiga 25a, Yevamos 35b and 41b, Gitten 42b, Yerushalmi Dmai 2:1, Shabath 108a, Tosfos Chullin 5a. Baba Metzia 114b.), interpret difficult verses (Rashi Menachos

45a), rationalize selected laws (Rashi Bechoros 24a), and reestablish smeecha ordination to the Sanhedrin (Radvaz, Maharal Chaviv, Tosfos Yom Tov). The smeecha ordination was terminated in 350 BCE at the time of Rabbi Hillel HaNasi the second and was since then lost until it will be restored again. May that time come today. As written in Malachi 3:24, before 'the great and dreadful day' Elijah the prophet will come (from Heaven to earth) to return the hearts of the sons to the fathers, and the hearts of the fathers to the sons. This may be referring to the fixing of family disunity that is a crisis in society and is referred to in Talmud Bavli Sotah 49 prior to the coming of the Messiah.

The Moshiah son of David identifies the true Cohaneem, Levieem and tribal identities by Ruah HaKodesh, but does not reveal who is a kosher Jew, a mamzer or slave, as Rambam's halacha on laws of kings 12:3 says 'in the days of the Messiah, when all of his kingdom rests and the all of Israel sits with him, their genealogical pedigree will be determined through his Ruah HaKodesh… and will identify who is from the tribe of Levi... and who is a Cohen… and who is from which tribe… but will not identify who is a kosher Jew or who is a mamzer or slave….'

In the laws of Sanhedrin 1:3, Rambam says that a Sanhedrin and prophet are needed to appoint a king. In the laws of Sanhedrin 1:7, Rambam says that a new king must be anointed. The prophet must be certified by the Sanhedrin and gives his prophesies to them (Rabbi Arie Kaplan 'Jerusalem the eye of the world' and 'handbook of Jewish thought' citing Rambam). From Malachi 3:24, which says that Elijah the prophet will return before 'the great and dreadful day', some wise Rabbis learn that Elijah will come before the Moshiah (Rambam laws of kings 12:2). This means that Elijah will be able to be the one who re-establishes smeecha to the Sanhedrin and with the Sanhedrin will be the prophet who appoints the Messiah king of Israel (Rambam Laws of kings 1:3). Other Rabbis learn that Elijah will not come before the Moshiah (Rambam laws of kings 12:2). In this case the Rabbis will have to re-establish smeecha to the Sanhedrin (Rabbi Arie Kaplan 'handbook of Jewish thought' chapter on Sanhedrin citing Rambam laws of Sanhedrin 4:11) and another prophet other than Elijah may appear with the Sanhedrin to appoint the Moshiah king. Elijah the prophet is supposed to proceed the Messiah according to Rashi. This may be the case whether the Moshiah comes hastened or in the final end time. Elijah the prophet is also supposed to proceed the Moshiah according to the Ramban. But, as stated before, by reason we can see that the Ramban is referring to the final end time (not hastened), because he also says that all the cities of Edom will be destroyed; which is the case of the final end time where the society has deteriorated so much that cities of Edom are so wicked that they cannot be redeemed and have no other alternative than being all destroyed in order to redeem the world. This is clearly the final end scenario; not the hastened scenario. The Radvaz, Maharal Chaviv, and Tosfos Yom Tov hold that Eljah the prophet will give smeecha ordination to the Sanhedrin. In my opinion, based on the reasoning just given, this is the case of the final end time. The Rambam rules, inconclusively though, that smeecha ordination may be reinstated by a scholar ordained by the majority or total consensus agreement of all the Rabbis of the land of Israel (Rambam Laws of Sanhedrin 4:11). This 'inconclusive' ruling may be based on the Rambam's other 'inconclusive' (same word in Hebrew for 'inconclusive' as before) ruling that, based on the different views of the sages, it is not sure whether Elijah will precede the Moshiah or not (laws of kings 12:2).

Rabbi Arie Kaplan's 'handbook of Jewish thought' chapter on Sanhedrin shows very clearly and conclusively that the Sanhedrin must be reestablished before the Moshiah comes.

In Peroosh HaMishnaiot, Tractate Sanhedrin, perek aleph, Rambam holds that the Sanhedrin of 71 elders must be re-established as a prerequisite prior to the coming of the Messiah. This is whether the Moshiah is in the final end time or hastened. In the final time, this is a Sanhedrin with Elijah as the head who has given them smeecha and teaches them all the unknown Torah laws that were lost in the exile until that time. In the hastened scenario this is a Sanhedrin where the Rabbis reinstated smeecha, the prophet is not necessarily Elijah, and we have to find the ancient anointing oil by our selves without the help of Elijah.

Maharatz Chajes notes that the statement in Talmud Bavli Eruvin 43b "*we tell the Beit din haGadol that Elijah has come*" reveals that there will be a 'Beit Din haGadol'; which is another term for the Sanhedrin; before Elijah comes. This supports Rambam's ruling that there will be a Sanhedrin before the Messiah comes, even if the Sanhedrin is at that point in time just a partially functioning Sanhedrin with questionable smeecha. It would be partially functioning because the Temple is needed for a fully operational Sanhedrin performing all the laws and the Temple is not yet built at that point in time. The Sanhedrin with smeecha anointed by Elijah the prophet will be able to anoint the Messiah king as a Sanhedrin and prophet are required to appoint and anoint a king (Rambam laws of Sanhedrin 1:3 and 1:7). The hastened Sanhedrin with another prophet who has found the anointing oil can also appoint and anoint the Moshiah. Then the Sanhedrin will be able to identify, anoint and establish the real Moshiah as king of Israel.

Even without Torah sources to indicate so, one can also see through logical reason the need for a Sanhedrin before Elijah or the Messiah comes.

Without a Sanhedrin there will be no way for the Jewish people to identify, greet, authoritatively certify and notify the world that this is in fact the real Elijah the prophet who is now here. The Rabbis need to be unified in a block of Sanhedrin unity so that their authority will be believed with indisputable credibility, without dispute by any individual Rabbi, that would put doubt on whether or not Elijah has really come and is here now. This would prevent the acceptance of Elijah. The same logic goes for the Moshiah. Without a Sanhedrin there will be no way for the Jewish people to identify, greet him, authoritatively certify and notify the public that this is in fact the real Moshiah who is to be appointed king. According to Rambam this person will not defiantly be the Moshiah though until he builds the Temple and compels the Jewish people to live by the Torah (laws of kings 11:4). These sources and logic mean that there must be a Sanhedrin *without smeecha given by Elijah* before Elijah the prophet comes so as to identify and authoritatively certify that this is in fact the real Elijah the prophet who is now here.

This issue of needing a Sanhedrin to bring the Moshiah is a critical issue because if there is no Sanhedrin when Elijah comes, and then later the Messiah comes, then how will the Jewish people know that he is Elijah if there is no Sanhedrin to clarify and authoritatively certify the issue? Will the Israeli government, or any other body of leadership in the world, be able, or even want, to identify, authoritatively certify and notify the Israeli public and the world that Elijah or the Moshiah has come? The answer is 'no'. Anyway, what's the point if there is no Sanhedrin to appoint the Moshiah king. The point is that Elijah will inspire the Jews to repentance (Mikroth Gidoloth Malchi 3:23), effect world peace between Jews and Gentiles, clarify doubtful halachos, interpret difficult verses, rationalize selected laws, reestablish smeecha ordination to the Sanhedrin, and to return the hearts of the sons to the fathers, and the hearts of the fathers to the sons. The Zohar Shemot chapter 7 teaches us that in the redemption period the wise men will surround themselves around

Moshiah Ben David but the unlearned masses of Jewish people won't really even know that this is the redemption period when it is happening.

These sources mean that in any case, hastened or final end time, that there must be a Sanhedrin before Elijah comes in order to identify and authoritatively certify to the public that Elijah has come.

We also learn that it is a commandment for all Jews in every generation to build the Third Temple (Rambam, laws of the Temple), and that a generation that doesn't build the Temple is like a generation that destroys the Temple (Talmud). There are Jews who would like to build the third Temple today, but the Third Temple can only really be built by the Messiah. Both Rashi (Talmud Bavli Sanhedrin 20) and Rambam (laws of kings chapter one) agree that the king from the royal House of David (the Messiah in this case) has to come back into power in order in order to build the Temple. They both say (Talmud Bavli Sanhedrin 20, laws of kings chapter one) that upon the Jewish peoples' coming into the land of Israel (the Rabbis say that this is when the majority of Jews are in the land), first we do the Mitzvah of appointing a king (Deuteronomy 17:14), then the Mitzvah of eradicating Amalek (Deuteronomy 25:19- may their memories be erased), and then the king (Messiah in this case) builds the Temple. Therefore, we need the Moshiah for a fully operational Temple, and for that to happen we need Elijah the prophet to return, and for that to happen we need to build a Sanhedrin.

Again, the Temple cleanses the spiritual impurity from the world that is blocking people from achieving their full blessing and potential in life and having a direct clear connection to G-d. The sacrifices in the Temple atone for our sins and bring great blessing and forgiveness for our sins from G-d. The Rabbis say that if the Jewish people and Gentiles knew the great blessing that the Temple brings, they would see to it that the Temple would be built today.

Sanhedrin is needed to bring the Messiah in Our Time

The Sanhedrin is the only body of wise judges capable of providing expedient, impartial, affordable, balanced, fair and true judgment. It is thus the foundation of a healthy, successful, happy, prosperous, wealthy and peaceful society that blissfully lives in wholeness with G-d. In practical realistic terms, the Rabbis will only have maximum power and authority to bring back the full Torah wisdom and respect for Torah and Torah rulings in Israel and the world, when they unify into a power block, a gang like group of wise sages, called the Sanhedrin. This Sanhedrin will be as the word of G-d itself. It will bring blessing to mankind. Even before Elijah or the Messiah comes, it will be emulated in other nations as a light unto the nations (Isaiah 49:6, 42:6) by a 'kingdom of priestly ministers' (Exodus 19:6) revered, feared, sought after for advise, and most of all loved and respected by all serious people in Israel and the world. Making the Sanhedrin is the next step in the salvation of Israel and mankind.

If you are a wise Rabbi then please note here from the beginning of this chapter: Maharatz Chajes notes that the statement in Talmud Bavli Eruvin 43b "*we tell the beit din hagadol that Elijah has come*" means that there will be a Sanhedrin (which is the Beit Din haGadol) before Elijah comes. Rabbi Arie Kaplan's 'handbook of Jewish thought' chapter on Sanhedrin shows very clearly and conclusively that the Sanhedrin must be reestablished before the Moshiah comes. In Peroosh HaMishnaiot, Tractate Sanhedrin, perek aleph, Rambam holds that the Sanhedrin of 71 elders must be re-established as a prerequisite prior to the coming of the Messiah. This supports the Rambam's law in Mishne Torah Laws of Sanhedrin 4:11 that the Rabbis of the generation will re-establish a Sanhedrin with smeecha.

Lesser Standards Required for Sanhedrin of this Generation

These Rabbis must meet the lowered requirements of Sanhedrin according to the lesser standards of our time (Rabbi Arie Kaplan's 'handbook of Jewish thought' chapter on Sanhedrin point 10:32). For instance, Rambam's requirement to know all seventy languages is not necessary if we only judge in Hebrew (and maybe English too if need be). Rabbi Yonathan Baitz Shlita said that the Rebbe is said to have once received a letter in Chinese, which he then translated and responded to himself, with the aid of books on Chinese. He had many books on many languages in his office. What the Rabbis of this generation must also realize is another point that Rabbi Arie Kaplan's 'handbook of Jewish thought' chapter on Sanhedrin also points out. This point (10:32 ibid) is that 'although one must be expert in all areas of Jewish law to qualify for ordination, now that the oral law has been committed to writing, it is sufficient that one be familiar enough with all the written authorities to render judgment in all cases'. This means that the Sanhedrin Rabbis don't have to know all the cases, laws, reasoning and sources by memory. They just have to know where to find the cases, laws, reasoning and sources so they can learn them in order to judge. When the Rabbis work together by delegating different areas of law to different Rabbis to become expert in and to teach the others in tutorials, then as a group they will all become experts in all the different laws very quickly so that they can judge cases that come before them.

History and Background of the Sanhedrin

We are commanded: *'Judges and police officers you shall appoint in all your cities which Hashem your G-d gives you for your tribes, and they shall judge the people with righteous judgment. You shall not pervert judgment, you shall not iniquitously favor one litigant over the other, you shall not accept a bribe for the bribe will blind the eyes of the wise and make just words crooked. Justice justice thou shall pursue so that you will live and possess the land that Hashem your G-d gives you'* (Deuteronomy 16:18-20). The judges must be *'accomplished, reverent of G-d (so they don't sin), truthful and hate iniquitous gain'* (Exodus 18:17-26), be taught the laws by Moses, appointed by Moses and go to Moses on difficult rulings that they can't decide.

Moses would lay his hands on the heads of the elders and Joshua to impart in them the spirit of wisdom and this laying of the hands, in Hebrew called 'smeecha'. Smeecha was thereafter passed down through oral declaration (Rabbi Arie Kaplan's 'handbook of Jewish thought' chapter on Sanhedrin) by the ancient Jewish elders, elders who were Bible prophets (Samuel, Elijah), judges, kings (Joshua, Solomon) and Talmudic sages, from generation to generation, until 350 CE when smeecha was terminated by pain of death by the Roman Empire. Smeecha is the laying of the hands on the elders that Moses did to impart the spirit of wisdom to them, and was thus carried over from generation until generation until it was stopped in 350 CE with Rabbi Hillel being the last to have smeecha. Since then we have had no smeecha to this day; unless Rav Josef Karo's smeecha in Tsfat circa 1500 CE was valid as per the Rambam laws of Sanhedrin 4:11. See Rabbi Arie Kaplan's 'handbook of Jewish thought' chapter on Sanhedrin for a discussion and sources on this issue.

The Talmud; in particular Talmud Sanhedrin; derives the laws from these and other passages where Rambam ruled many laws and rulings about our judicial proceedings and laws of judges and judgment regarding the Sanhedrin. These judges who judge Israel were called the Sanhedrin in the oral transmission from Mount Sinai; later called 'the Talmud'. 'Sanhedrin' is a term that was invented where 'Sanhedrin' is an Aramaic acronym for 'Sonei hadarath panim biDin', which means 'hating favoritism in judgment'. In Mishne Torah, laws of Sanhedrin chapter one, Rambam rules that in the land of Israel we Jews must have a Sanhedrin of seventy elders (plus one) to judge us.

We are also commanded that upon the Jewish peoples' coming into the land of Israel (the Rabbis say that this is when the majority of Jews are in the land), first we do the Mitzvah of appointing a king (Deuteronomy 17:14) and Rambam rules that this is the law (laws of kings chapter one). In the laws of Sanhedrin 1:3, Rambam rules that a Sanhedrin and prophet are needed to appoint a king. In the laws of Sanhedrin 1:7, Rambam says that a new king must be anointed (with the special anointing oil that Elijah can bring when he returns-may that day be now. Someone else can also retrieve the oil. Its location may already be known; but held secret for the right time.). From here we see that we need a Sanhedrin to appoint the Messiah king as well as needing Elijah the prophet to anoint the Moshiah king. Without a Sanhedrin we can not appoint the Moshiah king and can not even receive Elijah the prophet.

In chapter four of laws of Sanhedrin, Rambam rules that the Sanhedrin must have smeecha to rule as a Sanhedrin. This created a serious problem in forming a Sanhedrin since we have do not have the transmitted smeecha from Moses anymore in our times. The issue of smeecha is the main obstacle that the Rabbis see today in making a Sanhedrin. Rabbi Arie Kaplan's 'handbook of Jewish thought' chapter on Sanhedrin shows very clearly and conclusively that smeecha can be reestablished by the Rabbis before the Moshiah comes. Certain other requirements of the Rambam can be released for the lower standard of this generation (ibid). For instance, Rambam's requirement to know all the languages can be released if the Sanhedrin only judges in the languages which it knows, which in Israel is modern Hebrew to judge the Israelis, and maybe English too, to judge English speakers of which there are many in the world from all countries. Only two Sanhedrin members need to know a language to judge a case (ibid).

The previous chapter shows that we need a Sanhedrin to receive Elijah the prophet when he returns. So the question arises: How do we do this Mitzva to make a Sanhedrin if we do not have smeecha anymore? This seems to be the main problem today, along with unifying the Rabbis to respect each other and work together as a unified block. This will give the Rabbis more power in 'the real world', almost like 'a gang' has (lihavdeel). Since the time of Bar Kochba and Rabbi Akiva, circa 135 AD, when 24,000 students of Rabbi Akiva died for not respecting and begrudging each other, this has been a problem in the exile; lack of respect and unity among the Rabbis. Pri haTzadik, shevini 9, comments that ill feelings between Rabbis is the reason why they are falsely accused and vilified as it is written '*In the generation that the Messiah comes there will be false accusations and vilifications (Rashi) against the Torah scholars*' (Talmud Bavli Ketuboth 112b). Many praiseworthy Rabbis in the generation are working to fix this problem and are building unity through mutual respect from all the orthodox sects of Judaism. They are paving the way for Moshiah.

Past and Recent Attempts to Make a Sanhedrin

Some five hundred years ago, the writer of the Jewish codes of Laws that we now follow as the authority on law (the Shulhan Aruch), Rav Yosef Kara (zt'l) of Tsfat, accepted the Rambam's method of reestablishing smeecha but the chief Rabbi in Jerusalem opposed it and therefore smeecha was not accepted in that generation. Rabbi Arie Kaplan's 'handbook of Jewish thought' chapter on Sanhedrin gives sources of Torah essays on this debate. The fact that we follow Rav Karo's Shulhan Aruch to this day may support that the method of the Rambam of reinstating smeecha is correct. I believe that the problem that many Rabbis may have today with reforming the Sanhedrin is that the people of Israel have not requested it strongly enough; in addition to that they believe that the method of re-establishing the 'laying of the hands' (in Hebrew called 'smeecha'), mentioned by the Rambam in Laws of Sanhedrin 4:11, is not necessarily conclusive even according to the Rambam.

Another deterrent is the Rabbis of today's great humility in that they feel that they are not worthy of being on the Sanhedrin. I disagree. I think they are worthy. And in any case, we go by the lower standards of our generation (Rabbi Arie Kaplan's 'handbook of Jewish thought' chapter on Sanhedrin), and, what better option do we have? Society is in a stage of self destruction without the Sanhedrin. The Sanhedrin is needed to figure out what is the right thing to do, according to the Torah, considering all the elusively complex moral and ethical issues that only a Sanhedrin can figure out what is the right thing to do for the sake of the well being of the society and fulfill the will of G-d as the Torah teaches us to do. I reason that we must do the best we can and move forward with the best Rabbis of our generation. Even if we are still not perfect, it will still be better than having no Sanhedrin and leaving the generation to the mercy of the other bodies of law who are for sure making mistakes that are bringing destruction on society. The 'imperfect' Sanhedrin option is by far the better choice.

None the less, many Rabbis in Israel have formed what they call a 'New Sanhedrin' based on the Rambam's 'shita' (system of reasoning) by the year 2010. But, the Rabbis considered to be the biggest Rabbis of the generation have not agreed to this Sanhedrin; whether for some justified reasons or not is a matter or opinion, and the orthodox world holds that the opinion of the agreed upon biggest Rabbis of the generation (Rav Shteineman Shlita, Rav haGagol Keneivski Shlita, Rav Ohrbach Shlita, Rav haGadol haTzadik Avroham Stern Shlita, Rav Gideon Friedman Shlita, Rav haGadol Avraham Greenbaum Shlita, Rav haGadol Haim Kramer Shlita, Rav haGaon Yosef Trachman Shlita, the Aida Haredith Shlita, Beit Din haSepharedi Beit Yosef Shlita, Beit Din Rav Kaerelitz Shlita, etc.) is the opinion which is the right opinion that rules. Some have said that these are not really the biggest (Wisest) Rabbis and that we have been merely brainwashed by the orthodox media. This claim can be judged to see if it's true or not.

Objectively, what criteria must we use to determine who are the biggest Rabbis who are to be called the poskeem and Gadol haDor who make our halcahic and even national decisions for us? The answer that I heard and accept is that we determine who are the biggest (wisest) Rabbis by those who can answer questions that the other Rabbis could not answer. He must also have excellent midoth (character traits) such as love for Jews, love for Torah, love for Mitzvoth, seeing the good in others, humility, Bitachon (trust in Hashem), Emunah (Faith), purity, kindness, respect to others, patience, fear of Heaven so that he is meticulous in keeping the Mitzvoth and sinless, great at prayer, etc.. The biggest (wisest) Rabbi, the Gadol haDor, is he who could answer the questions that even those other big Rabbis could not answer and has the best Midoth.

Isaiah 1:*26-27 'And I will restore your judges as at first and your counselors as in the beginning. Afterwards you shall be called City of Righteousness, Faithful City. Zion shall be redeemed through justice (redemption shall come through practicing justice) and her penitents through righteousness'.* Some say that this passage along with Rambam laws of Sanhedrin means *'restore your judges as at first'* means that the body of 71 judges called the Sanhedrin must be restored first in order to prepare for the coming of the Messiah. Others say that Elijah the prophet must come and bring back 'smeecha' to form a Sanhedrin.

The New Sanhedrin can emerge to become the real Sanhedrin of Israel in time. I believe this will happen in reasonable pragmatic ways due to the need to fulfill the Mitzvah under the conditions of dhak hashaa or tsorech hashaa (emergency conditions) we face today. Most of the Gidoleem who did not join are mostly gone now and the other ones who are left are very old. The new generation gives hope.

I was active in making the Sanhedrin by supporting it and promoting it. In 2003, I saw the urgent need for proper Torah judgment to be upheld in Israel and the world, as a matter of pikuah nefesh, in order to save the country and world from many travails including Iran, terror strikes, poverty, immorality and the spread of sicknesses like AIDS. Therefore, I then acted and called to the people and government of Israel to make and support a Sanhedrin. I did this by mass email sends, posting pro-Sanhedrin message stickers all over Jerusalem and sending some 50 letters to qualified rabbis and judges in Israel trying to convince them to join. In January of 2003, I sent a letters to Beitei Din reasoning that they should join the Sanhedrin.

In 2005, a leading member of the Sanhedrin, Rabbi David Sears Shlita, asked me to be a member but I declined feeling that I am not worthy and wasn't viable until the real Gidoleem joined. In any case, I believe that I as the pre-kingship chezkat Moshiah must be respected as such for the Rabbis to back it and join. Maybe this will be with the coming of the new generation of Rabbis. In July of 2015 many children in the city where I lived at the time referred to me as the Moshiah in a non-mocking way. We accepted each other in mutual respect and love. They my people; I their king. I also accept the goyim as my people too; I their king, and will help them too as much as I can, as is humanly possible. The adults have had problems accepting me; ranging from ignorance, lack of time to read my book to see the truth about what is really going on here, arrogance and insane jealousy once they see who I really am. This has been the problem with the Rabbinate.

The need for a Sanhedrin is growing with the declining and deteriorating society in a state of self destruction due to lack of proper leadership and moral and ethical legal Torah judgments. I believe that at some point, maybe even now, people will be so aware of the need to have a Sanhedrin in order to survive, much less succeed and prosperity, that society will accept and support the New Sanhedrin, in spite of the doubts and risks, with or without smeecha from Elijah the prophet.

Worldwide State of Emergency: Sanhedrin Needed to Stop Wars, Economic Crash, Rising Disease and 'Natural Distracters' in the World

This issue of making a Sanhedrin to rule properly on law and order in society, with the proper balance, is an important issue, for the reasons that 'The world rests upon True Torah Justice…' (Ethics of the Fathers chapter 1), 'Perversion of justice, delay of justice and teaching the Torah law not in accordance with the Torah bring the sword (war, violence) to the world' (Ethics of the Fathers chapter 5), 'Failure to uphold capitol punishments for death penalty sins brings disease (cancer, AIDS, Ebola, viruses, dangerous bacteria) to the world' (Ethics of the Fathers chapter 5) and '*If you see a generation that many troubles come on them, go and check the judges of Israel, because all Divine retribution that comes to the world comes for no other reason than the judges of Israel*' (Talmud Bavli Shabbat 139a). From the above passages we can see how important the true Torah justice of a Sanhedrin is to the success, health, happiness and prosperity of Israel and the world. Our wars and diseases can be directly attributed to not having no Sanhedrin at the current time. The world needs a Sanhedrin to prosper, be healthy, be economically sound and be fully blessed, ultimately with the Moshiah as king and the third Temple that brings more blessing, atonement of sin, forgiveness, Heavenly mercy and prosperity to mankind.

Even two US senators recently remarked that 'the United States is going down the tubes. Only the Jewish Messiah can save us". If the US goes down the tubes, then Israel will loose its US support and things will be very difficult in Israel. Some may say that the country Israel would fall (Heave Forbid).

This is the direction in which we are now headed and if that happens the state of Israel ('state' means the current establishment; not the country of Israel), will fall and the house of David; who the state now denies (in Hebrew called 'kfeera') and rejects and even outlaws, along with the authority of the Torah, the Rabbis and Rabbinic courts; will emerge as the new kingship of Israel, accepted by both the Israeli Jews and most of the Arabs now residing in the land of Israel. The State of Israel will only stand if it changes direction and accepts and adheres to the authority of the Torah, the Israeli Rabbis and the Moshiah Ben David of the House of David, who has been in the land of Israel according to Rav Kadoori since 2001 and has passed his imprisonment stage of suffering in a prison mental hospital in Edom, which we know according to Rav haTzadik Dov Kook Shlita of Tiberius, who is quoted as having said: '*There are many people in mental hospitals who say that they are the Moshiah, and one of them really is*'. The New Sanhedrin has a web page.

The establishment of the Sanhedrin is the next step to bring the Moshiah which will mean: NO MORE WAR. May that time be now.

We Cant Know Many of the True Torah Laws Without a Sanhedrin

Rav Yosef Karo (zt'l), who wrote the codes of Jewish law that we now follow, said that some of the Jewish laws, the Halacha, is not clear. This is because we don't have a Sanhedrin and Elijah to rule on unknown laws. He supported the reinstating of the Sanhedrin and smeecha in his generation, which supports that this is the halacha, since his halacha of the Shulhan Aruch is what we rule by today. Without Sanhedrin there are many laws that we can not know. For example, Rav Eliyashiv (zt'l), Rav Ohrbach Shlita and Rav Fisher (zt'l) all disagreed on what is the blessing for rice cakes. One said shehakal, another mizonoth, and another haadama. The advantage of the Sanhedrin to transgressors of immorality is that the mere existence of the Sanhedrin will help make deadly venereal diseases such as AIDS and herpes go away (Ethics of the Fathers chapter five). The immense prayer power of the Sanhedrin will help cure people of terminal diseases and bring success and wealth to the world at large. The Sanhedrin also maintains the respect and dignity of transgressors so it does not allow them to be publicized so as not to commit the most grievous sin of slandering someone or embarrassing him in public. The Sanhedrin will protect people's rights to their life, limb, property, respect, dignity and good name, even of transgressors. The Sanhedrin will help peoples' happy marriage with or without children as well. Many blessing will come to the world with the establishment of the Sanhedrin. Again, the Sanhedrin is the only body of wise judges capable of providing expedient, impartial, affordable, balanced, fair and true judgment. It is thus the foundation of a healthy, successful, happy, prosperous, wealthy and peaceful society that blissfully lives in wholeness with G-d.

Sanhedrin Needed Now Regardless of Hastened Final End Time

In Peroosh HaMishnaiot, Tractate Sanhedrin, perek aleph, Rambam holds that the Sanhedrin of 71 wise elders (i.e. Rabbis) must be re-established a prerequisite prior to the coming of the Messiah. As seen from the above sources, if in the final end time, this is a Sanhedrin with Elijah as the head of the Sanhedrin, with the smeecha brought back by Elijah. If Ezekiel follows the chronological order of events, since Ezekiel 37:24; which says that the Moshiah becomes king; comes before Ezekiel chapter 40; when the third Temple is built; shows that the Moshiah becomes king before he builds the Temple. Rambam laws of kings 11:4 says that it is only possible to know for sure who the Messiah really ('Vadai Moshiah') if he builds the Temple. Since the Rambam says that we can only know who is the Moshiah for sure ('Vadai Moshiah') when he builds the Temple, and he can only build the Temple when he is king, then the question arises: how will the Sanhedrin and Elijah know who they should appoint king if he hasn't built the Temple yet and therefore they cant know with certainty whether or not he is really the Messiah? Elijah the prophet may know since he is a prophet, but, who the Moshiah is and when he comes have always been hidden so even he may not know. The Sanhedrin and Elijah may know through the identifying traits that this book gives over and logic. This issue is addressed through the identifying traits in the chapter of this book titled 'Pre-Kingship Character Traits that identify the Messiah before he becomes king'.

Merely as a speculative line of reasoning; not as a necessarily a proper halcahic line of reasoning to determine a ruling by any means, as I am not a certified posek; making a Sanhedrin based on Rambam's system may have some aspects of reasoning and justification on the basis of 'pikuah nefesh'. This is a Torah principle that permits one to violate certain Torah Mitzvoth in order to save the lives or souls of Jews and Gentiles. An example of this is a case where, although a Jew may be liable to the death penalty for desecrating the Sabbath, if he is really aware of what he is doing is a sin, a Jew is permitted to desecrate the Sabbath in order to save a Jews life or save him from a life of idol worship, which saves his soul. Another speculative line of reasoning to release certain halcahic requirements required to make a Sanhedrin may include 'Tsorech haShaa' (emergency measures; Talmud Bavli Sanhedrin 46 and Choshen Mishpat chapter two) where the tovei hair or 'Gadol haDor' (Shulhan Aruch Choshen Mishpat chapter two) or the tovei hair or 'Gadol biTorah' (Aruch haShulhan Choshen Mishpat chapter two) have authority to decide. There may also be argued an aspect of 'Shaa ait laasoth liHashem hafer et Torateacha' (Talmud Bavli Gitten 60a, Tamid 27b, Brachoth 24a and

63a, Truma 14b), meaning that a Prophet (as Elijah did when he did the sin of building an alter on Mount Carmel in times of the Temple) or the Nasi of the Sanhedrin (as Yehuda HaNasi did when did the sin of writing down the oral law in to Mishna) can release this necessity of certain halcahic requirements for the cause of a greater Mitzvah, like releasing this necessity smeecha in this case, for the greater Mitzva of making a Sanhedrin, since society is in a dangerous state of turmoil and near self destruction with out a Sanhedrin. But, this is not the reason since we don't have a prophet to decide rule way. I repeat, right now society is in a stage of self destruction and needs a Sanhedrin in order to serve G-d properly and be blessed with prosperity. This will bring health, economy, peace and happiness. It could bring a cure for cancer, AIDS and other afflictions that were currently do not know how to cure.

Again, according to the Pleisi in Beit HaSafek chapter 110 (Rav Yehudah Chayoon in 'When Moshiah Comes'), Elijah will precede the Messiah to announce his arrival only if redemption happens 'in its appointed final time', but need not come if the redemption is hastened. Again, in Igereth Teman, page 174, the Rambam says that prophesy returns before the Moshiah. This is full blown prophesy of 'Hazon vi mareh' (picture and vision) since we know that 'prophesy' through Ruah HaKodesh (Holy Spirit) to know the truth exists all though the exile (as per Hevroota citing Ramban and Chasam Sofer on Baba Batra 12a). Thus, another prophet, other than Elijah, may be the prophet with the Sanhedrin who is needed to appoint the Moshiah king as per laws of kings chapter 1:3. Logically, if we are to hasten the coming of the Messiah before the final time, which may mean that Elijah doesn't come before the Messiah to bring back smeecha and form the Sanhedrin (see chapter on Elijah the prophet), as shown, we must return completely to observing all the Torah commandments (Tshuva Shleima), learn Torah and be kind (to push away the midah of din) in order to hasten the coming of the Messiah, which includes enforcing Jewish law which requires re-establishing the Sanhedrin possibly even without smeecha from Elijah. The Sanhedrin must be accepted by the Jewish people of Israel living in the land of Israel; including Haredi, Hiloni, Dati Leoomi, Gentiles, Gentile Arabs and Jewish Arabs. Most Arabs in the land of Israel (AKA the 'Palestinians'), certainly those of them who are good people of good will, of which there are many, will accept and support the Sanhedrin since the Sanhedrin will be respectful, fair and kind to them. It will be the first ruler they ever had who will help them to prosper, whereas otherwise without a Sanhedrin they barely stand a chance to succeed or prosper in any thing. For and explanation of what are 'Jewish Arabs' see the chapter 'Most 'Palestinians' Come from Jews and Many May Still be Jewish'.

The Talmud Rules Conclusively that a Sanhedrin Is Needed to Bring the Moshiah

Talmud Bavli Eruvin 43b "*we tell the beit din hagadol that Elijah has come*" means that there will be a Sanhedrin (which is the Beit Din haGadol) before Elijah comes. This supports the Rambam's law in Mishne Torah Laws of Sanhedrin 4:11 that the Rabbis of the generation will re-establish a Sanhedrin with smeecha; even if the Sanhedrin is at that point in time just partially functioning because the Temple is not built yet; since the Temple is needed for the full functioning of the Sanhedrin. Again, this is a critical issue because if there is no Sanhedrin when the Messiah or Elijah comes, then how will the people know that he is the Messiah or Elijah if there is no Sanhedrin to clarify the issue? Also what does it mean 'the Messiah comes"? What does 'coming' entail? The people and certainly not the governments of the world will not accept the Moshiah with out a Sanhedrin.

In any case, whether in its final time (Has viShalom) or hastened (G-d Willing), it is a Mitzvah for us to make a Sanhedrin so as to know how to serve Hashem properly and bring back the authority of Torah and authoritatively certify that Elijah and the Moshiah have come and to appoint the Moshiah king. Who knows? Maybe we will merit the hastened Moshiah and have a prophet and the anointing oil to anoint the Moshiah king without Elijah as per the Pleisi in Beit HaSafek chapter 110 (Rav Yehudah Chayoon in 'When Moshiah Comes'). This will only happen if we make a Sanhedrin.

Logically, Elijah the prophet who is supposed to proceed the Messiah, according to Rashi and Ramban, cannot be identified unless there is a Sanhedrin to greet him and authoritatively certify that he is in fact really Elijah the prophet who has returned. This means that there must be a Sanhedrin *without smeecha from Elijah the prophet* before he comes. This means that we must make a Sanhedrin now in order for Moshiah (and Elijah) to come. Even if just Elijah were to come, the benefit to society would be immense.

Be clear on this point, not only can't the Messiah be identified without a Sanhedrin, but Elijah the prophet who is supposed to proceed the Messiah according to Rashi and Ramban, also cannot be identified unless there is a Sanhedrin to greet him and authoritatively certify that he is in fact really Elijah the prophet who has returned. This implies that there is a Sanhedrin *without the original ancient smeecha* before Elijah comes.

Talmud Bavli Megilla 17b/18a says that Jerusalem will be built first before (the Messiah son of) David becomes king as it is written "*Afterwards the children of Israel shall return and seek Hashem their G-d and David their king* (Hosea 3:5)". Building Jerusalem includes building the Sanhedrin that will await and identify Elijah and the Moshiah. The builders of the Sanhedrin are builders of Jerusalem.

These above listed sources mean that if the redemption comes hastened (G-d Willing), there will be a Sanhedrin of the greatest Rabbis of the generation who reestablish smeecha based on the Rambam's shita (method), who will identify and authoritatively certify the hastened Moshiah, where the anointing oil will be found by someone other than Elijah and a prophet other than Elijah will be proven to the Sanhedrin who will anoint the Moshiah king (with or even without Elijah's return). If the Moshiah comes in the final time, there will be a Sanhedrin before Elijah comes in order to identify and authoritatively certify that Elijah has come, then the Sanhedrin will learn from Elijah the unknown Torah laws (taikoo halachot) and receive the ancient anointing oil from him (Keriesoth 5), then the Sanhedrin of seventy elders and the prophet Elijah as head will be able to identify, authoritatively certify, anoint and establish the real Moshiah as king of Israel before he builds the third Temple. Then, after establishing the king Moshiah, we will be able to eradicate Amalek and then build the third Temple, in that order (Rashi on Talmud Bavli Sanhedrin 20 and Rambam laws of kings chapter one). This is the order of how these stages occur in the redemption.

The next step to bring the redemption is in our hands: to build the Sanhedrin and market it to the Israeli public. Yes, that is correct: we need to market it using today's modern marketing techniques which can market anything. That is part of the budget.

<u>The Power of Torah and the Messiah</u>

The Messiah, as any Jew, derives his power from Torah study and proper observance of the Mitzvoth (commandments) learned from the Torah. The codes of Jewish law, based on the Talmud, says that a Jew must 'toil' in Torah as his main occupation and only earn a minimum livelihood to sustain his learning as a general rule. It is forbidden for Gentiles to learn Torah specific to the Jews though; only their own Noahide Torah, which also gives them merit.

Let us explain. The Torah was created before the world was created and the letters and words of the Torah are the building blocks upon which the world was designed by G-d, the Creator. The Torah is the Will and Wisdom of the Creator and a Jew who lives in accordance with it is given mastery over nature in accordance with the degree in which he observes and learns the Torah and nullifies his will to the commandments (Ethics of the Fathers). Torah study is one of the pillars upon which the world stands along with kind deeds, Temple service, Peace, Truth and Torah Justice (Ethics of the Fathers chapter 1).

There are many examples of the power of Torah. In king Hezkiyahoo's time '*Our feet stood in war in the merit of the gates (a 'gate' is where the Rabbinic judges learn an detach Torah and judge) of Jerusalem that toiled in Torah*' (Talmud Bavli Macoth 10). This Torah study and prayer that king Hezkiyahoo sponsored in the synagogues and houses of study broke the enemy Sanchereb in his siege of Jerusalem (the ancient enactment of the war of Gog an Magog which will be continued and completed finally in the end times according to Ramban) where 180,000 of his forces were miraculously killed by a plague outside the walls of Jerusalem (Talmud Bavli Sanhedrin 94b).

Rav Pinchas ben Yair, a righteous Torah scholar, controlled the creations and commanded the river to split on the merit of his Torah because the creations are controlled by the Torah which is the basis on which the world was created and is run (Talmud Bavli Hoolin 7). He also said that '*Torah leads to carefulness (in keeping the commandments), carefulness leads to agility (in keeping the commandments), agility leads to being clean (of sin), cleanliness leads to keeping separate from sinfulness, separateness from sinfulness leads to purity (from evil spirits caused by sin; such as semen spilled in vein or touching the dead), purity leads to piety, piety leads to humility, humility leads to fear of sin, fear of sin leads to Holiness, Holiness leads to Holy Spirit, Holy Spirit leads to <u>resurrection of the dead</u>, and pity is greater than them all…or humility is greater then them all*' (Talmud Bavli Avoda Zara 20).

'*The Torah of someone who is a transgressor is poison of death, whereas the Torah of someone who is clean of sin (hagoon) is a medicine of life*' (Talmud Bavli Taanit 7). Therefore, we see that it is important to learn from someone who is free of sin. There are righteous people (in Hebrew called a 'Tzadik') like this who it is preferential to learn with but one must earn the merit and acceptance to learn with him. The Messiah is a Tzadik who learned from Tzadikeem, and thus his Torah is very healing, purifying, powerful, and gives him mastery over the material world and to others who learn from him.

The Messiah will have the best Rabbis to teach him.

The Messiah Will likely Be a Multi-Denominational Orthodox Jew

Orthodox Jews recognize that the Messiah will be an orthodox Jew. Every other sect or group may have those who delude them selves into thinking that their group includes the Messiah but only do the orthodox Jews live most properly by the Torah and this is a requirement to be the Messiah; living by the Torah commandments totally. Only the orthodox Jews do this so therefore the Messiah will be an orthodox Jew. This is correct that the Messiah is an orthodox Jew since the Messiah lives by the Torah as does any orthodox Jew. But, many orthodox Jewish people, unfortunately, think that he must be a member of their own sect, exclusively, in order to be the Messiah. This is not true.

Each orthodox sect embraces or emphasizes some parts of the Torah that the other sects don't embrace and these parts of the Torah are based on the writings of their leading Rabbis. The Messiah will collect all the main points of Torah truth of all the orthodox sects and unify them into one general all encompassing form of Torah that encompasses the ancient Torah that he will learn and teach by his special ways of hard work ('toiling in Torah'), insight and prophesy. He will see the good points and point of truth in every Jew and every orthodox sect and add them together to his more comprehensive Torah understanding and live by these aspects himself. The Messiah also has to be connected with every form of orthodox Torah Judaism, and to understand the mistakes, as well as the good points, of the cults in which the other Jews partake, such as Reform, Communism, Conservative, Atheism, Zionism, etc. in order to rectify them, where possible.

The Messiah has a Pure and Humble Heart

Ones' character traits are the foundation of his service to G-d and any defect in one of these traits inhibits his proper observance of the Torah commandments (Proverbs, The Gaon of Vilna, Even Shleima chapter one verse one).

The key to the Messiah's power is his proper observance of the Torah commandments. The key to his proper observance of the Torah commandments is good character traits and especially a pure and humble heart.

A person's fear of Heaven, love of G-d, evil inclinations, good inclinations, lusts, desires, arrogance, humility, slothfulness, diligence, hatred, love, all lay in the heart. Ones' heart, more then his mind, affect his actions, speech, thoughts and overall behavior. This is why the Torah refers to 'wisdom of the heart' and not head Also, in spite of those who say that the heart desires what the eyes see, it is also true that 'The eyes see what the heart desires'.

When G-d chose king David to be king He said: '*Do not look at his appearance or his tall stature, for I have rejected him. Man sees what the eyes behold, but Hashem sees into the heart*' (Samuel I 16:8). '*The Compassionate One (G-d) desires the heart*' (Talmud Bavli Sanhedrin 106). G-d wants a good heart; not a good head. Eisav had a good head but his evil heart over ruled it to he was wicked. A true Talmid Chacham must not just have a good head but must have good midoth (character traits) which lay in his heart, not his head.

A pure heart is the key to serving G-d properly. This is also the key to being the Messiah. In the people of Israel, the king is the heart, the Sanhedrin the brain, the people the body, the Army the arms and the Mosad the feet. For the body to act properly it must have a pure humble heart, a pure humble king.

'*Every haughty heart is an abomination to Hashem*' (Proverbs 16:5). Arrogance, pride, haughtiness, Ego all push away the Divine Mystical Presence of G-d (Talmud and Zohar in many sources). '*Humility is the greatest trait of them all and can lead to Holy Spirit and resurrection of the dead*' (Talmud Bavli Avoda Zara 20). The basis of the Messiah's proper Torah observance and study rests upon his humility in his heart.

The people learn from the king's example of purity of heart and humility. This is part of the function for the Messiah for Israel: to lead by example in purity of heart and humility.

We see that the foundation of the greatness of the Messiah lays in his highly pure heart and humility. He is king and as the heart of Israel, his heart must be pure and humble for Israel to be pure and humble.

A good book I read called 'A Heart to know Me' by Eliezar Yehudah Miller talks about the importance of heart in service of G-d. It is in the merit of this book that I write this chapter. Another related book is called 'Duties of the Heart'. Other good books to help character development are 'Orhot Tzadikeem' and the 'Tanya Igereth Tshuva' which was written by who I believe was the potential Messiah if his generation - the Baal haTanya.

The Importance of being connected to Righteous Jews for the Messiah to Come

Rav Nahman of Breslov (remembrance of the righteous is for blessing) brings out some essential points in his writings about what is needed to save the world and bring the Messiah.

He very astutely points out that in order for a person to serve G-d properly he must be 'connected' to a Righteous Jew (in Hebrew called a 'Tzadik') who he himself lives by the Torah and thus teaches and leads by example. Being 'connected' means seeking out and abiding by his advise.

A Tzadik is basically someone who lives by the Torah fully with almost no sins. A perfect Tzadik has no sins and does not even have an inclination for sin according to the Tanya. Rosh HaShana 16 says that one is judged a Tzadik on Rosh HaShana if his merits out weigh his sins. The first Rashi on Parshat Noah says that the main thing that makes a person a Tzadik is good deeds (not Torah wisdom as some may think). An evil person like Eisav can be wise in Torah but he is not a Tzadik.

He says that a Tzadik may or may not be wise in Torah and may not have learned much Torah (Sefer haMidoth) but the Shulhan Aruch says that to be a perfect Tzadik then one must know the Talmud and its halcahic reasoning well. He says that only by being connected to a Righteous Jew can a person really learn to serve Hashem properly. He also says the important point that in order for the Messiah to be revealed, people must be connected to a Tzadik, who he also says have Ruah HaKodesh or Nivooah, which is the only way that can reveal who the Messiah really is. This makes sense if you think about it also because only by being connected to a Tzadik will people be living by the Torah properly and thus merit the coming of the Messiah. People actually be able to know who the Messiah is through their *Tzadik's prophesy, Ruah HaKodesh (Holy Spirit) and true wisdom of seeing who is the potential Messiah of the generation.*

One can really only trust a Tzadik to know these things and must be connected to a Tzadik for these things to happen; serving Hashem properly and the Messiah of our generation being revealed in our generation while he is still alive and can still be the Messiah.

The Messiah Redeems Even the Worst Sinners if They Repent

The following passages from the prophets tell us that the Messiah will redeem even the worst sinners if they repent but that those sinners who don't repent are marked for punishments in the redemption period and will not be redeemed.

'*A redeemer* (Ibn Ezra says this means the Messiah) *shall come to Zion, and to those who repent of transgression in Jacob, says Hashem*' (Isaiah 59:20). Radak on the previous and following verses of Isaiah says that all of Israel will repent fully after seeing the miracles that HaShem performs. '*Zion will be redeemed through justice and her penitent through righteousness. And destruction shall come over rebels and sinners together, and those who forsake Hashem will perish*' (Isaiah 1:25-6-7-8). These verses show that the Messiah will redeem even the worst sinners if they repent but that those sinners who don't repent will be destroyed and perish.

More scriptures make these statements:

Amos 9:9-12 (9) '*Behold the eyes of the Lord Hashem are upon the sinful kingdom, and I will destroy it from upon the face of the earth, but I will not totally destroy the House of Jacob… (10) They will perish by the sword, all the sinners of My people, those who say: 'Not because of us will the evil approach any sooner'. (11) On that day I will raise up the fallen booth of David; I will repair their breaches and raise up its ruins, and I will build it up as in days of old, (12) so that they, upon whom My name is called (the orthodox Jews who live properly by the Torah), may inherit the remnant of Edom and all the nations, the word of Hashem, who shall do this'.*

Ezekiel 20:34 '*and I will take you out of the nations and I will gather you from the lands where you have been scattered' and 20:38 'and I will purge out of you the rebels and the criminals against Me, and I will take them out of the land of their sojournings, but to the land of Israel they shall not come.*'

Isaiah 1:25-28 "*(25) And I will return My hand upon you and purge away your dross as with lye and remove all your tin. (26) And I will restore your judges as at first and your counselors as in the beginning. Afterwards you shall be called City of Righteousness, Faithful City. (27) Zion shall be redeemed through justice (redemption shall come through practicing justice) and her penitents through righteousness. (28) And destruction shall come over rebels and sinners together, and those who forsake Hashem shall perish* (During the Redemption period, Hashem will kill all the unrepentant secular Jews and sinners among the corrupt 'religious' as He did in the holocaust and pogroms and AIDS, etc.." Radak identifies Isaiah 1:28 with Malachi 3:19 in which '*all the presumptuous and all who practice wickedness shall become like straw*' exterminated by the sun '*burning like a furnace'* (in hell) as part of Hashem's retribution for their sins. In Likootei Moran chapter 26 Rav Nahman of Breslov said that the wicked of Israel will have to be killed by the sword of Edom in order for the Jewish people to merit the land of Israel. The wicked sinners will be exterminated as part of the purification of human society as was done in the holocaust (Rav Shach zt'l) which also removed the opposition to the Zionists and paved the way for the state of Israel that paves the way for the Messiah, and the Israeli national religious Zionists say will come to rule as his seat and throne, but, the Haredim say the State of Israel must fall for the Messiah to rule since the State of Israel opposes the Messiah being king. The light of the Messiah heals the righteous and burns the wicked.

The above passages show that the Moshiah won't redeem everyone, even though he would want to if it were possible but since people have free choice it is really by their own will that they can decide to do the right thing. He redeems those who return to live by the Torah ways of HaShem, even the worst sinners, including even some big Rabbis, who become the pure and 'righteous remnant' of the people of Israel.

The 'footsteps', 'heels' and 'nine months' of 'birth pangs' before the Messiah comes

The Prophesies of the Torah often use the expressions of 'nine months' of 'birth pangs' before the Messiah is 'born' as a metaphor for the suffering of the Jewish people in exile that will precede and accompany the coming of the Messiah in the redemption period. This is symbolized metaphorically by the pain of a woman in childbirth (nine months is the time of childbirth). The 'nine months' of 'birth pangs' before the Messiah is 'born' are metaphors that represent the period of time in history that it takes for the Messiah to come, and the travail is called 'birth pangs of the coming of the Messiah'. It is not literally 'nine months' as some mistakenly believe. The period of history that comes at the end of the exile until prior to the coming of the Messiah is referred to the 'footsteps' or 'heels' of the Messiah (Rashi on Talmud Bavli Sotah 49b).

This "nine months" can be as long as two thousand years according to Maharsha, Rashi, and Biur HaGra to Brachot 8b. We see from the Maharsha on Talmud Bavli Sanhedrin 96a that 'The final two millennia (from 240 CE onward) is the period of travails of the Messiah, 'the birth pangs of the coming of the Messiah', when the Messiah can come and bring an end to the exile and suffering.'. From Jeremiah 49:22, 47:24, 50:43; Isaiah 54:1, 66:7; Micah 5:2 we see the use of the phrase 'birth pangs' as a metaphor for the travail of people in general and the Jewish people in exile until the Messianic redemption. We see from the statements in the Talmud "*Before Messiah comes, the kingdom of Aram will spread out in the world for nine months* (Talmud Bavli Yoma 9b)", "*The son of David (Messiah) will not come until the wicked kingdom of Rome (Edom) has spread over the entire world for nine months* (Talmud Bavli Yoma 10a)", "*The son of David (Messiah) will not come until the kingdom (Edom) has extended it's dominion over Israel nine months* (Talmud Bavli Sanhedrin 98a)" that the kingdoms of Edom and Aram will dominate the world and Israel during the period prior to the coming of the Messiah. In other words, the Jews and Gentiles in the world of exile are subjugated by evil Edomite and Aramite Gentile kingdom regimes until the Messiah comes, particularly Edom and Aram (the West and the Arab world ostensibly). This period of exile where the Jews are subjugated by Gentiles and evil and are waiting for the Messiah is metaphorically referred to in the Torah as the 'nine months' of 'birth pangs' before the Messiah comes.

Signs of the times before the Messiah comes: 'The Heels of the Messiah'

Although the prophets discuss the conditions of the world prior to the coming of the Messiah, the classic and most descriptive scriptures that depict the times before the Messiah comes, referred to as the 'heels of the Messiah', are from the Talmud. These quotes from the Talmud are often repeated verbatim in the Midrash, which is often the case between the Talmud and Midrash that quote the exact same scripture. This raises the question for those who question whether or not the literal meaning of the Midrash is true: If the Midrash is not literally true, then does that mean that the same passages found in the Talmud are also not literally true? The answer is 'no', and that the passages in both the Midrash and Talmud are always literally true but it depends on how one interprets them in their sometimes metaphoric meaning which must be elucidated by authoritative Rabbis upon whose source of interpretation we rely. As many do, one may speculate regarding which of these prophesies are fulfilled in our time. I've heard all sorts of ideas on the subject and there a number of books that discuss the topic. *Here are the key sources:*

Talmud Bavli Sota 49b and Sanhedrin 97a tell us: *'In the period which will precede the coming of the son of David (the Messiah son of David) insolence will increase and costs will soar'.* This statement literally means in Hebrew the 'heels of the Messiah' from Psalms 89:52. Rashi says that this refers to the final end of the exile. Talmud Bavli Taanit 7a says that among some six sins insolence, lashon hara and neglecting Torah study that cause droughts; which would cause food costs to rise. '... *The grape vine will yield its fruit yet wine will be expensive' (ibid).* Rashi says that people will be engaged in drinking parties so there will be a great demand for wine. '... *and the kingship will turn to heresy (ibid).* 'Heresy' means not believing in and respecting the Torah or the legitimate kosher (fit) orthodox Rabbis.

The world's dominant power (Edom) will be drawn after the beliefs of the Jewish heretics (Meleches Shlomo) and will spread these heretical beliefs throughout the world (Tifereth Yisrael). Some examples of these heretical leaders are Carl Marx who founded communism, Sigmund Freud who founded modern psychology, Messianic Jews, the gay rights movement, the pederast rights movement, Islam, Christianity, the Zionist occupied government (ZOG), reform and conservative 'rabbis', Jewish Harvard and Yale and other colleges' atheistic college professors (liberal, *conservative and center*), left wing atheist fascists, Yolo, Henry Kissinger, Council on Foreign Relations, etc.. Rashi on Sanhedrin 97a says that the prophesy that *'All of it has turned white, it is pure'* refers to that when the world has turned to heresy it will be time for the redemption.

Many of these heretical groups are filled with righteous Jews of good intention, but, none the less since they did not check what is the true people Torah halacha with the Gadol haDor they are thus heretics. For example reform Rabbis righteously marched with Dr. Martin Luther king (of blessed memory) for Afro-American rights in the 1950-60s at the risk of their own life but none the less they are heretics. Rav Nahman of Breslov says that a Tzadik can make mistakes that even kill people. Be careful! Check what the true Torah understanding and law really is before backing a cause or position because the road to hell is paved with good intentions. The big Rabbis see many things that we don't see, believe it or not, even though we are not 'in touch' (AKA Brainwashed by the 'education' system and biased by the media) because we don't watch TV, News paper, Radio, Internet, etc.. We must also remember that as Ethics of the Fathers teaches us 'don't judge someone until you stand in his place'; we don't really know what other people went through in life or what makes them the way they are so we really can't judge people. Only G-d really Knows and can judge; not man.

Talmud Bavli Sota 49b (and repeated in Talmud Bavli Sanhedrin 97a) continue: '*In the period which will precede the coming of the son of David (the Messiah son of David) there shall be no rebuke/proof*'. Rashi says that people won't reproach each other because they too will be iniquitous. '....*The meeting places will be used for immorality*'. This can mean 'pick up bars' but can have other interpretations as well. '...A*nd the Galilee will be destroyed (*probably in the war of Gog and Magog since the North is the best direction from which to attack Israel-'the evil shall come from the North'*) and the Gavlan desolated (*commentaries don't say that this is the Golan heights which logically in my opinion will be totally destroyed in the war of Gog and Magog along with the IDF's most heavily fortified position- the Northern Command which is under the mountain of Tsfat as every body knows*) ... and the people who live outside of Jerusalem will wander about from city to city and they will not be given grace'*. Rashi says these people are those who live on the borders of the land of Israel or the members of the Sanhedrin's courtyard. '... *And the wisdom of the scribes (*Kiddushin 30a says this means Torah scholars*) will decay/stink'*. This is from Jeremiah 49:7 'Council has been lost from the children. Their wisdom has decayed'. '*And those who fear sin will be despised (*or will melt away Psalms 58:8*) and truth will be absent'*. Sanhedrin 97a says that this means that the truth will be divided into flocks. Maharsha says that the generation will be so corrupt that the small numbers of truthful men will be forced to flee the towns and subsist in small secluded groups. '... *Youth will make the faces of the elders turn white'*. Rashi on Sanhedrin 97a says this means that they will shame them publicly. '*Elders will stand in the presence of minors*'. Rashi on Sanhedrin 97a says this means that youths will demand honor from elders as a sign of the insolence of the times. '... *The son derides his father. A daughter rises against her mother, a bride against her mother in law, a man's enemies are members of his own home. The face of the generation is like the face of a dog*'. Rashi on Sanhedrin 97a says this means they will be shameless or the literal meaning. Eitz Yosef says that this means that 'the face of the generation' refers to the wealthy who will lack compassion to the poor and will refuse them charity, like dogs who refuse to share their meat.

Rabbi Elchanan Wasserman in Kuntros Ikvos Meshicha quoting the Chefetz Chaim says that '*the face of the generation*' are the leaders (Bereishis Rabba 79:6) who, as demagogues, will first check to see if the views they wish to espouse will be popularly received, like a dog who looks back to see if his master follows. I believe that it could mean the literal interpretation (Rashi), that peoples' faces, which reflect ones' inner character traits, will literally resemble the faces of dogs, because people will be like dogs in their character traits. This is not necessarily in the negative sense and could mean 'like dog's following their hearts passion which are manipulated by their masters' who control them through the media and 'education' system. One can see these phenomena today.

Talmud Bavli Sota 49b and Sanhedrin 97a continue: "*In the period which will precede the coming of the son of David (the Messiah son of David) a son is not ashamed by his father* (knowing his sins and shortcomings). *Upon what can we lean? On our Father in Heaven*" (Talmud Bavli Sota 49b and Sanhedrin 97a). '... *The truth will be absent and he who flees from evil will ... be considered foolish by society....and honor will dwindle*' Rashi says this means that people won't respect one another (Talmud Sanhedrin 97a). The Talmud tells a parable on truthfulness whose moral is that telling a lie undermines the world (Maharsha) and that although it is permissible to lie in certain cases like to ensure peace (Talmud Bavli Baba Metzia 23b-24a), the lie may have non-positive repercussions none the less (Maharal).

Midrash Yalkoot Shimoni chapter 9 section 548 similarly also says: '*Rabbi Yehuda says that in the generation when the son of David comes the committee will turn to immorality, the Galilee will be destroyed and the Gavlan will be guilty and the people living outside of Jerusalem will go around from city to city, the truth will be in flocks going and sitting and will not reside in one place* (partial truth held by different groups where the whole truth is not found in any one group), *the wisdom of the scribes will decay/stink, and people fearful of sin will be despised, and the face of the generation will be like that of a dog, flocks and flocks in the* (spiritual) *desert as is said 'The truth will not be found.'.... And the vine (won't) give her fruit and wine will be expensive, and all the world will turn to heresy* (not believing in the Divinity of the Torah and not respecting the true Torah scholars even though these 'heretics' may be basically well intended but have been irresponsible and negligent in that they have not adequately researched what is the true and right thing to do and think according to the Torah usually from simply just not knowing any better or are 'intellectually lazy' possibly in part caused from not learning Talmud adequately. Again, the road to hell is paved with good intentions since people did not check to see what the real halacha really is and caused much damage as a result of their negligence) *and this is supported by Rabbi Yitzchak as Rabbi Yitzchak said 'The son of David wont come until all the word has turned to heresy'* (Midrash Yalkoot Shimoni chapter 9 section 548).

'In the generation when the son of David will come Torah scholars will decrease and the rest of the people's eyes will become worn out from grief and anxiety (i.e. social problems, money problems, marriage problems, health problems, problems with the youth, threat of war from Paras/Hamas, etc.). Many troubles and harsh decrees will come up in the world. Before one trouble is over another one will quickly come' (Talmud Bavli Sanhedrin 97a). This period of difficulty before the coming of the Messiah is known as the 'travails of the Messiah' (in Hebrew called 'Hevlei Mashiah') as an analogy to the suffering and travail of a woman in childbirth. According to the Maharsha on Sanhedrin 97b-98a this suffering is meant to force the Jewish people to repent before the Messiah comes. Radak on Isaiah 59:19 says that these tribulations will cause all of the Jewish people to repent fully and that all Jews will be saved. We hope this true. This suffering and tribulation is a result of the deterioration of the morals and ethics and Torah observance in society and paves the way to radical new change of the coming of the Messiah, like the way a kernel of wheat must rot in the ground before sprouting up (Aruch liNer, Maharal, Netzach Yisrael ch 32, Toras Chaim).

'That your enemies have taunted, Hashem, that they have taunted the heels (delay) of the Messiah' (Psalms 89:52) shows how the anti-Semites will mock

the Jewish people in the delay of the Messiah, using this as 'evidence' that the Messiah will never come (Radak).

Talmud Bavli Sanhedrin 97a goes on to tell us: "*In the period which will precede the coming of the son of David (the Messiah son of David) … Hashem will judge (redeem) His people when He sees that the (saving) hand is going and no one is being protected or helped* (Deuteronomy 32:36)'. From this verse we derive that '*The son of David won't come until the informers have become numerous*' (Talmud Bavli Sanhedrin 97a). This refers to those who inform on Jews to the foreign authorities, which may include the Israeli government since it is not really a Jewish government according to Torah law. When they become too successful G-d will bring redemption (Rashi). The son of David won't come '*until the students of Torah have become few*' (ibid) (Rashi notes here that the Torah scholars are Israel's true source of power and leadership), '*until the lowest denomination of money has gone from the purse'* (ibid) *(Rashi says this means the people will be destitute)*, and '*until the Jewish people despair of the redemption*' (ibid).Rashi says that this means that the Jews will be in such a dismal state that they will think that G-d has forsaken them and will despair of being redeemed. The Talmud here then notes that there are three things that come when one does not expect them: '*the Messiah, a find (of a lost object or something else good), and a scorpion'.*

Talmud Bavli Sanhedrin 98a says: '*The son of David will not come until a fish will be bought for a sick person and it will not be found*' *as it is stated 'Then I will make their waters settle and cause their rivers to flow like oil*'. On Ezekiel 32:14 Rashi says this means that waters will congeal and be unable to support aquatic life. On ibid 29:21 '*On that day I will cause power to sprout for the House of David'*, Rashi says this means the Messiah will come. The Jordan River in Israel is barely a trickle today. Ben Yehodah says this means that in those days food will be so scarce that even a sick person will be unable to find a fish. Maharal says that this means that the worlds decline prior to the redemption will be so comprehensive that it will effect even the aquatic creatures. Maybe this means that poverty will be so rampant that even a sick person will pay for his well needed food (the fish) and he will be not receive it because someone else who is starving or sick took it.

'The son of David will not come until the unworthy kingship has been ceased from the people of Israel… as it is written' He will cut off the shoots with shears… at that time, a gift shall be brought to Hashem, a people pulled and torn '(Isaiah

18:5-7)' (Talmud Bavli Sanhedrin 98a). There is a principle in the Torah called 'Baal haMea Baal haDeah' which means that the wealthy control society. Where many translations defines the translation as government I translate it as kingship or even better 'the establishment' because it is the wealthy 'powers that be', also called 'the establishment', in today's society who are 'the kingship' and dictate to the government what to do, not the other way around. This is how it really works in the USA today. The president and senate and congress and 'Supreme Court' etc. are mere puppets of the wealthy Eisav's in power. Eisav is Edom.

Professor of political science Paul Eidelberg said that Israel is an oligarchy where some fifty to three hundred or so ruling families control the country and choose the political leaders. The media is used to create a political smoke screen so as to make an illusion as to what's really going on. Rashi and Radak say that this means that before the Messiah comes the most petty vestige of the Jewish peoples' autonomy will be gone. The Messiah either comes 'like a poor man riding on a donkey' at the final time if the generation is guilty or hastened before the final time like the 'clouds of Heaven' if the generation is worthy (Talmud Bavli Sanhedrin 98). This means that the Messiah can come either 'hastened' before the final time if the Jewish people repent, or, in the 'final time' if the Jewish people don't repent. I look at this verse in terms of its possible meaning in the two cases of 1) the Messiah coming 'hastened' if repent fully and empower a Torah true Sanhedrin based government in Israel where there is no more unworthy kingship, or 2) if he comes in the 'final time', where the Jewish people don't repent and the society will be so deteriorated and corrupt that there will be only unworthy kingship with no real Torah kingship, just anarchy, before Gog and Magog attacks. We can learn from this that to hasten the redemption the Jewish people in Israel must empower a Torah government lead by the Tzadikeem (righteous Jews who really live by the Torah).

'The son of David will not come until the vile spirited (arrogant, haughty) are eliminated from the people of Israel… as it is written 'I will leave in your midst a humble and forbearing people and they will take refuge in the Name of Hashem (Zephaniah 3:12)' (Talmud Bavli Sanhedrin 98a). Talmud Bavli Sota 5a says that arrogance pushes away the Divine Mystical Presence of G-d and will return when arrogant people are removed from the Jewish people.

'The son of David will not come until all the judges and police are destroyed from the people of Israel' as it is stated 'I will turn My Hand against you, clean away your dross as with soap, then I will restore your (real Torah law enforcing-called the Sanhedrin) judges (Isaiah 1:25-26)' (Talmud Bavli Sanhedrin 98a). Yad Ramah says this means that there will be no judges no police and there will be a state of anarchy. Maharsha says this means '*the corrupt and ignorant judges*' as it states in Talmud Bavli Shabbos 139 that '*G-d will not rest His Divine Mystical Presence on Israel until the bad judges are eliminated ... if you see a generation where troubles and retributions fall on Israel then look to the judges* (for the cause of the problems)'. I look at this verse in terms of its possible meaning in the two cases of the Messiah coming 'hastened' or in 'its final time', which means that the Messiah will come hastened if we have only good judges and police who uphold the Torah law which is the foundation of rectifying society, and if he comes in the final time, the society will be so corrupt and immoral that there will be no good judges nor good police who uphold the Torah true law as G-d requires, thus anarchy. This Talmud passage then brings as a source: '*Zion will be redeemed through justice (Torah law upheld by the Sanhedrin in Jerusalem) and Jews will return to her through charity* (Isaiah 1:27). Yad Rama and Maharsha then go on to say that these judges (and police) who deter the coming of the Messiah are those who portray themselves as G-d fearing but in fact are really wicked. In any case we see from here that bad judges and police who fail to uphold the Torah law delay the coming of the Messiah.

'If you see a generation upon which many troubles come upon it like a river, expect the Messiah' as it is said 'When the troubles of Hashem's devouring Spirit come like a river, then a redeemer will come to Zion' (Isaiah 59:19-20) (Talmud Bavli Sanhedrin 98a).

'Put my coffin deep in the ground because there will not be a single palm in Babylon (located in the area of modern Iraq) *to which a horse of the Persians will not be tethered, and there will not be a single coffin in the land of Israel out of which a horse of the Medes will not eat straw*' (Talmud Bavli Sanhedrin 98a-b). Rashi here says that the army of Persia (Paras) and Media will vanquish Babylon before proceeding to conquer the land of Israel in the war of Gog and Magog. Their cavalry will be so immense that it will fill the entire country of Babylon. In the land of Israel coffins will be dug out of the ground to be used as feeding troughs for their horses. In today's terms, and the conditions and times may change, this would be interpreted as meaning that the army of Iran

will march through Iraq on their way to Israel to attack her in the war of Gog and Magog. Wikipedia claims that today Iran has over one million infantry ready to march, the world's largest infantry. Russia, Iran's military engineering backer, is said to have the largest stable of horses.

Although most people interpret the Bible prophesies of horses and donkeys as being metaphors for modern mechanized vehicles such as armored personal carriers, jeeps, trucks and tanks, there may be reasons that these modern weapons won't be effective (such as lack of non irradiated oil or other reasons) and animals may have to be used to carry the troops and supplies. Therefore, the prophesies of military animals coming in the attack of Gog and Magog (Ezekiel 38-39, Zachariah 12-14) may be literal or metaphoric. It doesn't really matter (unless someone is a relevant military planner).

"*The Messiah does not come until all the souls are vacated from the chamber of souls in Heaven*" (Talmud Bavli Avoda Zara 5a). The chamber of souls was created with the souls in the first six days of Creation and separates the angels from the Divine Presence (Rashi on Talmud Bavli Yivamoth 63b). The souls wait to be put into new bodies on earth.

'*In the generation that the Messiah comes there will be false accusations and vilifications (Rashi) against the Torah scholars... decree (against the Jews) after decree ... there will be plunderers and plunderers of plunderers*' (Talmud Bavli Ketuboth 112b). We hear in our times '*false accusations and vilifications against the Torah scholars*' when people libel us with comments like 'primitives', 'delusional', 'parasites', 'traitors', 'sexual deviants', etc.. Examples of decrees by Edom were the unjust anti-Semitic persecution and imprisonment of the Jewish hero Jonathan Pollard, the unjust anti-Semitic persecution and imprisonment of the kosher meat factory owner Shalom Mordechai Rubashkin, the forced evacuation of Gush Katif, the proposed Palestinian State, the Jewish building freeze in Yehuda and Samaria (the West Bank), outlawing of circumcision and kosher slaughtering of animals in various European countries. An example of plundering today is oil companies robbing oil that the Arabs robbed from the original land owners. Another example is record companies robbing artists and then being robbed themselves by Internet piracy and piracy from China. The list of examples goes on and on.

We see from these verses that if the Messiah comes in the final time that the society will be corrupt, deteriorated, unethical and immoral, which means Divine retributions of violence, poverty and disease for our sins (Ethics of the

Fathers) will be rampant. If we return to live fully by the Torah, then we can merit the Messiah coming hastened in our time. It is a realistic possibility, but we must repent fully and establish the potential Moshiah of our generation to be king for this to happen.

We all just have to take the first step of taking on new Mitzvoth (Torah commandments); one by one, step by step; starting with the Sabbath, then learning Torah, then another commandment which we like, then another one, etc., step by step, like a twelve step recovery program being coached by Righteous Rabbis and Tzadikeem. Then the Messiah will come in our time. Call your local orthodox Rabbi and Internet Rabbis for assistance.

The Seven Year Sabbatical cycle prior to the coming of the Messiah

Talmud Bavli Sanhedrin 97a and Yalkoot Shimoni Chapter 9 section 548 both describe a seven year Sabbatical cycle prior to the coming of the Messiah. This seven year period may, or may not, correlate to the 'seven years' of the Messiah's suffering and imprisonment prior to his being released from prison and fighting the forces of Gog and Magog as described in Yalkoot Shimoni on Isaiah 60. Ralbag says that the number seven is sometimes not literal but used to express 'many' so 'seven years' may mean 'many years', which means minimally three years, in the case of the Messiah's suffering.

Talmud Bavli Sanhedrin 97a gives us the sequence of the seven years:

1) 'First year it rains only on some towns,
2) second year arrows of famine set forth (Rashi says there is not an abundance of food anywhere),
3) third year there is a great famine where men, woman and children and the pious and people of good deeds will perish and Torah will be forgotten,
4) fourth year sufficiency but not a complete sufficiency,
5) fifth year great sufficiency,
6) sixth year 'Koloth' (in Hebrew this could mean voices, thunder, horn blowing, or reports) reports of the Messiah,
7) in the seventh year there are 'Wars of the Messiah'. By logic this seems to refer to the war of Gog and Magog that the Midrash says happens

in three attacks over the course of one year and ends in the plains of Jericho. Rashi here says that this refers to Gentile wars which we know also happen during the war of Gog and Magog according to the Midrash. See my book on the war of Gog and Magog for details.

Yalkoot Shimoni on Isaiah 60 says that the Messiah will suffer for seven years, be imprisoned, and when he gets released from prison '*Not one kingdom, nor two kingdoms come on him, but one hundred and forty kingdoms surround him'* and he may slay these wicked by the breath of his lips (Isaiah 11). This may imply that the Messiah will be released from prison at the start of the war of Gog and Magog just before the seventh year. Yalkoot Shimoni here also talks about seven years of suffering decreed on the Messiah which *may* mean a seven year prison term that would fall in the seven year period before the Messiah comes. He could even become king immediately upon release from prison, and then immediately after that, the 'one hundred and forty kingdoms' of Gog and Magog begin the attack all on the same day. As a general rule that prophesies for bad can be nullified by repentance, and that G-d upholds good prophesies in some way, if the redemption is hastened by repentance, then maybe this process of war is nullified and Edom will begin to serve him immediately as king instead of being destroyed by military, especially the capitol Rome (Rashi on Numbers 24:19) or other 'natural' means of Divine Retribution destruction such as floods, hurricanes, plagues, etc..

Talmud Bavli Megilla 17b says that 'wars are the beginning of the Redemption'. This may be referring to the war of Gog and Magog, but likely is referring to all wars prior to the different stages of the Redemption. For example the Talmud Bavli Megilla 17 and Sanhedrin 98 cite Ezekiel 36:8 that says that the beginning of the Redemption starts with the sprouting of the fruits of the and of Israel and the return of Jewish people to the land of Israel. In our times these wars would be WWI where Britain conquered the land of Israel (then called by the Roman name 'Palestine") from the Ottoman Empire, thus allowing the Balfour Declaration which gave the Jews the right to the land of Israel, and in WWII, where after the holocaust, international recognition of the need and right for a Jewish state became manifest and the Jewish people were granted the political right to rule the land of Israel as the next stage of the redemption. These wars affected the political changes in control of the land of Israel that allowed the Jews to assume a new political reality over the land of Israel. Today, with the war of Iran/Paras looming over out heads, there are many people in Israel *and Edom*/USA who see the need for the Messiah to be king of Edom, as well as Israel, for the sake of the survival of the kingdoms. This need may be merely perceived out of the selfish interest to survive the war of Iran and other grave dangers such as AIDS and social and economic deterioration that our countries face now for instance; not for the reason to serve G-d properly which is the right reason. The Messiah will try to lead the people to do the right thing (living by the proper Torah law, the 'halacha') for Hashem. Edom may just simply recognize the fact they need a good, truly righteous, leader who is the actual and true Messiah in order to save the world so that they wont die.

The Talmud continues to describe what will happen after the seven year period:

8) in the eighth year the Messiah comes. As all of the Messiah's enemies are destroyed in the war of Gog and Magog, as it is written: '*Those who escape from the sword of Messiah son of Josef will fall by the sword of Messiah son of David and those who escape from there will fall into the garbage bin in the war of Gog*' (Rashi on Isaiah 24:18). With all of his enemies dead, the Messiah's *reign and rule of his kingship are thereby fully secured over Israel and the whole of Edom which formerly controlled the world.*

Talmud Bavli Megilla 17 says "(full) *Redemption in the seventh … and what is seen to say healing in the eighth year… and a blessing of years in the ninth … and what is seen is the ingathering of the exiles after the blessing of the years*". This last war to be fought on the planet earth (may that time come soon) in the seventh year, the war of Gog and Magog, heralds in the redemption and marks what the Rambam calls 'the days of the Messiah' (laws of kings chapter 12). In the eighth year there will be no more disease and all those formerly sick will be healed by leaves (Ezekiel 47:12) that grow on trees that are watered by the new river of Jerusalem that springs from the Mount of Olives that splits open by an earth quake. In the ninth year the remaining Jewish exiles are ingathered to the land of Israel for Messiah as gifts to appease the new king, after the war of Gog, in addition to the first ingathering of exiles that marks the start of the redemption (Rav Saadia Gaon, Emuna vi Daat, chapter on redemption).

It is interesting to note that the Hebrew year, 5775 (Fall 2014 to Fall 2015), is the seventh the year of the seven year cycle and there are many wars in the world all of the sudden. Many nations are warring: the Syrian revolution, the newly declared Islamic State in Iraq (AKA ISIS, ISIL, Dayash), revolt in Egypt, the newly declared Kurdish State, the Russians warring the Ukrainians, the war in Gaza, Japan announced the she will enter back into the military theater in alliance with the West visa vie China after a non militarization policy for the first time since world war two.

The Third Gate of Edom will fall before the Messiah comes

'The students of Rabbi Yosi Ben Kisma asked: When does the (Messiah) son of David come? And he said ... when the gate (of Rome) falls, and it will be built and it will fall and it will be built and will fall and they aren't able to rebuild it until when the son of David comes' (Talmud Bavli Sanhedrin 98a).

Throughout almost the entire Talmud the term Rome is used for Edom when referring to the kingship of Edom since Rome was the emanation of Edom during the time period of history when the Talmud was written down by Ravina and Rav Ashi (circa 450 AD). This exile of Edom is the Jewish people's fourth, longest, most harsh and final exile. Daniel 7 refers to this exile of Edom as the 'fourth beast' and Daniel 11 refers to it as the 'king of the North'. Talmud Bavli Sanhedrin 98 teaches us that the third gate of Edom/ Rome will fall before the Moshiah comes. A 'gate' in the Torah refers to the place where the judges (i.e. the government) of the city sit. In essence, a 'gate' refers to the 'powers that be', or the establishment of wealthy and influential people that really run the government and tell the society it rules what to do.

This third 'gate' referred to here is ostensibly the kingship of Edom which is lead by their 'Nasi'; which translates as prince, president or king in different scriptural contexts; Gog (Ezekiel 38-39), which will fall in the war of Gog and Magog. Today Edom in the West does not have any kings; only presidents and prime ministers. This seems to be the fall of the third gate to which the Talmud is referring here. *'Hashem will destroy Edom through his people Israel'* (Ezekiel 25:14) which does not necessarily mean 'the *state of Israel' or the 'country Israel'*. The gate is likely located in Edom's capitol city which will be destroyed (Numbers 24:18-19); most likely in the war of Gog and Magog. Rashi and Rashbam on Numbers 24:18-19, based on Obadiah 1:18, say that there wont be a survivor of the 'house of Eisav'; which is not necessarily all of the Edomites. Talmud Bavli Avoda Zara 10-11 says that 'house of Eisav' that will be destroyed means those descendants of Eisav who are wicked in the ways that Eisav was wicked (murder, idol worship, stealing, rape, anti-Semitism, etc.). The Talmud here gives examples of two Roman Edomites; Caesar Antoninus and a Roman senator; who were righteous and went to Heaven for protecting and supporting the Jews at the risk of their own lives. The senator was actually killed by being buried alive for saving the Jews. Ramban says there wont be a survivor from every city (of Edom) in the world. This probably means any city in the world, that is an Edomite ruled enemy city of Israel, that poses a threat to Israel or the Messiah's rule will be destroyed in the war. This can be taken care of today easily by weapons of mass destruction (Nuclear, biological, chemical), which the state of Israel is *believed* to have, and the *people of Israel* have access to world wide as we serve in many armies, especially the US, Russian, Chinese, Indian and Persian armies. The Messiah even has followers in many countries who would be happy to do this job of destroying Edom's capitol for him. This does not necessarily mean a nuclear missile launched from the State of Israel, but could be as such if people are viewed as a threat to 'the people of Israel' in the land of Israel, or any where in the world, including the USA. If the people of Israel in the USA are attacked, then the attacker may be neutralized by even an unexpected 'wild card' vigilante force most likely from the USA itself.

When will the Messiah come and what determines his Coming?

The Vilna Gaon summarizes very well when the Messiah will come. He says "*In every generation there are possible final dates for the end of the exile and the Messiah to come, but the Messiah will surely come before the final end. These dates depend on the Tshuvah and merits unique to that generation. The ultimate end however, is not dependant on Tshuva, but on Divine Kindness as it is written 'For My own sake, for My own sake, will I do it. (Isaiah 48:11)' and on the merit of the forefathers, as it is written 'He remembers the charity of the forefathers and brings redemption to their children's children for His sake*' (the book 'Even Shleimah' by the Vilna Gaon Redemption chapter ten, part 9). The book 'Kol haTor' (written by a student of the Vilna Gaon and whose authenticity in representing the Torah wisdom of the Gaon accurately is not accepted by some Torah scholars, as per Rav Gideon Friedman Shlita, such as Rabbi Israel Eliyahoo

Weintraub (zt'l) in his book 'hatkifa bisaarath Eliyahoo' and Rav Moshe Sternbuach Shlita in his work 'Tshuvoth viHagaoth') chapter five claims that the Vilna Gaon said that 'the Messiah will come in a sinful generation without a doubt' which means that he will come at the last possible final time. I have never found any statement in the writings of the Vilna Gaon that I perceived as a mistake so I hope that this quote is not true and that the Messiah will come hastened before the final time or that the final time is now. I believe that this statement is incorrect because no one can know when the Messiah will or wont come because Talmud Bavli Pesachim 54b says that the time of the coming of the Messiah is one of the seven things that are concealed. It is a most secret thing in this world and also in Heaven. Therefore, I don't believe that the Vilna Gaon said that 'the Messiah will come in a sinful generation without a doubt' and that this is just a speculation of his student who wrote Kol haTor.

Daniel chapter 12:9-10 says that these matters of the end of days prophesies of the coming of the Messiah, the redemption and the war of Gog and Magog will be *'obscured until the end time'* and the wicked won't have understand *but the wise will understand.* Talmud Bavli Sanhedrin 97b says that the sages of his day weren't aren't able to calculate when the end time will be. Even the great Torah sage the Ramban attempted to calculate the end but was proven false. Rav says here (ibid) that *'all the ends (auspicious times in every generation for the Messiah to come) have passed and the Messiah's coming depends on repentance (returning to live by the Torah commandments) and good deeds'.* The Talmud Bavli Sanhedrin 97b says that what is preventing the Messiah from coming is the 'Divine Attribute of Justice', which might explain why the Vilna Gaon concludes that ultimately the Messiah will come as a result of 'Divine Kindness' (Even Shleimah), which overrules the Attribute of Divine Justice. By being kind we can arouse the forces of Heaven to reflect back our kindness and this too may arouse Hashem's kindness to bring the end.

Ultimately G-d decides when the Messiah comes, regardless of our meager understanding or wishes of when we think that time may be. Even if one knew the whole Torah and had prophesy, he still really can't know when the Messiah is coming because *this secret is hidden from man*, just as it was hidden from Jacob on his death bed when he gave the blessing to his twelve sons (Rashi), and prophesy can not reveal when the Messiah is coming.

The Messiah either comes 'like a poor man riding on a donkey' at the final time if the generation is guilty or hastened before the final time like the 'clouds of Heaven' if the generation is worthy (Talmud Bavli Sanhedrin 98). The 'clouds of Heaven' is a metaphor to coming fast in a miraculous way decreed by Heaven (Radak on Isaiah 19:1). Coming on a 'cloud' is a metaphor for multitudeness that humbles the creations before it' (ibid, Malbim, Mitzoodat David, Talmud Bavli Taanit 14). 'Like a poor man riding on a donkey' is a metaphor for coming slowly with great difficulty and opposition from the sins of people that oppose him and the others needed to bring him.

Talmud Bavli Sanhedrin 98 says "*Rabbi Yehoshua Ben Levi asked Elijah (the prophet)* when *is the Messiah coming? He said Go ask him yourself. Where is he sitting? At the opening of the city'.* Rashi says that this is the part of the Garden of Eden which is counterpart to the world and specifically in the part of the Garden of Eden that is counterpart to the city where he is bound; i.e. Rome, or the head city of Edom at the time. This could also mean that the leaders of Edom/ USA keep him oppressed through their agents in Israel. *'And what are his distinguishing features? He is sitting among the poor suffering of sickness' (ibid).* Rashi says literally 'diseased' and he is also '*counted amongst the diseased*' as is written in Isaiah 53 and '*he is desecrated by our crimes*' as is written in Isaiah 53 and 'our sickness he bore'. *'and all of them are bound in connection with* it *Say to him 'Shalom Aleichem' and they release and bind all of their bandages (for their wounds) all at one time, he ties one and releases one at a time saying maybe I will be needed and I don't want to be delayed in going concerning it* (Rashi: to redeem Israel*) …He asked him when he is coming He said 'Today'… (*The messiah didn't come and he said that the Messiah was a liar) …. *It was thus said to you 'Today' if you listen to the voice of Hashem* (meaning fully returning to living by the Torah and observing all of the commandments in the proper way, in Hebrew called 'Tshuvah Shleima')' (Talmud Bavli Sanhedrin 98a).

"*The Messiah comes today if you listen to Hashem's voice according to Rabbi Levi means that if Israel observes even one Sabbath properly then the Messiah will come immediately and they will be redeemed… and Rebbe says that if Israel does Tshuvah before the Holy One blessed be He for even one day then the Messiah will come immediately.*" (Yalkoot Shimoni Chapter 95 part 852).

Talmud Yerushalmi Taanit 3b says that "*if the people of Israel (the Jews) would do Tshuvah for one day, then the (Messiah) son of David would come immediately (as it is written in Psalm 95) ('I come) Today if you listen to His Voice'.* Rabbi Levi said that if Israel would observe one Sabbath properly then the (Messiah) son of David would come immediately.

'The students of Rabbi Yosi Ben Kisma asked: When does the (Messiah) son of David come? And he said … when the gate (of Rome) falls, and it will be built and it will fall and it will be built and will fall and they aren't able to rebuild it until when the son of David comes. They (the students) said: Our Rabbi, give us a sign and he said … when the waters of the cave of the Pamyas (AKA the Banyas) turns to blood and they turned to blood at the time of his death and he said to them 'dig me a deep grave (likely during the war of Gog and Magog when the bodies of the anti-Semites and their blood will fill the North of Israel, after which the Messiah comes) (Talmud Bavli Sanhedrin 98a).

'The yeshiva of Elijah taught that the world is destined to last six thousand years: the first two thousand years of nothingness'. Rashi here and on Avoda Zara 9a says that this means that the world was without Torah from the time of Adam until Abraham was 52 years old when he started to teach Torah to the world *(2220 BCE). The second two thousand years of Torah is a*ccording to Rashi is up to 172 years after the destruction of the second Temple which is the year 242 AD. Maharsha says that this period refers to a period when Torah flourished in the world, which ended with the death of Rebbe, after which Torah study declined severely. After that, *the 'third two thousand year period should have been the days of the Messiah but because of our transgressions which grew, those years of the Messiah were lost from us'* (Talmud Bavli Sanhedrin 97a).

'In the last Jubilee year the Messiah will come (this comes out to the Hebrew year 4,250 which is the Gregorian year 490 AD)….. Rabbi Eliezar said that if Israel does Tshuvah then they will be redeemed and if not then they won't be redeemed. Rabbi Yehoshua said if they don't do Tshuvah then they wont be redeemed and the Holy One blessed be He will stand up a king against them whose decrees are as harsh as Haman (i.e. wanting to murder all of the Jews. Hitler and Stalin are examples of this blessing (this is lashon maalia, a euphemism, for 'curse') fulfilled) until Israel does Tshuvah and return to good … as is written 'Return to Me (by Tshuvah) and I shall return to you (with redemption)' (Talmud Bavli Sanhedrin 97b).

These last two sources raise an obvious difficulty. We know that king Hezkiyahoo, who lived before 500 BCE, could have been the Messiah if he had sung praises to Hashem (Talmud Bavli Sanhedrin 94a), so, how could king Hezkiyahoo have possibly been the Messiah if he lived before the year 242 AD, which the above passages say was the beginning of the days of the Messiah? It implies that the Messiah can really come any time, independent of our merits, as the Gaon of Vilna pointed out.

"*The sons of Ishmael will attack Israel in three great wars, the third being the biggest, then the Messiah will come from Edom to the land of Israel* (Yalkoot Shimoni Isaiah Chapter 21)". From here we see that the ingathering of Jews to the land of Israel, and the three major wars of the sons of Ishmael; ostensibly fulfilled when the Arabs attacked Israel in the 1948 'war of independence', 1967 'six day war', and 1973 'Yom Kippur war'; may indicate that the Messiah will come from Edom to the land of Israel at some point after 1973, since these are the only three great wars of the sons of Ishmael against Israel that I know of in history. This Midrash raises an apparent difficulty that will be answered. How could the Talmud Bavli Sanhedrin 98 say that the Messiah can only come after the year 242CE or 490CE if these three wars of Ishmael only happened by 1973? A possible answer is that these three wars of Ishmael could have happened as early as 242CE if the time was right for the Messiah to come.

The above scriptures have lead today's orthodox Rabbis (*the only truly legitimate Rabbis as opposed to the heretical cults 'reform' and 'conservative'*) to believe that if the Jewish people return to living by the Torah commandments (in Hebrew called 'Tshuva Shleima'), and give acts of kindness, then the Messiah will come in our generation. That is why orthodox Jews and Rabbis invest so much time and money into bringing back Jews to living by the Torah and do so much kindness, in order to hasten the coming of the Messiah in our time. This is the real way to save the world. It is part of a spiritual war that is going on today between the regime of Satan and his servants (i.e. Amalek and Edom) and the Holy people of Israel together with the potential Messiah of the generation. It is a fight for world domination. There are many dead, wounded and prisoners on both sides already. Eventually, the righteous of Israel will stand and see Satan shamed before all mankind and eternity.

Since the Moshiah's coming depends on Divine Kindness, we can arouse this Divine Kindness by being kind.

Hastening the Coming of the Messiah

'If the Jewish people do not repent by returning to living by the Torah, then the Holy One, blessed be He, will appoint a king over them whose decrees are as harsh as Haman (in modern times these include Hitler, Stalin.) and the Jewish people

will be forced to repent and thus will G-d bring us back to the right path (living by the Torah)' (Talmud Bavli Sanhedrin 97b).

'If you see a generation that has great troubles come upon it like a river then expect him (the Messiah)... the generation is either wholly meritorious or wholly guilty... if they are worthy I will hasten his coming and if not he will come in the final appointed time .... If hastened he will come now in our day on a cloud of Heaven (Rashi and other commentators say this is a metaphor for quickly and miraculously) if they are worthy, and as a poor man riding a donkey (Commentators say this means slowly and with great material opposition) if they are not worthy' (Talmud Bavli Sanhedrin 98).

'If the Jews return to Hashem by living by His Torah (in Hebrew called 'Tshuvah Shleima'), the Moshiah will come (now before the final time)' (Rashi Talmud Bavli Sanhedrin 97). *'If people posses sufficient merit, then they will be redeemed before the pre-ordained time'* (Maharsha on Talmud Bavli Sanhedrin 98a). *"If Israel would return to Hashem by living by His Torah (in Hebrew called 'Tshuvah Shleima') for one day, then the (Messiah) son of David would come immediately (as it is written in Psalm 95 - 'I come Today if you listen to His Voice'.*

'If one Man or synagogue return fully (in Hebrew this is called to be a 'hozer biTshuva') to live by the Torah commandments then the Messiah would come immediately' (The Orah Chaim on Deuteronomy 15:5 (based on the Zohar Parshat Noah)).

'The Tshuvah of some individuals might be enough to save the whole of Israel and bring the Messiah for everyone' (Artscroll Ezekiel (36:32) page 560 note 1 on Radak, Margolios HaYam on Talmud Bavli Sanhedrin 97b based on Yoma 86b).

'If someone returns to Hashem, out of love for Hashem, in living by His Torah commandments, then all of his previous willful sins turn into merits' (Reish Lakish in Talmud Bavli Rosh HaShana 29). Tanya Igereth Tshuva chapters 4, 8-10 says that there is lower Tshuva and Higher Tshuva but only Higher Tshuva can nullify semen spilled in vein. Higher Tshuva requires learning Torah out of love which is a high level. This Talmudic passage in Rosh HaShana 29 demonstrates Hashem's ability to literally *change ones past.* This is like the theme of the movie 'Back to the Future'. For instance, if someone robbed a bank and killed someone there, if he does Tshuva out of love, then this bank robbery and murder could miraculously turn into a legitimate Beit Din (that is Hebrew for Jewish Torah law court) seizure of money and execution that are

deserved. Also, if someone had AIDS or terminal cancer, it could go away like it never existed. This could happen. Hashem is ALL powerful with NO bounds. He can do anything, cure anyone of anything. It is a principle of Torah that 'spirit over rides matter' and 'Holiness over rides the natural order'. It was said that the master cabbalist, the Baba Sali (zt'l), cured people of serious diseases with giving them water to drink, with special kavanoth.

Talmud Bavli Avoda Zara 20 tells of how a Jew can achieve a level of such Holiness through Torah observance that he is could even be able to resurrect the dead. We also learned in the Talmud (and Zohar) that 'Rabba created a man like being' and that the Talmudic sages knew how to create things through their wisdom and Holiness. From this we learn that *Holiness can overpower the material reality* that in truth is really subordinate to the spiritual reality. We live in a delusion thinking that the material reality rules over the spiritual. In fact it is exactly the opposite. See the chapter on the Power of Torah and the Messiah.

The power of Tshuva is so immense that it can bring one to the level of Holiness that overpowers the material world and can even change the past (Reish Lakish in Talmud Bavli Rosh HaShana 29).

The Chefetz Chaim (zt'l), one of Judaism's most recent Torah leaders who passed away in 1933 (the year my parents were born and that Hitler rose to power), on Sanhedrin 97b, pushed intensely for the hastening of the coming of the Moshiah. The first book that he published, also, like the Vilna Gaon's book, titled 'Even Shleima', which means 'fairness in business', encouraged the Jewish people to do Tshuvah on business ethics, which to this day is still a critical issue. The Gaon of Vilna ostensibly also saw the need to emphasis this point, in the 1700s, by also calling one of his main works 'Even Shleima'. This sin of lack of ethics in business is probably a main real reason why the world trade centers were blown up. Injustice caused by lack of proper business ethics literally starts wars and was the main real cause of the controlled demolition of the world trade center buildings; including stock fraud and Arabs bribing US government officials; as an FBI agent told me, through exchanging stock portfolios; to sell out Israel. Wars in Iraq over oil and Afghanistan for the heroin trade route are also an expression of this.

Slander (in Hebrew called 'lashon hara') is one of Amalek's (may his memory be erased) main weapons of evil and destruction of good peoples names and reputations. Lashon hara is one of the main sins that keeps the

Jewish people in exile and pushes away the redemption. Amalek will target the Moshiah as well as Israel with it. For instance he will label the Moshiah a 'mentally ill' and 'delusional' 'tyrant' and Israel 'war criminals' for killing Arabs in self defense. Rav Dov Kook haCohen Shlita of Tiberius said that "*there are many people in mental hospitals claiming to be the Moshiah. and one of them really is.*". According to this statement, this is the imprisonment of the Moshiah (Yalkoot Shimoni on Isaiah 60); imprisonment in a mental hospital.

In addition to 'Even Shleima', the Chefetz Chaim also wrote a book on lashon hara called 'Guard Your Tongue'. Lashon hara destroys the names and reputations of good people and keeps Jewish people divided and in strife unnecessarily. It makes people misunderstood and covers up our goodness from being seen by others. It murders our good names and has destructive results on our lives like breaking up relationships that are meant to be. It causes me, us all, society and other individual's monetary losses in the trillions annually literally. It is one of the reasons for the weakened economy (See Breslov Sefer haMidoth on Mamon). This is why Amalek (may their memory be erased) uses lashon hara; because it is so simple yet effective in destroying good people and it goes on with out being punished by man. It is written though, that one who disparages a Rabbi 'has no place in the world to come' and 'is given a disease for which there is no cure' (Talmud Bavli). This means that most Amalekites (may their memory be erased) have AIDS and gladly spread it, especially to the pure of Israel, if they get the opportunity, including pure children (Rashi on Deuteronomy 25). Based on Isaiah 53 and the Midrash cited up to here we infer that the Messiah is also damaged by lashon hara. My book on the final redemption and the ten tribes has a chapter that goes into full about Amalek (may their memory be erased) and his traits.

'*Torah study can hasten the Redemption (Gioola)*' (Talmud Bavli Sanhedrin 99). '*Messiah Son of David's coming depends on good deeds and repentance* (of the Jewish people)' (Talmud Bavli Sanhedrin 97a). "*The redemption will come only as a result of Torah study… and Kabbala*' (The Vilna Gaon, Even Shleima). '*One should study and fulfill the Jewish Law (in Hebrew called 'halacha') first before he learns kabbala. One who reverses this order will not be successful*' (The Vilna Gaon, Even Shleima, chapter on How to learn Torah). The Kabbala must be studied in order to help bring the Messiah, but the Kabbala should only be studied after one is adept in the rest of the Torah and living by the Jewish law (in Hebrew called 'halacha') first, being well learned and practiced in the

Talmud and halacha for the sake of Heaven (The Vilna Gaon, Even Shleima, chapter on Torah study). The codes of Jewish law (the Shulhan Aruch) on the obligation of Torah study for Jewish men bring the Rambam who says that the Kabbala should only be earned after one is well conversant in the rest of the Torah and lives by the Halacha and is morally pure lest he become like a 'wrinkled piece of paper'. The Halacha for Ashkenazi Jews and Sephardic Jews can differ. From these sources we see that learning the five books, prophets, writings, Talmud, Halacha, and then later kabbala when one is ready, can help bring the Messiah and the Torah should only be studied for the sake of Heaven and not for ulterior motives such as money nor honor. The Gaon in Even Shleima says that "*there are people who learn Torah and do Mitzvoth to show off and they are from the side of the Erev Rav and are destined for hell*". They are part of the false people pushing off the Moshiah.

The real Kabbalists (not the fake ones of which there are some) say that Gentiles' and unlearned Jew's learning of Kabbala acts as an opposition to the redemption and coming of the Messiah. It also damages the world and people who use kabala. This is one of the reasons why Kabbalists are opposed to the Kabbala from being translated from Hebrew, so to prevent those not learned from studying Kabbala. Any real master Kabalist ONLY teaches Kabbala to orthodox Jews who are worthy which includes *humility*. The Kabala learned by inappropriate people is used to create Armilus, the 'anti- Christ', via black magic and kabala employed by the other side in service of Satan. Its like giving nuclear weapons to Muslim Jihadists. This creation of Armilus, the 'anti- Christ', and how Moshiah 'kills' him, is explained in detail in my book on the war of Gog and Magog.

Again, the Talmud Bavli Sanhedrin 97b says that what is preventing the Messiah from coming is the 'Divine Attribute of Justice', which might explain why the Vilna Gaon concludes that ultimately the Messiah will come as a result of 'Divine Kindness' (Even Shleimah), which overrules the Attribute of Divine Justice. By being kind we can arouse the forces of Heaven to reflect back our kindness and this too may arouse Hashem's kindness to bring the end. Kindness is more important than most people realize.

From the above sources we see that Tshuvah Shleima (full repentance which includes coming to live by the true and complete Torah Halacha), Torah study and kindness can hasten the coming of the Messiah.

'*Rabbi Levi said that if Israel observed the Sabbath properly for even one day, the son of David would come immediately, because it is equated to all the Mitzvoth and he said from Psalms 95:7 'Because He is our G-d and we can be the flock He pastures and the sheep in His charge, even today of we head His Voice'. Rabbi Yohanan said that the Holy Blessed one said to Israel that even though I gave a limit to the final time of the end of days, if you do tshuvah (return to living by the Torah) even one day, then I will bring it not in its final season (Hebrew 'Onatah'; see end of the book of Daniel for this term), but today 'if you listen to His voice', and as we found regarding al the commandments, the son of David (AKA the Messiah) will come with the observance of one day of the Sabbath because the Sabbath is worth al the commandments in the Torah'* (Talmud Yerushalmi Taanit 3b, Midrash Rabba Shemot Parsha 28).

We learn on Talmud Bavli Megilla 17b/18a that Jerusalem will be built first before (the Messiah son of) David becomes king as it is written "Afterwards the children of Israel shall return and seek Hashem their G-d and David their king (Hosea 3:5)". The Vilna Gaon (circa 1770s) advised his devout students to make aliya (to ascend; in the sense of immigrating) to Israel, settle the land of Israel as part of the ingathering of the exiles, and build a Jewish infrastructure in the land of Israel, which will hasten the revealed redemption ("Kol HaTor" Chapter 5). Thus, we see that the Vilna Gaon advocated that the orthodox Jewish people return to Israel to build a Jewish infrastructure in the land of Israel to prepare for the Messiah. This was done one hundred years before the Zionist book "Lovers of Zion" was published in 1880. The 'first aliya' in 1882 was religious Jews. After that most of the Jews who made aliya to the land of Israel were not religious and thus the state of Israel became not religious as opposed to a religious state as it is supposed to be. Some believe that due to the failure of the religious Jews to move of Israel and build a Jewish infrastructure in the land of Israel in order to prepare for the Messiah, the mission of preparing for the Messiah fell to a lower spiritual level, and was given over to the secular Zionists, by decree of Heaven, where they built a Jewish infrastructure in the land of Israel to prepare for the Messiah. I believe this and see the good aspect of what hey have done. The IDF (Israel Defense Forces) is fit to be the Messiah's army, from the lowest to the top ranks; even if as such there is always room for improvement in many areas of the IDF such as the non politicization of rank promotion which should be based on competence alone. Non the less, the IDF is the most ethical army in the world. May Israeli soldiers have even died to avoid killing innocent Arab civilians who the terrorists use as human shields to protect themselves and make Israel look bad if the IDF accidentally kills some Arab civilians who the terrorists are using as shields. The media slander of the IDF is most always a grossly biased malicious anti-Semitic libel intended to incite people against Israel. For example, a 'war crime' is defined as 'killing unarmed civilians in time of war'. This is exactly what the Muslim terrorists do when they blow up Israeli busses or shoot rockets into the unarmed Israeli civilian populations. The terrorists are committing war crimes. But, when Israeli strikes back to defend herself, the media then libels Israeli claiming that Israeli is committing war crimes, not the terrorists. This is a very evil crime of anti-Semitic libel and support of murder of Jews that the media commits. The blood of their victims cries out from the earth. Be careful of what the media says. Its often not true.

Of all the Torah that I have learned in the past twenty years, I have found that the Torah enumerates five *specific impediments that must be removed and conditions that must be fulfilled for the Messiah to come hastened.* The following passages describe these conditions: "(Talmud Bavli Sanhedrin 98a) *the son of David (Messiah son of David) doesn't (won't) come until the 1) unworthy (non-Torah true) kingship is destroyed from Israel.... 2) (ibid) the vile haughty spirited are destroyed from Israel .... 3) (ibid) the bad judges and police are destroyed from Israel* (judges and police that enforce the Torah laws) (since Zion is redeemed through 'misphat' (Torah judgment) according to the Torah (Isaiah 1:27), which gives the Jews merit to inherit the land as per Deuteronomy 16:20 'justice justice thou shall pursue so that you will inherit the land'). 4) until *all the bodies are gone from the chamber of the souls* (a place in Heaven where souls are stored)(thus we need to be fruitful and multiply)' (Talmud Bavli Yivamoth 63b). This means that Jewish peoples' being fruitful and multiplying help bring the Messiah. And 5) until the Amalekite mixed multitude (characterized by greed, immorality, hypocrisy, honor seeking and lashon hara against the Moshiah and Hashem's Holy Service) is eradicated (The Gaon of Vilna, Even Shleima chapter on Redemption based on the Zohar Bereshit).

The Power of Repentance to Rectify Your Past and Turn Past Sins into Merits

Repentance and even more so 'full repentance' (in Hebrew called 'Tshuva Shleima') has the power to rectify your past and turn past sins into merits. This is because 'repentance from love' for G-d (in Hebrew called 'Tshuva meiAhava') fully erases any and all sins and even turns them into merits (Reish LaKish in Talmud Bavli Rosh haShana 29). Someone who fully repented from even the worst sins of his past, even 'abominations', as is the case with a Baal Tshuva (a repentant Jew), could be the Messiah. Even though many are familiar with the Zohar that says that 'there is no rectification for spilling semen in vein', and any have fallen into hopelessness from this statement, I would like to say a little known Torah principle that people need to know. Chapter four of Igeret haTshuva from the Likootei Amarim Tanya says that only 'lower repentance' does not rectify the sin of spilling semen in vein, but 'higher repentance' does rectify it. Religious people need to know this to avoid being overwhelmed by guilt and feelings of hopelessness for spilling semen in vein by which many are afflicted. Igeret haTshuva here also means that anyone could have been involved in any of the worst sins in his past, even 'abominations', but by 'higher repentance' from love for G-d, he erases them all, turns them in to merits, and goes on to the highest levels of being fully righteous, Holy, and even a 'chariot' who is totally nullified to the will of Hashem, as the Messiah will eventually be when he is most fully developed spiritually. Anyone can achieve this level. It is your free choice.

Misquoting the Rambam on Learning about the Moshiah and Redemption

Rambam's halacha on laws of kings 12:2 is usually misquoted as saying 'we don't learn these matters of the Moshiah and Redemption. We can't understand these matters and won't understand them until they happen.'. This is not exactly what the Rambam says here. There is a major error in interpretation. If you read the whole section of laws of kings 12:2, in it's context, you will see that what he says regarding the days of the Moshiah and prior to it, the coming of Elijah the prophet and the war of Gog and Magog, etc., is that: 'regarding the hidden things of the prophets ... where there are no sources to the Rabbis to resolve the meaning and mahloketh on them (my book has hidooshim that resolve some of these mahloketh)... one shouldn't spend his time on these hagadoth... nor to spend *too much time* on the Midrashoth and similar writings on these issues, and shouldn't make them the main part of his learning, because it does not bring one to reverence and love, and one shouldn't try to calculate the possible time of redemption, rather he should wait and ....

believe in every ting as we have clarified'. This does not mean not to learn about Moshiah and the redemption. It is a Mitzva to learn these subjects, especially regarding the aspects of the prophets which are revealed and not hidden and rife with mahloketh. The Rambam himself spent many chapters of his works on the Moshiah and Redemption. Obviously he does not mean not to learn about the redemption, Moshiah and the war of Gog and Magog. He teaches these subjects himself. Much is written about these subjects all through out the Tanach, Midrash, Talmud and Kabbala for us to learn, not to ignore. The great Rabbis of all times wrote books on these subjects for us to learn. It is just that we should not make learning these subjects 'the main part' of our Torah study. There is so much more to learn in Torah that we need to learn and this is only part of what we need to learn, but we should learn it. We are now in a different time than that of the Rambam, a time close to the coming of the Moshiah, as most Rabbis agree, and now need this 'heker viIyoon' to receive the Moshiah and make him king in our generation. In our generation where kiruv and hizook is needed, learning these subjects will bring more reverence and love for Hashem and His Holy Torah. It is a Mitzva now more than ever to learn this book. Without this book it is not possible to identify the pre-kingship Moshiah unless you spend twenty years like I did learning all of the Pardes and great books on these subjects with great Siaata DiSHamaya. With this book the Moshiah being identified and appointed king may be possible in our generation. Without his book, the real Moshiah is unlikely to be identified and appointed king in our generation, maybe impossible. As we learn from the Gomorra in Brachot: first learn, then discuss. Be wise. Learn this book. Teach it. Let's make Moshiah possible. This misquote has undermined the generations Daath Torah on Moshiah and the redemption. Please quote the Rambam properly from now on and correct others who make the well intentioned mistake that has such great blessing to quote the Rambam properly. It is a Kiddush Hashem and tikoon Olam to teach my book in the Beitei Midrash.

Unrealistic Expectations of the Moshiah

There are two main unrealistic expectations that make it difficult for people to accept the Moshiah.

The Rambam stated in Hilchot Tshuva chapter 9:2 that the Messiah will be '*wiser than king Solomon*' and nearly as '*great a prophet as Moses*'.

Since Solomon was the wisest man, and Moses was the greatest prophet of all times, who spilt the red sea and received the Torah, which was the greatest prophesy of all times, we have to look more closely at what this statement of the Rambam means and how it could possibly be.

Greater a Prophet than Moses?

For example, how can someone be as great a prophet as Moses who received the Torah, split the red sea and prophesied the ten plagues? How is that possible? The Messiah can not receive a greater prophesy than the Torah since the Torah is the greatest prophesy. The only way it is possible to be a greater prophet in one sense is that if he turns the whole world to accept the Torah and live by it, be king of the world and build the Temple. That is exactly what the Moshiah will achieve (Rambam laws of kings 11). In this sense the Moshiah is greater than Moses. But the Messiah will not be able to be on this level when the Sanhedrin makes him king. The Messiah will only be able to be as great a prophet as Moses when he is able to compel the world to live by Torah. This will only be after he is king and has the media and educational infrastructure at his disposal to teach the world Torah, and is in control of the judiciary to enforce the Torah laws. Only as king, when he is in full power and authority over the whole country of Israel, who has the majority of known Jews, will he be able to compel the (majority) of Jews there to live by Torah, and thus achieve 'chezkat haMoshiah', as per Rambam laws of kings chapter 11:4. More so, only after the war of Gog and Magog will he be in control of the world, education system, media and judicial system, as king of the world, and thus be able to spread Daath Torah to the world and compel the world to live by the Torah. Also, only as king will the Moshiah be able to build the Temple and achieve 'Vadai Moshiah' (ibid). So, it is an unrealistic expectation to think he would be on that level of prophet of Moses when the Sanhedrin first meets the Messiah and then later appoints him king. Don't expect the Moshiah to be as great a prophet as Moses even when he first becomes king. These are unrealistic expectations. You must look at the identifying traits outlined in this book that the Rambam does not list in order to identify the pre-kingship Moshiah. That is one reason why this book. My book, along with its additional specific detailed information of pre-kingship Moshiah, is needed to learn, in addition to the Rambam's laws of kings on the Moshiah, to bring Moshiah in our generation. It is a Mitzva to learn my book because it teaches about the Moshiah which part of the Torah that it is a Mitzvah to learn about. The chapter titled 'Misquoting the Rambam on Learning about the Moshiah and Redemption' explains the Mitzva to learn these subjects of redemption and Moshiah despite peoples' misquoting the Rambam to ignore them.

Wiser than Solomon?

And, how is a man going to be wiser than Solomon before the Sanhedrin reconvenes to learn the ancient Torah laws and understandings that one needs to know in order to be as wise as Solomon? When the Sanhedrin appoints the Messiah king, will he at that time be able to be as wise as Solomon? No. This is not possible at that time. He will only later be able to achieve that level of Torah wisdom after he learns the ancient unknown Torah laws and understandings with the Sanhedrin for many years, and that will also be only after Elijah returns and teaches us the ancient Torah laws and understandings that we have forgotten.

So, in the beginning of his life and even to the point of being appointed king, the Moshiah can not be as wise as Solomon at that point and can not be as great a prophet as Moses at that point either. Please disregard your unrealistic expectations and make Moshiah a reality. Don't be a fool. Be wise.

People have been misguided by unrealistic expectations of what the Messiah needs to be when he is appointed king. It is unrealistic to expect the Moshiah to be as wise as Solomon and as great a prophet as Moses before he becomes king. This misunderstanding makes it impossible for people to accept the Moshiah in our generation and make him king. This is in addition to the fact that there is no Sanhedrin to appoint him king, much less even recognize him, one of the reasons being is that they simply don't have the information of the Moshiah's identifying traits, that my book provides, at their fingertips.

These levels of greatness do not emanate until later in the Messiahs life and thus makes the potential Moshiah of the generation difficult to accept. It is an unrealistic expectation that the Messiah will be 'wiser than king Solomon' and nearly as 'great a prophet as Moses' before he is king. That is just simply not possible as I have shown here.

I believe in all the Rambam's statements totally, but, I must clarify them so that people will understand that the Messiah will be 'wiser than king Solomon' and nearly as 'great a prophet as Moses' only after the Messiah is in control of the world and his kingship is already fully established. Before that he will not be able to be on this level of Moses and Solomon. The criteria outlined in this book must be relied upon to determine who the potential Messiah of the generation really may be before he is made king, and then, and only after then, can achieve the levels of Moses and Solomon. The English reading members of the Sanhedrin and Rabbis in Israel who read my book will be able to identify who is Moshiah Ben David before he becomes king. They will be blessed with having had personally and directly brought the Moshiah in our time, if the generation merits it. May that time be soon.

Barriers, Enemies and Opposition to the Messiah

'*The evil forces ... represented by Amalek correspond to haughtiness and false leadership, which as we have seen (chapters 14-15) are a major impediment to the Messiah and messianic ideals*' (Likutei Halachoth, Orla 5:16, Rabbi Chaim Kramer Shlita 'Moshiah who what why when where?' pages 265-266). "*The leadership of the Jewish people will be corrupt demagogues in the time before the Messiah comes* (Rabbi Elchanan Wasserman and Talmud Bavli Sotah 49a)". '*Jews dedicated to the Torah and Mitzvoth could be opposed to the Moshiah*' (Rashab Rebbe, "With Light and with Might", page 61 ff). '*Our sins (of the Jewish people, religious and secular) prevent him (from coming)*' (Yad Rama & Talmud Bavli Sanhedrin 97a) where peoples sins will not only degrade the necessary preparations in society to build the necessary mechanisms to give rise to him, but, *they will also sin against him personally, without knowing who he is*, only to find out later, when he is finally revealed in this world, to their shame, if they are still alive, and defiantly they will find out in the next world, where all the truth comes out.

Traditional Jewish sources tell us that there will be many forms of great opposition to the coming of the Messiah, and to him personally as there was to king David and the redeemer Moses. This makes sense because the establishment of the Messiah's House of David as the world power will stop the rule of Satan over mankind and thus Satan will make every effort in recruiting every type of means and person available to try to stop that from happening, because when the Messiah comes, then Satan goes. With this also go Edom's rule and Amalek (may their memory be erased) will be eradicated. The Messiah 'slays the wicked with the breath of his lips (Isaiah 11) also refers to Armilus 'the Anti-Christ' (Midrash Zerubbavel) who he has to 'kill' in order to stop him from trying to take over the world and forcing people by pain of death to worship Satan. All rebels against G-d who refuse to repent (in Hebrew called 'Tshuva Shleima') die, including the Anti-Christ who only the Moshiah himself can slay. Only those who Hashem is with them, so that Hashem protects them, can stand up to Armilus. All others will fall to him until Armilus is slain by the Messiah. This is explained with the Torah sources in detail in my book on the war of Gog and Magog.

'*The sins of the Jewish people oppose the Messiah*' (Rashi on Talmud Bavli Sanhedrin 98). Every little sin we do trips up the necessary things that have to be in place for the Messiah to come. For instance, people may steal money, freedom, wives, and a good name from the Messiah which will prevent him from being fruitful and multiplying in the many ways that he needs to do so in order to be established as king. Who is going to back a poor, single, unfamous, persecuted man, 'mentally ill' 'ex convict' as king? How could that be? Peoples' arrogance, ego, conceit, baseless hatred and jealousy prevent the Messiah from being recognized and thus from coming (Rav Nahman of Breslov Sefer haMidoth and Talmud Bavli Rosh haShana). These character flaws in all of us also prevent the recognition of the Righteous leaders (in Hebrew called 'Tzadikeem') who are essential to bring the Messiah and make him recognized (Rav Nahman of Breslov Sefer haMidoth). These character flaws which distort our judgment of other people, and project our own inadequacies on to them, will also cause people to disqualify the Messiah on a personal basis, to his face and behind his back, as people are accustomed to doing to others. This is why the Moshiah of every generation does not surface above peoples' garbage pile of sins and bad character traits such as EGO which not only is an acronym standing for "Easing G-d Out', but also 'EMO' meaning 'Easing Moshiah Out'. As the Rambam says, there is a potential Moshiah in every generation, but we just have to open up our minds to accept him.

'*In the redemption period of history, the Jewish people will be confused, not know that it is the redemption, and there will be wicked people amongst the Jewish people who fight against the Messiah*' (Zohar Shemot 7).

The Torah enumerates five *specific impediments that must be removed and conditions that must be fulfilled for the Messiah to come.* The following passages describe these conditions: 1) '*the son of David (Messiah son of David) doesn't (won't) come until the unworthy (non-Torah true) kingship is destroyed from Israel* (Talmud Bavli Sanhedrin 98a), *2) 'the vile haughty spirited are destroyed from Israel' (ibid).... 3) the bad judges and bad police are destroyed from Israel (ibid)* (these are judges and police that don't enforce the Torah laws, since Zion is redeemed through 'misphat' (Torah judgment) according to the Torah (Isaiah 1:27), which gives the Jews merit to inherit the land of Israel as per Deuteronomy 16:20 'justice justice thou shall pursue so that you will inherit the land'). 4) until *all the bodies are gone from the chamber of the souls* (a place in Heaven where souls are stored)' (Talmud Bavli Yivamoth 63b). This means that Jewish peoples' being fruitful and multiplying help bring the Messiah. And 5) until the Amalekite mixed multitude is eradicated (The Gaon of Vilna, Even Shleima chapter on Redemption based on the Zohar Bereshit).

The Moshiah can't come until the petty government, the vile haughty spirited, the bad police, and the bad judges are all destroyed from Israel (Talmud Bavli Sanhedrin 98). Based on Tinkonei haZohar 144, cited in Hevlei haMoshiah bizmanainoo' by Rabbi Rafael Eisenburg HaLevi (of blessed memory), the petty government may also referred to as "the regime of the Erev Rav". According to Rav Rafael Eisenberg HaLevi (of blessed memory) in his book 'Hevlei haMoshiah bizmananoo', based on Tikoonei Zohar 144, "the regime of the Erev Rav" precedes the Messiah's kingship. Kol HaTor says that "Armilus resides in Edom and from there manages the regime of the Erev Rav". The Messiah can't come until all Erev Rav Amalek are eradicated (Even Shleima and Zohar Bereshit). Who are they? They obviously have the traits of Amalek (may their memory be erased) so they are difficult to identify since like snakes they are cunning and shrewd in deceiving people from knowing who they really are. Lashon hara against the Holy Rabbis is one of their trademarks. A good detective with access to intelligence or siata dishmaya (Heavenly Assistance) may be able to find some of them and deal with them based on the traits outlined on them in the chapter on Amalek (may their memory be erased) that is found in my book on the war of Gog and Magog. Someone with proven authentic prophesy or Holy Spirit is the only real way I can think of to identify who as an individual Amalek really is.

Again, the Talmud Bavli Baba Batra 12 says that since the destruction of the first Temple, prophesy was taken away from the prophets (who were not wise-Rashi) and was given to wise (prophets), odd balls (the definition of 'odd ball' is an unresolved discussion in Talmud Bavli Megilla 3b) and children. Hevroota on Talmud Bavli Baba Batra 12a, citing the Ramban and Chasam Sofer, says that this form of prophesy is prophesy through Ruah HaKodesh

(Holy Spirit) to know the truth through the vessel of wisdom in our mind; not full blown prophesy of 'Hazon vi mareh' (pictures and visions) and 'hida' (riddle) that the Bible prophets such as Isaiah, Ezekiel and Jeremiah had. This is an interesting statement since we know from the Arizal and Rav Nahman of Breslov that prophesy comes through the sfeeroth of hod and netzach and ruah HaKodesh comes through malchoot. Ramban here also says that prophesy can be given to the pious who are not sagaciously wise, as in the case of prophesy being given as an agency like Yona the prophet. Around the same time that the Sanhedrin of the Knesset Gidola took away the evil inclination for idol worship (Talmud Bavli Yoma 69b), the last prophets, Haggai, Zechariah and Malachi, all died in a single month in 313 BCE (Rabbi Arie Kaplan's book called the 'handbook of Jewish thought'). That is when prophesy is said to have ended. In Igereth Teman, page 174, the Rambam says that prophesy returns before the Moshiah. This prophesy that returns is full blown prophesy of 'Hazon vi mareh' (picture and vision). For a thorough coverage of the history and principles of prophesy and ruah HaKodesh from ancient times to our times see Rabbi Arie Kaplan's book called the 'handbook of Jewish thought'.

The opposition to the Messiah comes from peoples' sin, heresy, jealousy, lack of faith, arrogance, Edom, Amalek, Erev Rav, wicked Gentiles and Jews, and even some people who don the appearance of being 'religious'.

There is a war for power, influence and control of the Jewish people between the Messiah and the wicked Erev Rav and Edom who are in power before he arrives on the scene; unless they choose to serve him as king instead. These wicked pseudo Jews are in addition to the wicked anti-Semitic Gentile enemies of the Messiah, who know that by keeping the Moshiah subjugated and oppressed, as the true leader of Israel, they are also in fact keeping the whole people of Israel as a nation, and mankind, subjugated and oppressed as well, and thus by keeping themselves in power, which is their goal. Many of them may have top University PhDs in political science, psychiatry, economics, war, religion, etc. which helps them in masterminding this plan. The Gematria of 'politica' (Hebrew for politics) is equivalent to that of Amalek (may their memory be erased) which shows a connection whatever that may be. As secret government organizations such as the KGB, FSB, MI 6, FBI (Fourth Beast Incorporated), NSA, CIA and the Iranian secret police professionally do (see the YouTube video "Jimi Hendrix the last 24 hours" on the CIA's operation Chaos that killed him and John Lennon), it is a very simple tactic of undermining and taking down the true leaders of Israel in order to undermine and take down the Jews as a whole people. They do this with every nation they rule. That is one way they maintain their power and control. The arrogant stupidity of the unlearned people and their vulnerability to accept slander (in Hebrew called 'lashon hara') about the Messiah undermines his credibility and authority, and thus facilitates this subjugation. Many of the people in these organizations defect to the side of the Messiah and can cause their governments as well to come to the side of the Messiah. This will be the case if the Messiah is hastened before the final time.

As shown in previous chapters of this book, Isaiah 53, brought down by Talmud Bavli Sanhedrin 98a and Rashi there, tells us that the Messiah will be a scapegoat who is oppressed and afflicted for other people's sins. Before he comes into this world he offers him self up for this purpose. Yalkoot Shimoni on Isaiah 60 says the same in more specific and clear terms, including the Messiah's imprisonment. Isaiah 53 is a resoundingly clear description of the opposition to the Messiah where the Messiah is rejected and cast away by the corrupt society that scapegoats him and imprisons him by framing him as a sinner who is sick because of his own sins. The Zohar Shemot 7 tells us that wicked people among Israel will fight against the Messiah and Talmud Bavli Avoda Zara 3 tells us that there will be converts (but not all converts) will abandon their loyalty to the war for Israel due to fear of death in the war of Gog and Magog. We see it in practice in our times in the land of Israel and the USA with heretical organizations who act with out the advise of nor the authority given by nor grace granted by the real Rabbis of the generation nor the Moshiah of the generation.

If you think about the reality of the true nature of a system that is corrupt and hates Torah Jews who are living by G-d's Torah ways, then you can understand why they would be so opposed to the Messiah, who opposes everything they stand for. The *Messiah will be amazingly victorious* in the end despite the great opposition. He may often resort to his ability to '*slay the wicked by the spirit of his lips*' (Isaiah 11) in order to defeat them, cleanse their abomination from the land and establish the righteous royal House of David as the new kingship of Israel. One day the king Messiah may give medals, and certainly, G-d will give medals in some sense to all those good people who righteously and gloriously bring to repentance and stop all the enemies of the Moshiah now.

Talmud Bavli Sotah 49, Ketuboth 112b and Sanhedrin 96-98, that describe the social conditions prior to the Messiah, give us an indication as to how the corrupt, wayward, immoral, irreverent society is likely to treat and regard the Holy and righteous Messiah son of David. These sources show us that on a good day they will disregard him as no one important, and on a bad day he is in prison being derided, mocked and attacked. The society must stop this for the Moshiah to come and redeem Israel with full redemption (Gioola Shleima) hastened in our times. Also, the Messiah, as someone who fears sin, the Talmud teaches us is also someone who is despised by the majority of the sinful people of his time at first, at one time or another; as a Torah scholar, he is accused and prosecuted, and plundered as well ('*In the generation that the Messiah comes there will be false accusations and vilifications (Rashi) against the Torah scholars... decree (against the Jews) after decree ... there will be plunderers and plunderers of plunderers'* (Talmud Bavli Ketuboth 112b)); as a man of deed, he will be disregarded; as a scholar and nobleman (a prince from the royal House of David) he will be for a time 'the stone that was despised' until this despised stone 'has become the cornerstone' *(*Psalms 118:23 'The stone that the builders despised has become the cornerstone' refers to the Messiah according to Rashi on Micah 5:1*)*. As the devout orthodox Jew, likely a Haredi Jew, the most misunderstood, media libeled, and thus despised kind of Jew today, and holy man that he is, the heretical governments of the world, especially Edom (the West), including the petty Jewish government, also in Israel, filled with corrupt, wicked, self interested demagogues, will certainly disregard him and persecute him until they repent or are stopped by others. They will also probably hate him and will try to murder him (see the chapter 'murder attempts on his life are part of his fate'). There is *serious* opposition to him. No other person could survive this opposition unless G-d was with him as is written is one of his traits as per Talmud Bavli Sanhedrin 93b. Otherwise he would not be able to survive. So we see that still, none the less, '*Hashem is with him'* (Talmud Bavli Sanhedrin 93b) and they will loose all and he will get all including awesome wives who raise great children with him and wealth.

The Vilna Gaon describes the opposition to him from the Jewish people (Even Shleima chapter on redemption), which make it very difficult for him to assume the throne of kingship, and may even require going to war with the corrupt Erev Rav and other wicked Jews in power in order for him to assume the throne.

The Torah tells us that moral decay destroys society and creates the situation of calamity and anarchy that prevails before the Messiah comes if he comes at the final time due to our failure to repent and we are all judged in the category of 'guilty' ('Haiv') and not meritorious ('Zoche'); whatever that means in terms of what criteria G-d uses to judge us to determine if we as a generation are 'guilty' or 'meritorious'. '*If you see a generation with great troubles that have come on it, then go and check the judges of Israel, because all the Divine retributions come to the world only for the reason of the (bad) judges of Israel as it is said in Micah 3 'Please come hear this the heads of the House of Jacob and the officers of the House of Israel that commit abomination (of injustice) in judgment (court judgment and executive government judgment) (*This injustice has caused destruction in Zion*). … The Holy One blessed be He wont rest His Divine presence on Israel until the bad judges will be destroyed from Israel*' (Talmud Bavli Shabbath 139)". These bad judges oppose and oppress the Messiah as well. '*The Messiah won't come until all the corrupt and ignorant judges are removed from Israel*' (Maharsha on Talmud Bavli Sanhedrin 98a). As cited in Isaiah 53 and Yalkoot Shimoni on Isaiah 60, corrupt judges and likely police in Edom and Israel frame the Messiah to prison, which obviously constitutes major opposition to the Messiah and his ability to redeem Israel and the world. But this suffering too will pass and he will move on to redeem the world and return the Kingship of G-d to Man with the ancient understanding, health, happiness, peace and prosperity to all mankind, with us jubilantly and blissfully bringing sacrifices to G-d in His Temple in Jerusalem.

As the Vilna Gaon in Even Shleima chapter on redemption says '*The Messiah won't come until all the vile haughty spiritedness is removed from Israel*' (Talmud Bavli Sanhedrin 98a) also represents the arrogant, rude, false leaders who set a bad example for the Jewish people and Gentiles as well, may oppose the Messiah as well, but may also support him in many cases as well since they see that they will only be redeemed if they support him.

'*Before the Messianic era, it will be impossible to know the halacha (application of Jewish law) clearly*' (Rabbi Josef Karo (the remembrance of the righteous is a blessing), the codifier of modern Jewish law accepted by world Jewry since the 1600s). This confusion will make it difficult for the people to understand the Torah well enough to clearly identify the Messiah. If there is no Sanhedrin then it will be impossible to identify the Messiah and establish him king as per Talmud Bavli Eruvin 43b where Maharatz Chajes notes that the statement "*we tell the Beit din haGadol that Elijah has come*" means that there must be at least some form of Sanhedrin body of Rabbis in Israel before Elijah comes, if not a fully appointed Sanhedrin. This supports Rambam's point of view in Yad Sanhedrin 4:11, even if the Sanhedrin is at that point in time with out smeecha and just a partially functioning Sanhedrin because the Temple, which is needed for a fully operational Sanhedrin, is not built. Again, not only cant the Messiah be identified without a Sanhedrin, but Elijah the prophet who is supposed to proceed the Messiah according to Rashi and Ramban, also cannot be identified unless there is a Sanhedrin to greet him and authoritatively certify that he is in fact really Elijah the prophet who has returned. This implies that there is a Sanhedrin *without smeecha* before Elijah comes.

As part of the oppositional barriers to the Messiah, people will question the importance of his deeds that he performs which constitute the '*signs and wonders*' that identify him. The confusion of many people, caused by their own ignorance of what the Torah says is the Messiah, and also the doubt purposely cast on him by the slander of the mixed multitude and Amalek to destroy his name and great reputation, will make it difficult for people to properly identify him; especially through Amalek's slander of the Messiah.

There will not be 'sign on his head' that says that he is the Messiah, and since most people will be confused and not know how the Torah defines the Messiah, most people will not be able to identify him, and doubt and denial of who he really is will surround him. The only way to identify him is to study what the Torah says and to see who may be qualified to be the Messiah based on the Torahs identifying traits.

'*Sins of the Jewish people prevent the Moshiah from coming*' (Rashi Talmud Bavli Sanhedrin 98). This gives power to Edom, Amalek (may his memory be erased) and the Erev Rav to rule over us.

'*Why doesn't the Messiah come? Because people are having relations with virgins in Nehardia on Yom Kippur*' (Talmud Bavli Yoma 19b).

'*The Messiah son of David doesn't come until all the bodies are gone from the chamber of the souls* (a place in Heaven where souls are stored)' (Talmud Bavli Yivamoth 63b). This means that being fruitful and multiplying help bring the Messiah.

'*The son of David (AKA 'the Messiah') wont come until the exilarch leader in Babylon and the president of the Sanhedrin in the land of Israel are gone*' (Talmud Bavli Sanhedrin 38a). This condition was fulfilled a log time ago.

Every generation that pushes away the Moshiah of his generation has a price to pay; once it was pogroms, recently it was holocaust, and now it is AIDS, the threat of Iran attacking the world, Hamas in Gaza, Hizbola in Lebanon, wars, terror, poverty, spiritual darkness, bad TV, bad food, bad jobs, poverty, bad religion, depression, strife, hunger, etc..

Rambam says that every generation has a person who is the potential Messiah. Orgianized religion's failure to recognize and support this true potential Moshiah in any particular generation, including this generation, inherently proves that they are not being fully honest and meeting their full potential to serve G-d. It's a shame, but can be rectified. In religion, there are way too many ego tripping men with grossly exaggerated over estimations of themselves in their delusions of grandeur and don't want to recognize the real potential Messiah, often times thinking that they are the Messiah. This book helps identify the real potential Moshiah by his pre-kingship traits (Talmud Bavli Sanhedrin 93b, etc.). That is one purpose of this book; to sort out the real potential Moshiah from the false ones.

One might think that orgianized religion would want to back the Messiah. So what's the problem? Why isn't orgianized religion identifying and rallying to back the real potential Messiah of the generation who is here right now living in our generation? Why has orgianized religion failed to rally to back the real potential Messiah of the generation in every generation of the exile of Edom? The simple answer is that until now organized religion has been lost in the dark regarding how to identify the real potential Moshiah of the generation since it has not had a book like this that can help them identify the real potential Moshiah of the generation so it was not possible to do so. Now it is.

Another problem is that we need the orthodox Jewish Rabbis, from top to bottom, to respect each other and unify into a Sanhedrin that will be ready to authoritatively certify that Elijah has come, or, if hastened in our time, as the Pleisi says, possibly even with a prophet other than Elijah, to appoint and anoint the Moshiah as the chapter on Sanhedrin shows. The society must support the Sanhedrin.

The Mixed Multitude Regime prior to the Messiah

'*Before the Moshiah comes there will be a regime of the reincarnations of the mixed multitude ruling Israel*' (Rav Rafael Eisenburg (the remembrance of the righteous is a blessing) in 'Hevlei haMoshiah bizmananoo' based on Tikoonei haZohar 144). '*The Messiah son of David doesn't come until the petty government is destroyed from Israel*' (Talmud Bavli Sanhedrin 98) is also interpreted in the Zohar (in the book 'Chevlei haMoshiah bizmanainoo') to mean the mixed multitude regime ruling Israel.

The mixed multitude (in Hebrew called 'Erev Rav') are people from Egypt, during the time of the Exodus from Egypt, who thought they wanted to be Jews and Moses wanted to bring under the canopy of the Divine Presence as converts from Egypt. After Moses was on Mount Sinai with G-d for forty days in order to get the Torah, and since they thought he delayed from returning and thought that Moses would not return, they then broke down to their old ways of idol worship. Through black magic the Erev Rav created and then worshiped a 'Golden Calf 'at the foot of Mount Sinai saying 'these are our gods who brought us out of Egypt'. This caused the whole Jewish people to fall since we did not rebuke them for building the golden calf. In Talmud Bavli Beitsa 32 the sages told a story that said that there was Erev Rav in Bavel (ancient Babylon). The Zohar teaches us that their reincarnated souls are put in the leadership of the Jewish people in every generation and keep the Jewish people in exile. They cause disaster and exile in Israel in every generation (Zohar Bereshit).

There is a general rule in Torah that says that the more Holy and good something is, the more it is opposed by the side of evil (in Hebrew called the 'Sitra Achra'). This evil includes Satan and his realms of demons, in addition to the evil inclination found in most of us, Amalek (may their memories be erased) the mixed multitude false leaders among us, and wicked people. It must be remembered that the dark forces of the evil side and the husks of spiritual impurity associated with peoples' own evil inclination (in Hebrew called 'the Yetzer haRa') are what motivate, entangle, warp, pervert, and manipulate people and groups against G-d, Torah, Israel, and the Messiah. This is part of Satan's attempt to prevent the Messiah from establishing the Holy Throne of G-d and his Davidic rein in this world; which includes the third Temple and Sanhedrin. This is part of G-d's plan to give us the free choice to overcome the evil and by thus gain merit to be rewarded and go to Heaven. Without the evil there would be no free choice. Tshuvah Shleima and nullification to Hashem can cleanse us of these husks of spiritual impurity that block our souls from the light. The third Temple and Sanhedrin will act as a drain that cleanses these husks of spiritual impurity that block our souls from the light and bring us to full blissful, happy love light all of our days. This only comes with the Messiah.

Part of the most effective barrier that opposes the Messiah is the enemy within, including the evil inclination found in each of our hearts, which is our real worst enemy, since Hashem only reflects back onto us our service of Him, and no evil would befall us if we serve Him perfectly.

'Before the Moshiah comes there will be a regime of the reincarnations of the mixed multitude (in Hebrew called 'Erev Rav') ruling Israel' (Rav Rafael Eisenburg (the remembrance of the righteous is a blessing) in 'Hevlei haMoshiah bizmananoo' based on Tikoonei haZohar 144). *'Armilus will sit in Edom and rule the mixed multitude regime in Israel'* (Kol haTor). Armilus is a leader of the anti-Semites who leads the enemies of Israel against Israel and the Messiah by recruiting the enemies of Israel found amongst the wicked people within the people of Israel. Armilus is a Frankenstein like demonic monster that the Amalekites create through black magic, witchcraft, kabbala and sefer hayitzeerah. Gog (Ezekiel 38-39) also leads the anti-Semites against Israel. Armilus and Gog are explained and identified in full detail, with the sources, in my book on the war of Gog and Magog. In today's terms, for example, this could mean that Armilus directs the United States State Department Israel Department, and rules and manipulates it's puppets in the Israeli government and Jewish 'leadership' from there through the CIA that are stationed in Israel and the world's Jewish communities. He could also be some one out side of the government who manipulates the government, possibly the Vatican, or the UN, the World Bank, all of the above, and many other parts of the establishment. Another current popular theory says that he runs the system through the Church through one of the eight Masonic sects in the Vatican who had access to the statue of the virgin in the catacombs from which they used black magic to create Armilus. Gog gathers many goyim to attack Israel. See my book on the war of Gog and Magog for the full explanation of how this works based on the Torah sources.

The Zohar teaches us that there are five types of Erev Rav. These five types of Erev Rav are called: Neffilim (fallen ones), Giborim (mighty), Anakim (giants), Refaim (demons) and Amalekites. The souls of these people come from the husks of evil spiritual impurities that remained from the time of the flood. In Zohar Bereshit 28 it is written that the mixed multitude causes the exiles of the Jewish people. The Zohar says that 'The Neffilim come from the fallen angels Aza and Azal, who fell from their holiness and fornicated with woman because they were fair, and Hashem gave them their portion in this world and not in the next. The Giborim, mighty ones, rob the children of Israel, shattering their work, and build synagogues and Yeshivas, putting the scroll of the Torah and a crown upon its top, in order to give themselves a big name, and not for the sake of Heaven. Anakim, giant ones, belittle those of value, bring the world back to a state of without for and void. Refaim, demons, abandon the Torah, abandon those who study the Torah, and abandon Israel in time of distress, and even if they have the power to save them they do not want to do so, and instead do favors to those who worship idols. Amalekites became the heads of Israel from the time of the fourth exile of Edom (the exile in which we now live) and are men of Hamas against Israel' (Zohar Bereshit). In Hebrew 'Hamas' means many things including violence, treachery, betrayal, robbery and false testimony. These are the Amalekite Erev Rav's character traits as well as those of Amalek (may their memory be erased). Rashi on Deuteronomy 25 says that Amalek (may their memory be erased) likes to seduce the pure of Israel into the abomination of man lying with man to make them impure.

Since we are in the exile of evil Edom; what the Torah teaches us is the final and most enduring exile; the Zohar teaches us that the heads of the Jewish people are Amalekite Erev Rav and that the final redemption of Israel depends on the destruction of the Amalekite Erev Rav (in Hebrew 'Erev Rav Amalek'). Some of the Holy Rabbis of today hold that we are now living in the final redemption period nearing 'the coming of Moshiah'. Whatever that means must be clarified as this book intends to do. Rav Yitzchak Kadoori HaKadosh (the remembrance of the righteous is a blessing) was quoted by the Israeli newspaper Yidioth Ahronoth circa the year 2000CE as saying that the Messiah son of David was already in Jerusalem, as we know that the Messiah comes from Edom (most likely the USA part of Edom which is the leading part of Edom today) as earlier chapters show.

The Gaon of Vilna, in Even Shleima perek on Gioola, says that 'the Messiah can't come until the Erev Rav of Amalek (may their memory be erased) are eradicated'. By reason we can also see that the influence of their heretical ideas and impurity must be cleansed from our brainwashed minds and society at large. They have had a long term damaging effect on society throughout the exile of Edom where they and their bad religions and heretical ideologies have ruled to the detriment of us all. 'Amalek' (may their memory be erased) is described in depth in my book on the war of Gog and Magog but we will summarize here.

Amalek (may their memory be erased) are the evil race of men that have souls from the primordial serpent that seduced Eve and deceived her into eating from the fruit of the tree of knowledge of good and evil. Amalek (may their memory be erased) are thus literally the devil incarnate in this world. They attack the weak amongst the Jewish people (and Goyim) especially when Israel sins (see Rashi on Deuteronomy 25); especially for the sin of doubting G-d or cheating in business (Commentators, Rashi cites 'hekesh' on Deuteronomy 25 to connect Amalek with cheating in business or doubting G-d). In addition to their main character traits of greed, immorality and injustice (also characterizing the Erev Rav), Amalek's traits are more particularly characterized by speaking slander in order to set Jews apart from one another by dissension, strife and disunity. They target the Holy with slander, such as Rabbis, in order to destroy G-d's authority in the world by putting doubt into peoples' Faith in Hashem, Rabbis and Torah. They are also characterized by committing treachery against Jews (and Gentiles), arrogance, throwing off the yoke of Heaven and seducing others to do the same. They empower heretical ideas and movements that contradict the Torah, seducing pure Jewish men into having immoral relations with other men, witchcraft, and in particular they like to fight against and target the righteous and pure people of Israel with slander, injustice and murder in order to destroy their names and lives, often using other Jews to do so. It is a Mitzvah to eradicate all of Amalek and their ideas and spirit from the world. These traits are leaned from the Vilna Gaon in Even Shleima and Kol haTor, Zohar Bereshit 28 and Rashi on Deuteronomy 25. It must be noted that not all people with traits of Amalek are Amalek, or with traits of the Erev Rav are Erev Rav. Many people have some of these traits to some extent or another, but can repent to cleanse them out of him. Only a true Tzadik or wise Rabbi who is morally pure, filled with good deeds, and wise in Torah, is truly able to know, by Holy Spirit (Ruach HaKodesh) or Prophesy (Nivua), who is really Erev Rav or Amalek (may their memory be erased). We must relay on these Tzadikeem and wise Rabbis for advise and guidance on what to do with these people identified as Amalek or Erev Rav.

To help understand more clearly the underlying causes of failure of the Jewish people in every generation, the Vilna Gaon, in his book Even Shleima, chapter on Redemption, elucidates for us the problem of the influences of

Ishmael, Eisav, and the mixed multitude amongst the Jewish people. By identifying the problem we can fix the problem through repentance, returning to live by the Torah and removing the Erev Rav from power by empowering only the Sanhedrin and the Moshiah to judge and govern us, or at least only righteous Torah Jews, Tzadikeem, until that time comes. The Vilna Gaon (ibid) says that *'The Jewish people have three kinds of spiritual impurity mixed in with them: Ishmaelites, Esavians, and Erev Ravians. The Messiahs, son of David, and son of Josef, will appear and separate the Ishmaelite and Eisavian impurity from the Jewish people. But, this will be insufficient until the Jewish people are cleansed of the Erev Ravians. They are the proud wealthy who cling tightly to Jewry and Jewry learns from their behavior … and (their bad influence can only be) cleansed off through the hardship of exile. The corrupting generational decline allows the mixed multitude to become ever stronger and the true Torah leaders must decree new restrictions and preventative measures to amend the breaches made by the mixed multitude.... There are five character traits (or types) of Erev-Ravians among the Jews: 1) quarrel mongers and slanderers (in Hebrew slander is called 'lashon hara'), 2) lustful people, 3) hypocritical people who are not what they pretend to be, 4) those who seek honor as a means of fame, 5) those who chase after money. The quarrel mongers (and slanderers) are the worst of all and are called Amalekites. The Messiah son of David cannot come until they are eradicated from this world. All arguments that are not for Hashem's sake originate from these people who rush to lead and to take glory and credit for themselves'*. The Amalekite Erev Ravian's slander breaks down most Jew's Faith in G-d, belief in Torah and belief in them selves and their own sense of self esteem, self respect and self worth. This is the goal of Amalek (may their memory be erased). They are very successful in our generation and there is and domino effect to their slander that causes it to spread everywhere unless stopped by the Rabbis Shlita. This slander also break up the mutual respect and thus love between Jews and thus breaks up the unity of Israel. Thus they stop the Messiah. Their biggest accomplishment in every generation is intelligently slandering the two Messiah's as well, thus causing people in the generation to disregard and ignore the two Messiah's. This is what is happening now. This has caused a plague of lack of self worth and self respect beliefs that has skyrocketed and people turn to life coaches and therapists for help. In the book 'the eight chapters', the Rambam is quoted as saying that 'if one is sick he goes to a doctor. If he is sick in the soul (Holeh Nefesh), he goes to a wise sage (Chacham)'. For a example, an example of intelligent slander might be lashon hara posing as the 'professional opinion' of a life coach, therapist, judge, policeman, clergy, leader, respected public figure, etc.. The Satanic evil inclination system of the evil side of the world (the 'Sitra Ahra') that is also a part of us that is found within us incites people to do this slander. This intelligent slander makes the slander seem 'kosher', believable and acceptable to people. The lashon hara may even be from a well intentioned Tzadik (haShem Yislach viYirachem) or Rabbi Shlita (haShem Yislach viYirachem) with good intentions who is projecting out his own low self esteem, lack of self respect and lack of sense of sell worth on to other people including the two Moshiah's. Thus the two Moshiah's (Ben David and Ben Josef) of the generation are pasuled (disqualified) in people's minds and the Rabbis Shlita ask: Where and who are the two Moshiahs of our generation? He's sitting right in front of you Rabbi Shlita. In the 1700's, the Vilna Gaon and Baal haTanya had the traits of and referred to themselves as the Moshiah Ben Yosef (the head) and Moshiah Ben David (the heart), respectively. If they met it would be the meeting of the head and the heart, which is need for us to be whole and in balance with Hashem, ourselves and each other. When the Baal haTanya went to meet the Gaon of Vilna, lashon hara kept them from meeting. Rabbis Shlita say that if they had met the Moshiah would have come. Both Moshiah's understand this and forgive all those, and pray for all those, who were mislead by their yester haras to err in this matter. For those who made this mistake, don't worry, everything will be okay. You are forgiven. You are okay.

The Vilna Gaon (Even Shleima, chapter on How to Learn Torah, point 17) also points out that '*there are people who do good deeds and Torah commandments and learn Torah in order to show off. These people are from the side of the mixed multitude (in Hebrew called the 'Erev Rav') and are destined for hell*'. '*In the exile most of the clergy are not Hagoon (clean of transgression)... and oppose the righteous Tzadikeem* (including the righteous Messiah of the generation)' (Rav Nahman of Breslov Likootei Moran chapter 12). '*A clergy member who is not clean of transgression, his teachings are like a poison*' (Talmud Bavli Taanit 7). '*It is a Mitzvah to respect clergy, but when one of them lacks good character or is not respectful of Mitzvoth then he should be regarded as the petty '(zol') or common ('kal') of the people*' (Shulhan Aruch Yoreh Daah 243:3). "*People from clergy of not good character and are unfit to teach are called 'Demons'. They destroy the honor and authority of Torah in the world and cause people who learn from them to become atheists and to hate the morally pure religious and righteous Tzadikeem of Israel*" (Rav Nahman of Breslov from the book "Advise" by Rav haGadol Avroham Greenbaum Shlita, chapter on controversy and strife section 8, and chapter on Honor, point 10, 11, 12).

In spite of problems we in the clergy all have as flesh and blood people with an evil inclination, that causes us to sin sometimes, as well as a good inclination that causes us to do good; Mitzvoth; there are many fully righteous orthodox Rabbis who don't sin at all and are advising people well on the proper path of Torah Mitzvoth, including the seven categories of Noahide Torah laws for Gentiles. We all hope that these Rabbis and their followers help bring the Messiah in our generation. The generation would be wise to listen to the fully righteous orthodox Rabbis and this will only bring blessing to the world and individuals who listen to them. You should be supportive and in consultation with your local orthodox Rabbi where ever you live. If you don't have one then get one or use the Internet or the telephone book to find one. You may contact me to refer you to a good Rabbi as well.

Jewish leaders who don't listen to the big orthodox Jewish Rabbis of our generation are the false leaders of the Erev Rav who cause disasters to befall us and keep us in exile. They steal the budget and support from the best orthodox Rabbis and Tzadikeem to whom the support is really due, thus supporting false leaders and thereby damaging (Has viShalom) the Jewish people and the honor of Hashem, and push away the Moshiah and redemption of Mankind in that generation. An example of this is when the people don't listen to the big Rabbis, the Gidoleem, on who to vote for in Israeli elections. Even intelligent Israelis delude themselves into thinking they know better than the big Rabbis and mess everything up in the leadership of Israel by voting into government unworthy Knesset members. This allows the Erev Rav to rule over us. This is how the disrespect for the biggest orthodox Jewish Rabbis of our generation and Gadol haDor pushes off the Messiah. People don't realize it, but, among these Rabbis is also the potential Moshiah himself who they are not respecting. We must listen to the fully righteous (no sins) orthodox Rabbis.

'*The Messiah son of David doesn't come until the petty government is destroyed from Israel*' (Talmud Bavli Sanhedrin 98) is also interpreted in the Zohar (in the book 'Chevlei haMoshiah bizmanainoo') to mean that these five types of mixed multitude behavior and traits must be eradicated from the positions of power among the Jewish people in order for the potential Messiah of our generation to be esteemed and respected and thusly to be established king and served properly. Otherwise, until then, not only will the Erev Rav, but also their traits, will oppose the potential Messiah of our generation. Many of these people will sin against, rob, slander, scapegoat, and oppress the potential Messiah of the generation, which endangers him personally and opposes his redeeming Israel. In addition, many of these people from the mixed multitude may not like the Messiah because *they think that they are the Messiah* as part of their delusional ego trip and thus disrespect the Messiah.

The Messiah does not wish the deaths of the Erev Rav and prays for them to repent and become good. No one has to die. Everyone can repent. Only Amalek has to die, and have speculated that if Amalek converts to Judaism then he is a Jew who is no longer Amalek and thus does not have to die. I don't know if this is true. In any case, those who don't repent will be sorry.

In Likootei Moran, Rav Nahman of Breslov says that it is the job of what he calls "Moshe Moshiah' to make a 'biur' ('sorting out', clarification or separation) of the Erev Rav. The Ramchal in Gnizei haRamchal Kinath Hashem Tzivaoth, chapter on Moshiah in the Gate of Rome, says that the Messiah suffers and undergoes great trials and tribulations, in 'the Gate of Rome' (see the Gaon of Vilna on Apitha diKarta on Sanhedrin 98 who says that the Messiah sits in the gate of Rome in Heaven), which according to the Ramchal means that the Messiah is suffering in imprisonment, so as to atone for Moses regarding the Erev Rav and thereby make a biur ('sorting out'). This is part of the Messiah's job to clarify and sort our among the Erev Rav who is a Jew and who is a Gentile, Noahide or idol worshiper, and can be saved and who can't. All can be saved if we repent fully; in Hebrew called Tshuvah Shleima.

The Messiah of the generation depends on the merit and support of the generation. *'The House of Jacob will be a fire, the House of Josef a flame, and the House of Eisav for straw, and they will ignite them and devour them. There will be no survivor to the House of Eisav, for Hashem has spoken…'* (Obadiah 1:18). Talmud Bavli Avoda Zara 10-11 says that '*the House of Eisav*' refers specifically to the descendants of Eisav who live in his wicked ways but not the righteous ones. May we see the righteous ones of Eisav support the Messiah of the generation and bring down those opposed to the Messiah, like the burning of a house of straw. May the righteous of who Eisav lead Edom, America and the West, back the real Moshiah of our generation as it is written 'the older Eisav will serve the younger Israel' (Genesis 25). May this be part of the hastened

Moshiah in our time; Eisav USA serving the Moshiah who will save them and be their benevolent and righteous king that they always wanted to govern them for their own good. As two American senators came out in 2014 and said: "America is going down the tubes. Only the Jewish Messiah can save us", this shows that even leaders of Edom want the Moshiah since they recognize that America will fall unless the Moshiah saves them.

One of the many things that the Messiah and his flock will do is to see to it that the corrupt government and bad religion of the Erev Rav regime will be cleansed and replaced with righteous, ethical, morally pure people who live by the Torah under the advise of the fully righteous Rabbis of the generation; those who listen to the Gadol haDor and will form a Sanhedrin. This will be the end of the opposing Erev Rav regime and pave the way to the Messiah in our time. May that time be now. Amen.

Most 'Palestinians' Come from Jews and Many May Still be Jewish

Most Rabbis with whom I spoke don't know who are the *'Ishmaelites' and 'Esavians'* spoken about by the Vilna Gaon in Even Shleima cited in the previous chapter. It is obvious that they exist though, since the Gaon gave them importance when he mentioned them. Who are they?

Genetic research by Professor Ariela Oppenheim of Hadassah University in Jerusalem indicates that eighty percent of the Arabs living in the land of Israel come from Ashkenazi Jews who migrated to the land of Israel and then assimilated into the Muslim and Christian Arab culture. The YouTube documentary "Hidden Palestinian Jews' gives details including a news documentary shown on Israeli TV. The documentary shows that many Arab villages and tribes in the land of Israel, including many Bedouins, say that they come from Jews and some even say that they are still Jewish. There are many cases of this in the land of Israel. Some of these towns only intermarried with people from their own town which means they are still Jewish. Many Jewish customs and traits are still maintained among the Arabs of the land of Israel, such as Jewish stars on their graves. The 'Palestinian' 'Arabs' are the smartest and most educated of all the Arabs, which is yet another indication that many of them are really Jewish, or at least part Jewish. Many of them look like Jews. They also seek just revenge for what they feel are crimes committed against them by the Zionists and this can also be a Jewish trait as well as Gentile trait so case of terrorism and extreme violence is no proof one way or another.

This finding is supported by historical records that show that most of the 'Arabs' living in the land of Israel today actually come from Ashkenazi, Middle Eastern and Sephardic Jews who emigrated to the land of Israel in the last thousand years. They converted to Islam and assimilated into the Ishmaelite culture. Many of them look Jewish and act Jewish, including the identifying traits of modesty, generosity and mercy, as cited in the Talmud as three identifying traits of Jews. Many Arabs have these traits, which is an indication, not proof, that they are really Jewish. In the time of the Arizal in Tsfat, Israel, circa 1500 AD, he commented that most of the land was occupied mainly by Ishmaelites only numbering in the thousands by my estimation, with only a minority of Jews living in Jerusalem, Tsfat, Hebron, Tiberius, and maybe some other settlements. He called it 'the exile of Ishmael', a term not found in the revealed Torah. Many Jews who migrated to the land were compelled to assimilate into the Ishmaelite culture and eventually lost their Jewish identity and became know as Arabs. We can see the same process of Jews loosing their identity with the Westernized Jews in Israel who have lost their Jewish identity and are called hiloneem. Many of them can prove their Jewish ancestry to the Rabbinate, though, so they are still considered Jews by Jewish law, even if many are not spiritually Jewish anymore. Ironically, in Israel, these 'Arabs' are called '*Ishmaelites*', which is the term that the Gaon of Vilna uses to describe a type of Jews in Even Shleima. Most people think that the Arabs are from Ishmael, which may be only a small minority of them, since only a few thousand of Ishmaelites were noted in the land five hundred years ago before Jews started immigrating to the land from abroad. These were Jews who returned to the land of Israel as part of the ingathering of the exiles during the beginning of the redemption period. Thus, most of the so called 'Palestinians' seem to really come from Jews who were culturally Arabized and many may still be actually really Jewish, although there is no Halachically accepted proof of this in most cases. Thus they are viewed as Gentiles by the Rabbis who decide who is Jewish.

It appears that the '*Ishmaelites*' spoken about by the Vilna Gaon in Even Shleima are the Arabized Jews in the land of Israel who are more Ishmaelite than Jewish.

The West is Edom, which is Eisav's rule. Thus, the Western culture is Eisav's culture. It has traces of other Western cultures such as England, also some values ancient Greece and Rome. There is also a strong influence of the Jewish people, especially in America, which is called a secularized 'Judean Christian' society, not a secular Christian nor secular Catholic society. 'Secular' is an aphorism for throwing off the yoke of Heaven. Thus we have Edom, Eisav's culture. The *'Esavians'* that the Gaon of Vilna cites in Even Shleima are mostly the secular Westernized Jews who are more like Eisav in their cultural traits than those of a Torah true Jew. Some 'Torah Jews' though are also Eisavian despite their outward appearance and Jewish customs. In Israel the Eisavians are called 'hiloneem' but some Esavians are also 'religious', including all the sects of the Haredim and Dati Leoomi. Many of these hiloneem are great Jewish souls who have been born into low places and will return to living by the Torah. Jews who return to Torah are known as 'Baalei Tshuvah' and this is a movement in Judaism. We hope that all the hiloneem will become Baalei Tshuvah, be redeemed and go to Heaven.

Most of the hiloneem today are still recognized by the Rabbis as Jews though. But as time goes on, unless they become Baalei Tshuvah, there will be less and less recognition of them as Jews. In this case they can end up like a Westernized version of the 'Palestinians'; Jews who have lost their Jewish identity and status as Jews because they blended in with the Western culture of the Gentiles. Just like the Jews who converted to Islam are known as 'Ishmaelites', the assimilated Westernized Jews in Israel loose their Jewish identity more and more as time goes on and many are even converting to Christianity. There are some thirty thousand in Israel today, and growing with the help of missionaries. The Torah views this as severe and could warrant harsh Divine Retribution as was the case when the Jews of Germany were moving to convert to Christianity and their souls were saved by the holocaust before they could do so. The hiloneem in Israel, and many secular Westernized Jews abroad, are what the Gaon of Vilna called 'Eisavian Jews' in his book Even Shleima. We will see what happens to them in time. We hope and pray and make great efforts that they will become Baalei Tshuvah and be redeemed with the rest of Israel. This book will help stop the spread of missionaries in Israel and all English speaking lands, and will hopefully bring them back to Torah Mitzvoth (Commandments) with Thsuva Shleima (Full Repentance). This can help hasten the redemption, but at least will help save the souls of many Jews and Gentiles too, who we also want to be included in the redemption.

These two groups; the Ishmaelite Jews and Eisavian Jews, cited by the Gaon of Vilna in Even Shleima chapter on redemption; are the majority of Jews in Israel today. Like Eisav and Ishmael they are in conflict; brother against brother, Jew against Jew. It is an unfortunate case of culture clash of Epic and tragic proportions.

Our self deceiving egotistical petty frivolous nonsense opposes the Messiah

People are supposed to respect, love, be king to and see the good in others, and ourselves. We are supposed to be positive in our thinking, grateful for all we have and don't have, trust in G-d that everything is for the best and have Faith in every word of G-d as it is brought down in the Torah as well as believing in the righteous orthodox Rabbis. This is healthy and good.

In the exile we have a problem with these positive healthy attitudes. This is part of the mental prison of exile in which most people imprison themselves. It hurts themselves and others who they don't respect, love and see the good in.

Much of the following paragraph is paraphrased in modern terms from Rav Nahman of Breslov's collective writings and when I say this I am looking at myself in the mirror, as we only see in others what we see in ourselves (Baal Shem Tov, Talmud Bavli Kiddushin 70). When we see a problem in another, it is Hashem telling us a message that we must rectify something, including in ourselves. When we see something in others that we don't like, we should not hate or get angry at the other, but pray and work on ourselves to fix what is inside us that made Hashem show this to us. Our self deceiving egotistical (in Hebrew called 'Gaiva') petty frivolous nonsense and circum locative rhetoric that we repeat in our minds, and convince ourselves to believe, and espouse to others, instead of true Torah understanding, is what makes us blind to not seeing other peoples truths that they tell to us and that we are supposed to see and recognize. It causes us to drift off into a world of our own imaginations that is not reality, not Torah and not connected to G-d. This also blinds us to our faults and good points, and those of others. We all do this to some extent. This also opposes the potential Messiah of the generation for it blocks us from accepting him and seeing his truths that he is trying to teach us to make the world better and bring the final redemption. This Gaiva, lack of respect, and lack of kindness at the root of the problem. How do we fix this? Humility, respecting everyone, being kind, learning Torah, recognizing the great orthodox Rabbis of the past and current generations, returning to live by the halacha (Jewish law), seeing the good in ourselves and others that G-d gave us, being Truthful and accepting and doing the advice of true Tzadikeem (that's Hebrew for Righteous Torah Jews).

There are two famous morals taught by the Chefetz Chaim in Yeshivas. The first is a story of a man who wanted to fix the world. He tired to fix his country and saw that he could not. Then he went to his city to fix it and saw that he could not. Then he went to his family to fix them and saw that he could not. Then he realized that the only one he can fix is himself. I believe that we must fix ourselves but even when we are not perfect can help others to fix themselves as well. The second moral is that a man found a piece of paper with a picture of the world on one side and a picture of a man's face on the other. But, the paper was ripped into many pieces so he couldn't see the picture of the world as it was meant to be. He tried and tried to put the picture of the world back together but could not put it back together. So, instead, he put the pieces of the picture of the man's face back together, and then the picture of the world on the other side looked fine.

Ancient Examples of People who opposed the Moshiahs of Past Generations

A historic example of opposition to the anointed of Hashem, the potential Moshiah of his generation, is actually notated the Torah itself for all generations to learn from.

The righteous king Hezekiah, the anointed king of the House of David in the first Temple period, was the potential Moshiah of his generation. But, there was a wicked, arrogant, immoral opponent to him named Shevna. Shevna's Yeshiva (a Yeshiva is a Torah learning academy) was more numerous than the Yeshiva of the righteous and morally pure king Hezekiah. Shevna sought to usurp his throne and spoke lashon hara (slander) against the righteous king Hezekiah. Rashi on Talmud Bavli Sanhedrin 26b says that Shevna and his Yeshiva were impure by having forbidden immoral relations with man and were pleasure seekers, not toiling in Torah as is needed to be great in Torah.

Thus, their Torah did not last. Eventually Shevna was plagued by Hashem and ended in a cruel and unusual death by the sword of the enemies of Israel. The immoral people of the Yeshiva of Shevna were blemished in their observance of the Covenant (in Hebrew called 'Pgam haBrith'). They literally couldn't think straight, had delusions of grandeur, and this coupled with their arrogance, prevented them from accepting and appreciating the king Hezekiah, the true potential Moshiah of that generation. The point that we learn from this is that the true potential Moshiah of this generation also has the same problems with the same type of people today.

There were many examples of basically kosher Jews who opposed Hashem's Divinely anointed leaders such as Moses and king David. These examples may be mirrored in at least some aspects by some people as well in our times as part of the opposition to the potential Messiah of our generation. This includes lack of respect and obedience to our Torah leaders (the Gidoleem, Tzadikeem and Rebbes) who are the Moses and king David, Moshe Moshiah, of our generation (Likootei Moran 2).

Why do we mourn on the 9th of Av? Because ten princes of ten tribes in Moses day asked Moses for permission to spy out the land 'to see if we could conquer the land' that HaShem had already promised we could conquer. They lacked Faith in Hashem's promise, and Moses' kingship, to deliver us as a nation to the Holy land. Moses permitted them to go spy out the land as a lesson in personal growth; hoping that they would reconnect their Faith to affirm their Belief in Hashem's promise to bring us into the promised land, or if not then face the punishment as a consequence for their denial (kfira) of G-d and Moses. They failed the test. They brought back a libelous evil report to the people of Israel saying that we were too weak and small to conquer the land. In the spies report of the land they said that we were 'like grasshoppers in their eyes'. This incited a lack of Faith among the people. The people then cried due to this report. HaShem then said 'because you have cried for no reason, I will give you reason to make you cry on this day of the 9th of Av in history'. All of the following tragedies commenced on the 9th of Av: the destruction of the first and second Temples, the Spanish inquisition, WWI which lead to the WWII holocaust, etc.. The Rabbis say that the ten spies did not want to go into the land because they would loose their stature as princes once they entered the land. They say this as a metaphor to Jewish leaders who want to stay in America and other places outside of Israel where they can have honor and material comfort on the 'merit' of living out side the land. This is the story of the ten spies who questioned Hashem's promise and Moses' authority.

Another example of rebellion against the true leader Moses is Korah. He was a Levite who out of jealousy for the mantle of leadership questioned Moses' authority and even had the hootspa (Gaul, nerve, disrespect, haughty conceited disrespect for what is good and right) to ask why we had to wear Tzitzit?

Another example of rebellion against the true leader Moses is the Erev Rav. The Erev Rav were constantly trying to stone Moses and undermined his name and authority by asking questions like "Why have you brought us out of Egypt? To kill us in the desert?'.

Another example of slander against the true leader Moses is his sister Miriam. She criticized Moses for marrying a beautiful woman (called dark or black in the scripture which means beautiful). She got leprosy and was put outside the camp. She repented. Moses then prayed for her and she was healed.

Another example of opposition to the anointed of Hashem was King David, Hashem's anointed 'Moshiah' of that generation. He was constantly slandered, rebelled against, targeted for murder, derided, and opposed by people in his generation, as the Psalms indicate. 70,000 Jews died of a plague in David's generation for speaking slander against him. Examples of rebellion against the true anointed leader king David was were/are numerous.

1) 70,000 people who spoke slander against him died of a plague
2) The wise Sanhedrin head and his teacher Achitophel planned a revolt against him
3) His son Absalom revolted against him for the throne.
4) His son Adonyahoo revolted against him for the throne.
5) Saul's head of the Sanhedrin and chief general, Doeg the Edomi, a descendant of an Amalekites convert (Midrash), who killed all the Cohaneem at Nov and advised Saul not to kill all the Amalekites, slandered David behind his back and incited king Saul to be enraged with murderous jealousy and hatred for David to the point where Saul persecuted David and sought his blood.
6) Saul's daughter Michal, David's wife, libeled David for dancing before the ark immodestly and she died childless.

7) Shimi Ben Gera slandered, cursed and mocked David at his time of weakness when he was fleeing from his son who was trying to take the throne by force with an armed militia.
8) Uriah the Hivi took David's wife Bat Sheva from him. Upon Uriah's slaying Goliath, David mistakenly said that he could have any Jewish girl for this (Midrash), and G-d then said "ohYeh? Any Jewish girl? How about your soul mate Bat Sheva!". G-d then gave Uriah Bat Sheva to wife. Later, David had an affair with Bat Sheva when Uriah was away at war and divorced from her for the duration of the war so as to not make her an aguna if Uriah would be missing in action. David got her pregnant. He ordered Uriah to come to Jerusalem and stay there to make it seem as if Uriah got her pregnant. Uriah did not listen to David and returned to the war. What people forget is that Uriah did not return to the war as an act of nobility, but was part of a rebellion against David and as such did not respect David when he told him to stay in Jerusalem to cover up for David's impregnating his rightful bride soul mate Bat Sheva. Since Bat Sheva was not married at the time, the Rabbis say (Talmud) that any one who says that David sinned is making a mistake. As king David had the right to kill Uriah for rebelling against him which means also just simply not obeying what David told him to do. Even though Uriah was a rebel and David did have a right to kill him, this incident was still considered not good for a Tzadik on David's level even though he didn't sin.
9) There are more examples believe it or not including rebels amongst once loyal priests and a chief general.

I don't know if the above examples of rebellion against Moses and David can reflect the problems that the Moshiah has in our time since most people today do not seem to be really conscious of what they are doing is wrong. But, their may be some aspects of these past problems; jealousy, arrogance, pride, seeking honor, greed, etc.. Today, most people sin because we lack understanding and think that we are right even when we are really wrong. Sometimes we sin because we lack self control. In any case, to solve this problem, it is a Mitzvah to give support only to kosher, morally pure orthodox Rabbis, Jews and their Yeshivas and to only support and recognize those organizations and bodies that follow the advise of the biggest Rabbis of the generation. The guidance of the kosher orthodox Rabbis ensures that what we are supporting is really truly good, and some rebel group that causes Jews to sin and push off the redemption. We hope that the potential Messiah of the generation and his Rabbis and people who are with him will succeed in this Holy mission.

Whether religious or secular, everything considered, today in Israel, everybody and every group is doing their part to do some aspect of good that is necessary in helping bring the Moshiah and the final redemption.

Slandering Rabbis, Torah and Israel in the Media Undermines the Moshiah

One of the most detrimental things done today to oppose the Moshiah is to destroy the credibility of orthodox Jews and the authority of Torah, particularly in Israel, the USA, and the West, or anywhere. This happens when the media publicizes the sin of a Torah Jew, or Rabbi, where the sin is considered reprehensible to society. This pushes masses of people away from Torah and Rabbis. It is usually orchestrated with intelligent design on the part of some anti-Torah or anti-Semitic goy or self hating Jew in the media with the purpose of destroying peoples' Faith in the authority of the Torah and the Rabbis. Rabbis are only human; flesh and blood; and sometimes sin like everyone else due to being trapped by the evil inclination that can get the best of us at times. This sin of a Rabbi does not mean that the Torah is not true and that Rabbis are 'bad', but the damage that this does to the authority of the Torah and the Rabbis and thus society is atrocious and catastrophic. This is an example of how the wicked Erev Rav and particularly atrocious Amalek works through lashon hara (slander). He poisons peoples minds with it on purpose with the calculated purpose of destroying good and the good names of good people like orthodox Rabbis. We must reject and protest against such slander just as spitting out the poisonous venom of a snake. The Media is guilty for doing this and also guilty for not publicizing all the good that Rabbis and orthodox Jews do for G-d's honor, the honor of Torah, morality and ethics, and all the vast kindness (in Hebrew called Chesed) that they do for Jews and even goyim sometimes. As the Gaon of Vilna says that good and evil are mixed since the destruction of the Temple (Even Shleima), although the media does good for reporting a lot of news, it also does bad in terms of slandering Rabbis, Torah and Israel, and not reporting the good things about us.

On the morning of 18 November 2014, two Palestinian men from Jerusalem entered Kehilat Bnei Torah synagogue, in the Har Nof neighborhood of Jerusalem, and attacked the praying congregants with axes, knives, and a gun. They killed four Rabbis while praying and a Gentile Israeli police officer. They also wounded seven other male worshippers. The TV news media CNN reported the Palestinian Muslim terror attack as 'an attack on a mosque in Jerusalem'. This was a blatant lie. When people protested CNN refused to correct the sin they made. This is a grave sin. The media has committed many such grave sins, over and over again, against believers in G-d; especially Jews and Israelis, but also against Muslims when they are in a weak position (like the Iraqis) and are unable to defend themselves. This is Amalek in the media; attacking the weak, slandering the innocent, lying to cover up injustices and pervert justice, atrocities, greed, government corruption, spreading abomination via the media, etc.. The disrespect the media has for Rabbis is usually more subtle. It usually takes the form of totally ignoring them and the important things they have to say to the society to guide the people in the proper ways. Just as the media is wicked for this, the media is also wicked for slandering Israel and Rabbis and not showing them and the Holy Torah due respect.

Pro G-d, pro Israel, pro morals and ethics, pro Torah News media like Fox news is better though, even if it still has room for improvement by voicing the word of G-d through the leading Rabbis of the generation on issues.

The Media is meant to teach Torah by Holy orthodox Rabbis and the potential Moshiah of our generation on all major moral and ethical issues (such as what the Torah really says is right and wrong on a particular issue, the Sabbath, Noahide laws, abortion, human rights, gays rights issues, injustice in the courts, stealing, fairness, kindness and respect to others, ethics, morality, etc.). The Rabbis and potential Moshiah of our generation have been denied this. This is opposing the Moshiah and the salvation of mankind. It is part of the darkness of Edom and Amalek at the head.

If the real, best, righteous orthodox Rabbis were given voice over the major news media, it would add wisdom, insight and understanding to the problems and conflicts of the world society. This would pave the way for mutual respect between peoples and peace.

The Destruction of the Messiah's Opposition

Referring to the transgressors of Israel and the Gentiles in the end of days it is written: '*Those who escape from the sword of Messiah son of Josef will fall by the sword of Messiah son of David and those who escape from there will fall into the pit in the war of Gog*' (Rashi on Isaiah 24:18). Not all transgressors are enemies of the Messiah, but all enemies of the Messiah are transgressors. From here we see that the final stage of destruction for the Messiah's enemies are in the war of Gog and Magog.

The best way for us personally, right now, to destroy the enemies and opposition of the Moshiah, is by *fixing ourselves* and doing 'Tshuva Shleima' (completely returning to live by the Torah commandments) and making yourself a friend, backer, guard or supporter of the Tzadikeem (Righteous), the poor Rabbis and the potential Moshiahs of your generation (while they are still alive will live a long good life). Being kind and respectful is an essential part of this Tshuva Shleima.

The ways in which Messiah's opposition will be destroyed include:

- '*Tshuva Shleima*', meaning full repentance, committing ourselves totally to live by all of the Torah Mitzvoth, is the key to hasten the redemption right now. *Tshuva Shleima*' includes doing all the Torah Mitzvoth properly as we should. By returning to live by HaShem's ways written in the Torah (in Hebrew called '*Tshuva Shleima*'), and learning Torah, we thus pave the way and remove the obstacles of sin that obstruct the Moshiah from coming (Talmud Bavli Sanhedrin 98). '*Tshuva Shleima*' includes maximizing our love for Hashem, love and kindness and respect for all people including Gentiles and Jews and all of G-d's Creations, Torah learning, Mitzvoth, charity to the poor, especially righteous poor Torah scholars.
- Reish Lakish says that by correcting ones ways (and character traits) by repentance out of love for HaShem '*even his willful transgressions will be transformed into merits*' (Talmud Bavli Rosh HaShana 29a). Correct, Hashem can change the past! Here's your chance to change your past. Take it. He is G-d; He can do anything.
- *Learning Torah* daily if possible in the name of Heaven and thus filling our 'Daath' (Understanding) and behavior with the understanding

and ways of HaShem, cleansing ourselves of sin and fixing ourselves by Tshuvah Shleima in every aspect and way possible.

- Demanding only the Torah law by the law of the land in which we live, as ruled by the Rabbis, and eventually the Sanhedrin and House of David be our official senior executive ruling bodies and courts in Israel and all the countries. This helps remove the obstacles to the Moshiah and pave the way for the full redemption to be enabled to occur (Rashi Talmud Sanhedrin 98).
- Being kind to all people and respecting and seeing the good in every person and judging people favorably including yourself all the times as G-d has given us all the gift of life for the time being until we move on to the next world.
- Not just seeing the good in others, but *also pointing out the good in every person all the time* (The Chefetz Chaim Foundation and Rav Nahman of Breslov Likootei Moran 282). This will empower the good in the Jewish people (and Gentiles), help the good inclination to overpower the bad inclination, and motivate us to do more and more good until it becomes our habitual behavior and natural inclination.
- Think positively (the Rebbe) and trust in G-d that all is good and will be good. Everything is going to be okay.
- Attitude of Gratitude always.
- Arrogance, Ego, haughtiness, and conceit constrict ones wisdom to the point where he is a fool who thinks that he knows it all, disrespects people who are wiser than him and reject and disparage the Rabbi and Tzadikeem, including the potential Messiah of the generation. These flaws may even cause one to be on an ego trip where he thinks that he is the Messiah himself, and men often do, causing much destruction in the world. These blemishes in character must be rectified. Pray to G-d for Help to do this. He will help.
- *Work on being humble*, grateful, loving and appreciative of what you have and your lot in life. Peoples' arrogance, self deceiving ego-centrism, self-centeredness and selfishness, baseless hatred, jealousy and sins prevent the Messiah from coming (Sefer HaMidoth and Rashi on Talmud Bavli Sanhedrin 98 and Rosh HaShana).
- According to the book Kol HaTor, Moshiah Ben Yosef (Josef in English) paves the way for Moshiah Ben David, and by *upholding and living*

by Ben Yosef's traits we too can help pave the way. His traits include: righteously judges people, *upholds true Torah justice*, the Covenant of Peace like Pinchas did to Zimri and Cozbi, the sword of salvation, war against Amalek (may their memory be erased), upholds justice in the courts. *Good police and good judges who enforce the Torah laws are certainly part of the process of bringing the Messiah and in addition to being a pillar of the world, are in the aspect of Messiah son of Yosef and the Messiah himself.* People who do these things will probably meet the Messiah and may also merit working with the Messiah on a personal basis to establish justice in Israel and the world.

- The Arizal and Gaon of Vilna say that we must pray that Moshiah Ben Yosef be spared death (as it is written that he could be 'pierced through' Zachariah 12:10 as per Talmud Bavli Succa 52a this refers to Messiah Ben Yosef) by the hands of Armilus by praying everyday the Amida's "Kisei David" the *intent/devotion* (in Hebrew called 'Kavana') that Ben Yosef be saved and Armilus be destroyed. I like to take this prayer even one step further and to *pray with the Kavana that the Messiah Ben Yosef (and his camp) of our generation, who ever he is, succeeds in all ways and successfully paves the way for the Messiah and establishes and supports the Messiah son of David's thrown in Jerusalem soon in our time.*
- We must pay any monetary damages and appease those who we have hurt.
- We must be fair and honest in business and commerce.
- Pray to *Hashem*, the G-d of Israel, for everything. For more effective prayer, start the prayer with recognizing His awesome greatness and praising Him at the beginning of the prayer. Then pray for *others needs first*, and *then your needs*. The Amidah, Shimona Esrei, eighteen blessings, prayer is an excellent template formula for prayer. It was written in ancient times by prophets and Sanhedrin. Also Tachanoon by king Hezkiyahoo is very powerful. It got him fifteen more years of life when he was ruled to die by a prophet.
- Giving charity, especially to poor orthodox Jews. The best charity is giving to worthy Torah scholars and brings the most blessing and is the most elevated form of charity (see Shulhan Aruch laws of Tzadka). See your local orthodox Rabbi for assistance in this. Sending charity to

Israel, especially Jerusalem, also Beitar Illite and other poor religious cities in Israel is most elevated and blessed.

- Get married to you true love soul mate and bring as many children into the world that you can, especially if you are Jewish, and give them caring, loving child hoods with good Jewish or Noahide educations if you are Gentile, and hugs and kisses every day (if they want the hugs, but not if they don't like being touched). Guard your children from all dangers and guide them to do good things like kindness, good deeds, skills, prayer, charity, seeing the good in others and educating them to be good people who live by G-d's laws.
- Be Friendly to and Respect All people, including Jews, Goyim, including Arabs, so as to weave a thread of love and kindness and respect through all peoples and embrace our destiny as the Jewish 'kingdom of priestly ministers' (Exodus 19:6) who are a light unto the Goyim (Isaiah 49:6, 42:6) who teach the nations of the world the Noahide Laws.

The Messiah's Last Enemies will Perish in the war of Gog and Magog

'*Those who escape from the sword of Messiah son of Josef will fall by the sword of Messiah son of David and those who escape from there will fall into the garbage bin in the war of Gog*' (Rashi on Isaiah 24: 18). This means that in the final redemption period of history, the Messiah and his people Israel have many enemies who are killed in stages. First their enemies are killed by the Messiah son of Josef, then by the sword of the Messiah son of David, and those who escape that will be killed in the war of Gog and Magog. After that there will be no more blocks of major enemies for the Messiah. Maybe their will be individual enemies who will be brought judgment by the Messiah as king of the world.

People who are bringing the Moshiah

The people who are bringing the Moshiah include everyone who does good deeds. This especially includes Jews who are properly living by the Torah laws (the orthodox Jews) and Gentiles who are living by the Noahide laws. But, every good deed, act of kindness, prayer or Mitzvah (Torah commandment) that any body does, Jew or Goy, helps bring the Moshiah. People who repent bring the Messiah. People who pray bring the Messiah. The builders of Israel, people who serve in the IDF, Mosad, Shabak, the Israeli military system, good police, good judges and the Torah learners are bringing the Messiah. The good police, good judges, good public defenders, good public prosecutors and good government officials who uphold social justice and good social policy in accordance with the what the Rabbis say to do in our times according to the Torah are bringing the Moshiah.

In the people of Israel, the king is the heart, the Sanhedrin the brain, the people the body, the Army the arms and the Mosad the feet. For the body to act properly it must have a pure humble heart, a pure humble king. The Mosad are the unsung heroes of Israel. As the foundation they are the feet that move anywhere in the world to support Israel and do what they have to do to make the reality of Israel.

The Zohar teaches us that the final redemption will come on the merit of the youth (in Hebrew called 'Noar'); just as the redemption from Egypt came on the merit of the righteous woman of Israel who saved the Jewish babies from Pharos deadly decree of death. Is there anyone today in Israel who may be a twenty year old, thirty year old, sixty year old or even an eighty year old 'youth'? I think that the majority of Israelis are youthful and are part of this youth who are bringing the Moshiah.

The immense suffering of the people in Israel, travail, poverty, fear of terror and war, and general difficulties of living in Israel gives the Jewish people much merit to bring the Moshiah. It is a big Mitzvah to support Israel; especially the Torah Jews in Israel and the defense. As the chapter 'The Power of Torah and the Messiah' shows the Torah learning and observance is bringing the Torah and building Jerusalem in preparation for the Moshiah to come. As we have seen in previous chapters, Tshuvah Shleima is key. But, ultimately, as we have seen in the chapter on 'When will the Messiah come and what determines his Coming?', since the Moshiah's coming depends on 'Divine Kindness', we can arouse this Divine Kindness by being kind. This includes being kind to all, including Arabs so as to make peace with them as it is a Mitzvah of 'Rodeif Shalom' (pursuing peace).

Misconceptions of What and Who the Messiah Really Is

The following is a list of widespread misconceptions and nonsense which contradict what the Torah actually teaches us. Some are critical mistakes which are a matter of pikuah nefesh need to be corrected. Unfortunately, in a small number of matters, dogma has replaced daath Torah. The Torah of all the various Orthodox Jewish sects of this generation is quite excellent, a pillar of Truth and Holiness in the world in my opinion, deserves reward, and is helping bring the Gioola Shleima and Moshiah to Israel. I am sure these people of truth will help correct the misconceptions. Yasher Koacha!

The Common Misconception	The Reality the Torah Prescribes
1) "Everybody will like the Moshiah and he will be nice to everybody"	Wicked will try to destroy the Moshiah and he will slay them by the spirit of his lips-Zohar Shemot 7 & Isaiah 11
2) "Moshiah will take care of that"	Moshiah cannot come until the bad judges bad police, petty government, Inflated ego wicked and Erev Rav Amalek are destroyed from Israel(Sanhedrin 98,Gra Evn Shlma ch Gioola)
3) "Moshiah will save everybody"	Moshiah will come to Zion *for those who repent*-Isaiah 59.
4) "There's no Nivoah today"	Nivooah returns before the coming of the Moshiah-Rambam Igereth Teman 174. Baba Batra 12 says that the wise, strange people and children can have a level of prophesy. See Chasam Sofer.
5) "We're all from the two tribes of Yehudah and Benyamin"	In this redemption, first the ten tribes of Israel return to the land, then Yehudah in the war of Gog and Magog-Malbim on Ezekiel 37-39 and Mica 5, Gra EvenShlaima ch Gioola. This means that most of the people in the land of Israel today (including the Palestinians, who are mostly from Islamized Jews) are from the ten tribes.
6) "Moshiah must be a chacham who is anointed by Elijah"	Moshiah will be established by the Sanhedrin and a Navi and anointed-Rambam Hilchot Mlachim ch. 1:3,7.

7) "We must wait for Moshiah before we can move to Israel"	Jews must settle the land of Israel prior to and in order to prepare for the coming of the Moshiah-The Gaon of Vilna. Megilla 17b-Jerusalem is rebuilt before Moshiah comes.
8) "Zionists caused the Holocaust"	The halacha directs us to settle the land of Israel; teaching the Torah not according to the halacha brings the sword to the world.-Rmbm hilchot Mlachim ch Aleph, Avoth 5:11. reward and punishment hits those to whom it is relevant. The Jews who stayed in Europe were punished with death. The Jews who moved to Israel were/are rewarded with life. Zionists didn't cause the holocaust. G-d did it for His reasons not all known-The Rebbe. As a general rule though it was caused by our sins-Rav Shach; although Tzadikeem and innocents can also be taken in this type of situation when the angel of death is given power over the masses.
9) "We need Sanhedrin in order to execute people today"	Choshen Mishpat 2, 425 regarding rodfei dam, rodfei Zachar & transgressors of Gilui Araiot may permit in some cases by 'Gadol haDor' or Tovei haIr. Aruch haShulhan says 'Gadol biTorah' can decide.
10) "The Rabbis must support that a person is the Moshiah"	Sanhedrin appoints the Moshiah which is comprised of the majority, not all, of the Rabbis. He must also be anointed with the anointing oil by a real prophet authorized by the Sanhedrin.
11) "All Torah study is good for us"	One must be Hagoon in order to be permitted to teach Torah or learn in the Beit Midrash; Any teacher who is not hagoon, his Torah is poison and it is a Mitzvah to ignore him-Yoreh Dea hilcot Torah 243,Tanit 7.
12) "The Third Temple will float down from the sky" ("Rashi" Succa 41)	Moshiah, an artesian, will build the third Temple.

	-Rashi Succah 52b, Rambam Meleachim 11, Aruch liner, Rov Poskeem
13) "ten year maximum age gap for marriage"	A kitana may marry a zakein – Shulchan Aruch Evn Ezra 2:9 Rasha fathers playing G-d and bullying their daughter's in marriage matters destroys her and her zivoog, clal Yisroel, pushes away the Moshiah and the Schina - Sota 17.
14) "We don't know much about who the Moshiah really is. (how many people in any generationmeet this description? Not hard to spot.)	Moshiah is a musician, man of war, understanding, attractive, an oppressed scapegoat imprisoned for our sins, an engineer, from Edom (the USA), pursues social justice-Sanhedrin 93&98,Succah 52, Midrash Raba Shemot 1:26,Isaiah 11,Yalkut Shimoni Isaiah60
15) "We're all in galut now"	'Galut' is defined as the 'exile' from ones land. 'Shibud Malcuyot' is what people intend to express. We are in the process of leaving the galut of Edom and the Gioola is coming in stages until the full redemption when we will be totally out of galut and in full Gioola.
16) "What's you're hashkafa in Yiddishkeit?"	Rashi Brsht 18:16 "All Hashkafa in Torah is wicked". Hashkafa limits ones field of vision to the point where it pushes out many Torah truths and other good things. Moshiah will bring the Torah atika back to Israel (NOT Yiddishkeit, which in addition to Torah, unfortunately, includes a mixture of Jewish and many Gentile ways of Europe)- Rav Nahman of Breslov.
17) "We should get rid of the Arabs"	We should be kind, friendly, respectful and even charitable to the Arabs in order to make peace with them. Many Israeli Arabs are really Arabized Jews who returned to the land of Israel in kibbutz galuyot and therefore have a right to the land as Jews. Other Gentile Arabs will take the Noahide oath and be permitted. It is wiser and more

	righteous to speak words of peace with the Arabs and forbidden to incite nor antagonize them or any Gentiles.
18) Moshiah builds the Sanhedrin	The Sanhedrin is made before Eliyahoo comes-Maharatz Chaoth Eruvin 43b. Rambam Sanhedrin 1:3. Kerithis 110 Beith Safek. Moshiah may or may not be involved with forming the Sanhedrin. It is not clear.

Rambam: Islam and Christianity Pave the Way for the Messiah

In laws of kings chapter 11:4 the Rambam says that the religion of Ishmael (Islam) and Jeshu (Christianity) were brought to the world by G-d 'to pave the way for the Messiah and rectify the world to serve G-d'. As the Talmud tractate Avoda Zara on idol worship teaches us, in ancient times idol worshippers were evil people who not only worshipped idols but would murder, steal, and commit all forms of immorality including bestiality as part of their custom. They were evil people who would murder a Jew at any opportunity and it was a Mitzva for a Jew to kill them when ever possible.

We can see that *most* Goyim in the world today have come along way since then. Islam, Christianity, and especially modern American Judeo-Christianity are largely responsible for this improvement. Modern American Judeo-Christianity even supports Israel, morality, ethics and G-d in the world. In this the Bracha 'haRav Yaavode et haTzaeer' is fulfilled.

In the year 280 AD, "Rav Chiya Bar Abba said in the name of Rav Yohanan that Gentiles outside the land of Israel are not idol worshippers. Rather it is a custom of their fathers that is in their hands" (Talmud Bavli Chullin 13b). ArtScroll notes here that this means that the Gentiles didn't really have ideological devotion to idolatry and this seems to still be the case to this day even though there may be traces of idol worship in Islam and Christianity, which neither religion would want to admit. In any case most Muslims and Christians believe in the One G-d who created the world in spite of theology of trinity that is 'a custom of their fathers that is in their hands'. Most of them are well intentioned people who mean to do good and go to Heaven. In addition to basically believing in One Invisible, Monotheistic, All Powerful, All Knowing, Fair, Just, Merciful and Kind G-d, that is in the ball park of what the Torah defines as G-d, the adherents of both these religions believe in many other Torah principles that they learned from the Torah. These principles include that they want salvation, believe in a moral ethical model of laws based on the five books of Moses that by necessity must rely on the Jewish oral law, and, they want to go to Heaven. In comparison with the ancient religions of idol worship, these religions are very Jewish and based on many Torah principles in many ways despite some of their contradictions to the Torah and denial of some Torah precepts (May G-d have mercy). Thus, we can see Rambam's statement that Christianity and Islam are paving the way for the Gentiles to a higher service of G-d, as stepping stones, eventually to reach the highest level of service of G-d for them which would be in the guidelines of the Noahide Laws as shown in the beginning chapters.

Jesu of Nazareth said that he has come to establish the Torah which includes the five books of Moses ("Do not think that I have come to abolish the Law or the Prophets; I have not come to abolish them but to fulfill them." Mathiew 5:17). The Koran recognizes Moses as 'a prophet' and thus recognizes the five books of Moses as the truth that we must follow as well. Thus, both Christianity and Islam recognize the five books of Moses to be the source of laws that people must follow. These five books of Moses and the oral transmission (the Talmud) that explains the five books are called the Torah. This means that Christianity and Islam recognize the Torah as the basis for all the laws that they must follow. The Torah says that the Torah laws were given to us for eternity to keep, and Talmud Bavli Megilla 2b-3a says that the laws of man are only derived from the five books and not from the prophets. We learn the seven Noahide laws that the Gentiles must keep from the oral transmission from Mount Sinai, and was recorded in Talmud Bavli Sanhedrin 56-60, and explained in the chapter in this book on the Noahide Covenant. Therefore, both Christianity and Islam would agree that the seven categories of Noahide Covenant laws all apply to Gentiles for all times with no alteration nor changes. Since Jesu and the Koran recognize the Torah of the prophet Moses as the truth, then any statements that contradict any part of the Torah are thus not true, and people are not obligated to believe in, nor abide by, these statements that contradict the Torah. The Moshiah lives by and teaches the Torah so therefore Christianity and Islam will support the Moshiah. This will bless them with the best in this world and the next world in Heaven, when they are elevated to the higher form of service of G-d in the keeping of the ancient, pure, unadulterated Noahide Covenent laws. Thus, the Gentiles will be brought closer to G-d through the Moshiah. They too will be redeemed. They will also be able to come make sacrifices in the Temple and be forgiven for their sins along with the Jews.

There are many great people who I have met who are believers in the religions and ideologies of Christianity, Islam, Buddhism, Hinduism, Atheism, Communism, Humanism, etc.. But these many good people are misguided by false precepts, too many to list here, that are against the Torah, and thus are not as good people as they would be if they followed the Torah fully. Only the Torah guides a person in the right ways with the right balance of what G-d really wants in how a person serves Him. Only the Torah knows the finer details and nuances of what to understand and what to do practically in any situation. All people who follow these Torah ways will receive the maximum blessing when they follow them properly as guided by a good, righteous, morally pure, orthodox Jewish Rabbi. The Gentiles will thus rise higher to their real potential and blessing when they live by the Noahide laws as guided by a good orthodox Rabbi, preferably a Tzadik, and ultimately the Sanhedrin headed by the Moshiah.

Religious and ideological precepts that go against the Torah are not good. They mess people up and bring damage, wars, disease, poverty, sadness to the world. They act as a barrier between man and G-d and mislead people to make errors. These errors are often accepted as religion but are really not good and undermine peoples' proper service of G-d and their full connection to Him. These errors in religions and ideologies have mislead Gentiles (and Jews) into sins, including anti-Semitism (also self hating Jewish anti-Semites), which has brought Divine Retribution from Heaven on them. We saw an example of this Divine Retribution of Hashem when the USA and Europe coerced Israel to expel 10,000 Jews from their homes in Gush Katif, Gaza, in August, 2005. Some 10,000 Jewish Israeli men, woman, children, elderly and sick were forced out of their homes and communities in Gush Katif. Their businesses and all that they built up were destroyed. Many people, entire families, were left without work and became homeless refugees in Israel. Just as soon as the Gush Katif was totally evacuated and destroyed as a settlement of Israelis, Hashem punished Europe with heavy storms, floods and fires that killed many people and caused billions of dollars in damage. In addition, shortly thereafter, Hashem hit the USA with a massive hurricane 'Katrina' that wiped out New Orleans killing some 10,000 people there, the same number of people who were expelled of the Gaza strip. The number of those hit in each case was ten thousand thus showing the measure for measure nature of Hashem's Retribution. Coincidence? No way. You can verify these statements online in the records of the news media on the Internet. All the pieces of the puzzle are there for you to put together.

People must realize that religion is man made and the Torah is from G-d. Man made religions and ideologies are holding many good Gentiles and Jews captive and are misguiding us to make mistakes. Many good Jews and Gentiles have been deceived, damaged and even killed by false religious beliefs. Too much tragedy and disaster has come out of these man made religions. It must stop. The Good Gentiles who want the full truth will revert back to Noahide Covenant and the good Jews who want the full truth will return to living by the Torah commandments in full as soon as they realize what is going on. In 'The End' the rest may be laid waste so be careful to try to live by the full truth.

The solution for the Gentiles is to reject their man made religions and ideologies and to embrace the Noahide Covenant fully, and for the Jews to live by the Torah as guided by the righteous orthodox Rabbis. Thus we of the brotherhood of man will all be blessed to have a good life in this world and to go to Heaven. May that time be now. Amen.

The Zionists must accept the Messiah to fulfill the Zionist Dream

The Zionist dream of the Jewish people being 'a nation living in our own land free of Gentile subjugation' can only be fulfilled with the re-established House of David as the monarchy kingship of Israel with the Messiah son of David as king. Only the Moshiah can end the Gentile subjugation (Rambam laws of kings chapters 11-12 and Talmud Bavli Brachot 34). Until then the Jewish people in Israel will never have full success and be free of subjugation from foreign Gentile powers such as America and the Arabs. The Arabs of the land of Israel (AKA 'the Palestinians') will only accept Israel under a righteous Davidic king who is strong, fair, respectable, moral, ethical, sympathetic, respectful, understanding and kind to them. The Messiah is also the savior of the Arabs in this sense. He is also a spiritual savior because under his kingship the Jewish people will be guided to live properly under Hashem and His Torah and will be much more successful in the Mitzvoth and the blessing that comes with this. With the Moshiah as king, more people will go to Heaven in addition to having the wealth of happiness here on earth under the Messiah's kingship. Israel's economy will also pick up in a serious way and there will be more wealth and a higher standard of living for all people in Israel. The world economy will also increase. Everybody's rights will be protected. The Temple will bring great blessing to Israel and mankind. The sacrifices will purify the world of the husks of spiritual impurity. People will be forgiven and go clean.

"*The sons of the lawless men will rise up to establish a vision but they will stumble*" (Daniel 11:14) is interpreted by Rashi and Rambam to be referring to Jesu the Nazarine and his disciples. The book 'Prophesy and Providence' by Rabbi Meir Simcha Sokolovsky says that this verse refers to the Zionists. As a general Torah principle both opinions would be true, because any group of Jews who establish a vision that is against the Torah is bound to fail eventually. In this case, when this happens, and it will happen, the House of David will become the kingship of Israel. The good parts of the Israeli government system will fall into place under the kingship of the Moshiah, while the bad parts will fall by the way side. It is only a matter of time.

May the kingship of the House of David return to Israel soon and the righteous remnant of Israel move forward to build the Third Temple.

May you merit the best of this world and the next world (the highest of the Heavens), and do what you must to achieve that true success, which means becoming perfectly righteous. Don't despair. Keep trying over and over again no matter how many times you fall. 'A righteous man falls seven times and get up'. The real winner falls many times, but keeps getting back up and being a good person no matter how hard he/she has been hit. May you merit Tshuva Shleima-Full and complete repentance and thus perfect service of G-d.

Christianity and the G-d of Israel's Infinite Mercy, Grace and Forgiveness

I have had the pleasure of meeting many really good and righteous people who are Christians. I wish them the best of this world and Heaven.

I want to explain my Torah view of Christianity to people, especially Christians. Most Christians support Israel, G-d, morality and ethics, which helps save Jewish lives and will help bring the Messiah regardless of all else considered. Thank G-d for these Christians who support Israel. G-d bless them all. I often meet really great people who are Christians in Israel where I live, like recently Zack and Paolo, and am inspired by them; especially the idealistic young ones and some of their wise elders. They, as the good Jews, are a blessing to the world wherever they live, often times coming from America from where I come.

We see that the USA is in dire trouble due to the immoral and unethical behavior there, but that righteous Christians are a pillar of Faith in G-d, Torah based laws of morality and ethics there. The good Christians and religious Jews there give at least part of America hope of being saved from the Divine Retribution there. In the past twenty years in America we have seen many hurricanes (Katrina, Sandy), floods, fires, tornadoes, AIDS, Oklahoma city building bombings, world trade center bombings, etc.. We know that this is caused by our sins. Due to their goodness, charity, righteousness, and support of G-d, Torah based law and Israel, I see much good there among the Christians. I care about them and want only good for them. I feel that we are basically on the same side, the side of G-d, despite theological differences. I've also met many excellent people who are Atheists and Muslims. I also wish them all, as I wish for all people, the best of this world and to go to Heaven, even with our mistakes and sins.

To have both worlds, though, requires that we are totally righteous and that we get our service of G-d right with as few deviations from His true laws as possible. We should strive for total truth in the proper way to serve G-d so as to please Him as much as possible. Let's use our minds to see what is true and false from what they told us. May G-d help us.

When looking at the mistakes religious people make, one Rabbi I learned with in Yeshiva jokingly commented that the Messiah will come despite the religious. He was referring to all religious people, including Jewish people, in this comment. I'll be directly honest and upfront and say that my hope is that all the Gentiles will become Noahide who live by the seven Noahide laws and the Jewish people, including those who are Christians, Muslims, Atheists, etc., will all return to orthodox Torah Judaism which is what G-d really wants from us. This is the truth. This will bring the world great blessing and wealth and bring the full redemption and the real Messiah to be king. This book proves this; especially in the sections 'G-d Created and Sustains the World', 'The Divinity of Torah', and 'The Noahide Covenant'.

Although I don't believe in man made religions, I want to stress again, as I stated in the introduction of this book, that nonetheless I respect all people regardless of their religions and think that every religion has great people even though their religion is man made and filled with mistakes and untruths. Despite this, G-d still loves us, and in any case these people of all religions do good things and they will go to Heaven despite their mistakes. We're all only human; flesh and blood. G-d put them in false man made religions for His purposes.

As pointed out in a previous chapter, the Rambam (laws of kings 12) says that Christianity is paving the way for the Moshiah. I can't disagree, but also want to point out that 'Religion is made by man. The Torah is from G-d'. The Torah believes that the woman born man Jeshu really existed circa 300 BCE but not as the man defined by Christianity. We also believe that he never claimed nor pretended to be the Messiah.

There are many man made false religions filled with untruths that misguide even the best and most well intentioned people. People have been mislead into believing in these false man made religions and denied connection with the Torah and Noahide Covenent through ignorance, misinformation and bad education passed down from their fathers. This has often been with good intentions by the many millions and millions of good people who are Christians, Muslims, Atheists, etc. and sometimes not, especially when Eisav, Ishmael, Amalek (may their memory be erased), Erev Rav and the wicked among us Jews and Christians are involved, always masking their true hidden evil purposes for greed, sex and power, always guised as good, so as to trick the people they rule over.

For people who don't know who originally founded Christianity, his name was the original Hebrew-Aramaic name 'yeshua', which is short for yehōshu'a (Joshua), just as Mike is short for Michael (as quoted from the Jewish Messianic apologist and missionary, the hurt, abused and confused, but brilliant Jew, and supporter of Israel and Torah morality and ethics, Dr Michael Brown; May G-d have mercy). The Aramaic yeshua became the Greek jesous, then Latin Jesu passing into the German and the English Jesu of Nazareth. As I stated in the introduction, as a Jew, I am not allowed to say the name of a being that some people worship as an idol so I can't say his true English spelled name nor mislead other Jews into doing so. Here's the quick summery based on correlated Jewish, Christian and historical sources: Jesu was an orthodox Jew born in

Bethlehem, Israel. According to most, but not all Christian and non-Christian scholars, he was born in the year 0 AD. His birth was chosen to mark the year zero for the Western world of Edom back in the day when it was called Rome.

In the time of Jeshu, there was a Roman Empire rule in the providence of Judea. The Roman rule of subjugation was cruel, merciless and imposed forced taxation of the Jews by the foreign Roman power. Many Jews suffered greatly from this subjugation, wanted to revolt, were desperate for a savior; the savior the Messiah son of David; and eventually broke out into a war with Rome, incited by Jewish Zealot ruffians, and forced the rest of the Jewish people to go with them against the will and advise of the Rabbis (Talmud Bavli Gitten 56a).

The two most power social groups in Judea at the time (not the democrats and the republicans) were the Pharisees and the Sadducees. The Pharisees were people, as their name in Hebrew means, who separated them selves from the corrupt Roman Edomite society and were the common masses of Torah religious orthodox Jews lead by the Rabbis of the Talmud. Jesu was a Pharisee who studied with these Rabbis to be a Pharisee Rabbi The Gospels noted his rebuke and protest against corruption among the Sadducees, but as a polemic referred to them as 'Pharisees' to hide the early Christians participation in the Messianic Judean revolt against Rome; against the advise of the Rabbis. This made people think he wasn't a Pharisee himself, but he really was. The Pharisees are similar to the Haredim of today, who try to separate ourselves from the Western Edomite society to protect our souls and morality. The Sadducees were the ruling class of pseudo Erev Rav Jews of the day, who rejected the oral transmission (the Talmud), and worked as the local proxy Erev Rav regime for Rome, who was occupying the land of Judea and was subjugating her for taxes. Jesu could not have been a Sadducee since they were part of the system he was trying to overthrow, and, there again, points out to his being a Pharisee, even though he may have had criticisms against some of the lesser moral and ethical people of his Pharisee sect, but his rebuke was really mainly directed towards the Sadducees, which was covered up in the polemic of the Gospels in order to hide the Christians revolt against Rome, who would kill all such revolutionaries against Rome.

Islam tradition says that Jesu was conceived when a Roman soldier who was part of the occupying force of Judea raped his mother, Hebrew name being Miriam (AKA Mary) who was married to a man named Josef. The birth, as Taboo, was hidden by being born in a barn. Rape was probably common by the Roman occupiers as was killing Jews and other people there subjugated very often 'legally' by public crucification. Many of the biggest Rabbis of the time, like Rabbi Akiva, were crucified by the Romans for the 'crime' of teaching Torah. Jews never used crucification as a form of death penalty which shows that Pharisee Jews who hold by the oral tradition were not involved in crucifying Jesu. Crucification is forbidden by oral tradition (the Talmud) so the Pharisees could not have done crucified him. Maybe the Erev Rav regime of the day, the Sadducees, was involved.

As most Jews at the time, Jeshu and his eventual followers were Torah observant Jews; today called Orthodox Jews. His quote "Do not think that I have come to abolish the Law or the Prophets; I have not come to abolish them but to fulfill them." (Mathiew 5:17) alludes to his belief in Torah as a Jew. Jesu grew up as what we would now call an 'ultra-orthodox' or Haredi Jew, learned Torah with the Pharisee Rabbis of the Talmud, whose tradition is now carried by the sect called the Haredim who wear black and white clothes and black hats and fury round 'shtreimels'. As the story goes, and happened to not less than a few students, Jesu got caught by his Rabbi looking at a girl, had a falling out and misunderstanding with his Rabbi, Satan entered the situation, he moved to the Galilee area and taught his understanding of Torah in Nazareth and the sea of Galilee (now called the Knereth) area to simple Jews from around 20 CE until 33 CE. He lead revolt against Rome and according to the Gospels seems to have had Messianic ambitions along with his followers. The revolt on Judea was brewing against Rome, only later, after his death to break out into full scale war. Popularized Roman Christianity gives 33 CE as the year for his death.

The 'New' Testament claims that he was a charismatic leader who impressed people with his great oratory ability, Rabbinic Torah knowledge that he learned from the Pharisee Rabbis (paraphrase quote Gospels 'I have come to establish the Torah'), public performance of magical miracles (the art of which was known by many Pharisee Rabbis of the time) and the permissibility of 'freedom' from Torah. *If* he was really born in the year zero as the religion says, then extrapolated sources (Gospels, Josephus, Talmud) and logic indicate that he was affiliated with the highly anti-Roman atheistic Essene and Biryoneem (strong armed) cults and lead what some people believed to be a Messianic rebellion against the Roman rule (quote Gospels 'I have come to bring the sword' and had violent war like followers who were 'sons of lightning', 'Iscariot' (hidden knife assassins), etc.). They wanted to free Judea of Rome's' cruel and merciless occupation, subjugation and taxation of Judea, and were desperate for a savior; AKA, the Messiah

In the year 33CE he went to Jerusalem to celebrate Passover and was murdered there by the Roman occupation government by crucification (as they did with all rebels) for trying to overthrow Rome and establish the Messianic kingdom of the House of David as the government in Judea. The 'holy grail' was the Jewish Kiddush cup he used to make a blessing over the wine for Passover. You can but one at any Judaica store.

Jesu was crucified by Rome for the capitol crime with the title on his crucifix 'king of the Jews', which for Rome means he was killed as a rebel against Rome and challenging the kingship of Caesar (Eisav). During the same century in Judea many other thousands of Jews were also crucified by Rome, even big Rabbis who were Holy martyrs. Millions were murdered by the sword in the war against Rome from 66 CE until 70 CE, the Romans destroyed the second Temple in Jerusalem. They enslaved the surviving Jews, including children, who were sent back to Rome for 'pleasure,' and many committed suicide by jumping off the transport ships. The commonwealth of Judea was destroyed, and many of the great Rabbis of the time were later also crucified for the 'crime' of teaching Torah in public and some of them are known in Judaism as 'the ten Martyrs'. In 70 CE, with the fall of Judea, the Sadducees disappeared and the Pharisees continued on to this day as we are all descendents of the Pharisees, including Jesu and his original followers.

Roman history says that Nero was the first to label this new Jewish Messianic sect 'the Christians', accused them for burning Rome (which they probably did as they were part of the Jew's revolt against Rome) and decreed death penalty on them, including feeding them to the lions and burning them alive in Gladiatorial coliseums in Rome. They were a part of the Judean revolt against Rome. The main followers of Jesu in the first century wrote accounts of the new sect's 'history', beliefs, propaganda and polemic that are now called 'the Gospels'. Most of the early Christians were also executed by the Romans for being part of the revolt against Rome. As a matter of practical necessity, the Gospels acted as a polemic to hide the Christians revolt against Rome so as to try to save their own lives and allow the religion to continue and spread in Rome.

You must understand the founding of early Christianity in its broader historical context as a Jewish Messianic sect that was part of the Jewish peoples' war against Rome, Some 65 years later, circa 135 AD, another Messianic revolt was attempt by Bar Cochba and the city of Beitar and all the residents of the city; man, woman and child; were massacred by the Roman legion stationed there.

The sect of Messianic Jews grew, recruited Gentiles, and eventually was accepted by Rome, circa 325, under Emperor Constantine's' Mycenaean council, as the new official religion of Rome, called 'Christianity' until this day. Rome brought the local Roman citizen's idols into the new official religion so it would be accepted by all. At this point Christianity was totally deformed and taken away from its original concepts of Messianic Orthodox Torah Judaism and became a Gentile idol worship religion exploited for Roman Empire political and imperial purposes. Other scriptures associated with Christianity were later written or adopted from Jewish and Gentile sources for reasons that I didn't looked into.

The original Christianity started out a Torah based Jewish Messianic sect of Jews in Judea circa 20 to 33AD. But, by the time it had later found its way into the Roman Gentiles' hands in Rome, certainly by 325 CE at the Mycenaean council, the Romans had mixed into Christianity so many foreign Gentile idol worship practices that it didn't even look like the original Christianity any more. Rome made Christianity the official religion of the Roman Empire in the Mycenaean council circa 325 in Rome's' attempt to unify the Empire which was falling apart and becoming vulnerable to internal revolt and foreign overthrow. Rome had to add the idol worship rights into Christianity so as to mass market it to the idol worshipping Gentiles of the Roman Empire. What is the 'real' Christianity is a matter of opinion or debate by it's members. But, one thing is for sure, the form it takes now was certainly not the original intent nor form of the original Torah based Jewish Messianic sect of Jews in Judea circa 20 CE to 33CE.). When questioning if there is idol worship in Christianity I believe in the statement by Rabbi Chiya in the year 280 CE. "*Rav Chiya Bar Abba said in the name of Rav Yohanan that Gentiles outside the land of Israel are not idol worshippers. Rather it is a custom of their fathers that is in their hands*" (Talmud Bavli Chullin 13b). That ArtScroll here notes there that this means that the Gentiles don't really have ideological devotion to idolatry. This seems to still be the case to this day, especially considering that the Great Knesset removed the evil inclination for idol worship from the world in ancient times. Therefore most Christians really are not idol worshipers, they just have received a custom from their fathers that most of them don't really whole heartedly believe in, thank G-d, but I find that they generally do believe in the Noahide Covenant and can accept it as the real truth.

I grew up as an atheist assimilated Jew who literally knew nothing about religion. I was innocent and naïve. I knew how to play guitar, science, sports, and war. Every thing else did not seem to matter to me. I knew nothing about politics, social skills or religion. I only wanted the truth with no concern how people would react to it or the consequences fro saying true things. To this day, like most Haredi Rabbis, I find politics a hassle and ridiculously frivolous waste of time. The Gematria of 'politica' in Hebrew equals Amalek (may their memory be erased). One day, I asked my mentor, Leah Fine (of blessed memory), if 'Jesu really existed or if he was a myth?' I also asked if he was the Messiah. I got yelled at by my mentor who I guess was hurt, felt fear and was angered by that question. Being yelled at was no satisfactory 'answer' to me though. So, I set on the investigation path. To my surprise, I found that Judaism not only didn't deny that Jesu existed, but affirms that he existed historically. That impressed me since I thought that his existence would just simply be denied by the 'competition' (Judaism). I researched the history of Jesu and wrote a college research paper on him at SUNY Purchase for Professor Lee Schlesinger, concluded that Jesu was an 'ultra religious nationalistic Jew who tried to over throw Roman domination of ancient Judah', and lost the war, along with the rest of the Jews (for the time being). That was in 1981. The paper disappeared. I lost it.

The question still remained though: Was Jesu the Messiah? My 1981 research really didn't address that issue but I felt that he wasn't because how could he be the Messiah if he died before completing the mission to establish the Torah kingship of the House of David, save the Jews from gentile persecution, establish the Torah word of G-d and save the world? I was not aware of any Temple eat that point so building the Temple did not even come up as an issue, and it is a main issue needed to be the Messiah. But, still, I really did not know enough Torah to answer that question because I did not know what the Torah says is the Messiah. The focus of my research was to determine who Jesu was, just who was the historical character, not who is the Messiah. Like many people I thought maybe he was he like a cartoon character? One of the seven dwarves? The question was not if he was the Messiah, just if he really existed, so the question of the Messiah issue remained unresolved. I didn't care what the answer to that was so I left it unaddressed in 1981. I just wanted to know if Jesu really existed historically and got my answer.

Now, with this book, and being the most knowledgeable Rabbi in the generation on the subject, the question of who and what the Messiah really is can be addressed properly and fully to the finest point in detail of truth, the true truth, of the subject.

Torah sources in this book conclusively show that Jesu the Nazarene; the person who Christianity purports as their so called 'Messiah'; was not the Messiah, never could have been the Messiah, never will be, and never even came close to being the Messiah or bringing any part of the true Redemption of Israel, which includes the Torah word of G-d being accepted and lived by among all people in the world, including the Gentiles, living by the seven Noahide laws, peace on earth, no disease, Torah justice and freedom of the Jewish people from Gentile subjugation, the Messiah son of David of the royal House of David as the established and recognized king of Israel and the entire world, the third Temple build and in full operation, the return of the Sanhedrin as the chief court of Israel and the world, and the Jews return to the land of Israel. No one in history has ever even come close to accomplishing these monumental feats. Therefore no one was ever the Messiah. Jesu never accomplished any of these requirements. And if you say he didn't achieve these requirements to be the Messiah the first time he came, and that he will come back later a second time and fulfill them then, because he was killed before achieving being the Messiah the first time, well, then you could say that about anyone. That's a weak excuse and pseudo-explanation. It's nonsense. Christianity is a man made religion. The Torah is from G-d and is the real truth. No one has been the Messiah yet, but he will come in the future at some time.

If you look at it really truthfully, by the sources in my book on the Messiah, you see that according to the Torah *the real Messiah is invincible. No one can kill him and he can kill anyone and every one including the Anti-Christ.* For the real Messiah there is no second coming. The real Messiah does the job the first time around.

Look at who the Messiah is according to the Torah sources that define what the Messiah really is. He will take on the whole world and win. Although he accepts suffering and imprisonment on himself to cure and atone for the sins of the Jewish people (Midrash on Isaiah 53), in order to fulfill his goal of freeing the Jewish people from spiritual and political bondage, he is a deadly and highly dangerous man of war also quite capable of righteously and justly *'slaying the wicked with the spirit of his lips'* (Isaiah 11) with out using the art, craft and science of war, of which he is also a master. He doesn't use this power on everyone. He judges with great and meticulous care and skill (Isaiah 11). He has Holy Spirit, Wisdom and prophesy so that he is able to detect anyone trying to hurt him, or any other Jew or Gentile for that matter, and he can kill any or all of the wicked who deserve it with prayer. Anyone who would try to kill him would surely be slain by him (or others) or forced to accept the Torah and the Messiah would go along his merry way. The real Messiah literally *can't* be killed, and, he can kill anyone who he wants to kill. He can wipe out or better yet conquer an entire country and rule over it with an iron fist or soft gloves. He will finish the job of redeeming Israel and being the Messiah before he dies. If not then he's not the Messiah but just a fictitious man made mythological figure.

The Talmud Sanhedrin 63b teaches us that "*The Jews knew that there is no substance in idolatry and engaged in idolatry only to permit themselves to overt immorality*"; i.e. 'orgianized' religion. We find this adage true today as well. I found that most Christians (Jews for sure and maybe many Gentiles too) turn to this religion as a means of trying to excuse (and atone for) their immoral or unethical behavior that they cant control and for which they feel a sense of overwhelming shame ('Bound by Shame') that needs to be pacified or rectified to make it go away and not be felt. Whether they cant stop or don't want to stop their immorality is hard to tell on an individual basis. As Ethics of the Fathers teaches us 'don't judge someone until you stand in his place'; we don't really know what other people went through in life or what makes them the way they are so we really cant judge. Only G-d really Knows. I am not judging. I am only looking at the good. I try to put my self in other peoples' place and take their side, as much as possible. It's Satan's job to persecute people and point out the bad so as to incite G-d to punish them; not my job. I prefer to take peoples' side and intercede for them, including Christians, who I feel are basically good. I write this book also to bring Christians to a higher level of service; the Noahide Covenant for Gentiles and Torah Covenant for Jews.

Is Jesu g-d as Christianity espouses? G-d is the Creator and King of the world who controls everything, is omnipresent and all Knowing. Can a man do any of these things that G-d does? No man can do any of these things.

Therefore no man can be G-d. Good people have been misguided about this issue of G-d. He is One and can not be divided into parts but includes everything in Creation. By calling or worshiping any one of His Creations, anything or anyone, other than G-d Almighty Alone as One, is idol worship and is strictly forbidden by the Noahide Covenent and Torah for both Gentile and Jew. May G-d have Mercy. G-d is All Merciful and All Forgiving AND Atoning for our sins without intermediary.

Another important point for Christianity is that the proper way to pray to G-d is directly without any intermediaries, but the Rama says, in Mishna Brura 156, that a Gentile is permitted to do what is called worshipping an idol 'in partnership' with G-d (in Hebrew called 'Shitoof Avoda Zara'). This is believing that G-d gave independent power to a thing or person and worshipping G-d through that thing or person in 'partnership' with it. Jews are forbidden to do Shitoof Avoda Zara though, so we must be careful of this.

Also, the Torah is the quintessential scripture that defines G-d so any denial of the Torah by any man made religion is in some ways a deviation from the proper G-d to worship and path to follow which is the Noahide laws for the Gentiles (see the book The Path of the Righteous Gentile by Chaim Clorfene and Jacob Rogalsky for details of the Noahide Covenant and seven Noahide laws which is the proper path and set of G-d given laws for Gentiles) and 613 Torah commandments for Jews.

In any case, I want to remind people, or reveal to people here, that believing in or praying to a false god, idol, religion, a cult, won't really help solve the problem. It could just makes it worse, or maybe it could help make it better of people still basically follow the Torah. It's best to pray to G-d directly without intermediary. He does not need intermediaries. He Hears every word and Knows every thought an demotion we feel in our heart. He mostly wants our heart as well as our following the right rules; which is the Torah as interpreted by the righteous orthodox Rabbis of our time.

As we understand, we need atonement for our sins. That is the purpose of the third Temple we wait for the Messiah to build; to atone for our sins by animal sacrifices. In the absence of sacrifices Hashem accepts prayer and repentance as we learn from the Prophets. This need for sacrifices to atone for our sins is part of the nature of people; all people: Jews, Gentiles, Christians. Most people looking for rational truth don't accept Christianity because it just simply doesn't make sense. People usually go to Christianity because they have a deep inner guilt that they need to atone for some sin (as is natural and most people have) and think that Christianity is the only way to atone for that sin, to 'cleanse the blemish', to sooth the guilt. They are brainwashed to believe that Jesu died for their sins and that only he can cleanse or atone for their sin. This is not true, but, this is a reason people join the religion today; other maybe than for political or economic reasons.

We must ask the question: Do people need Jesu for forgiveness and atonement of our sins? People need atonement for our sins but only G-d is All powerful and can atone for our sins. Jesu can not forgive nor atone for our sins. Only G-d can do that and He does. The G-d of Israel is not the all punishing non forgiving G-d of the five books of Moses that many people misperceive. The G-d of Israel is more forgiving and merciful than people realize. He is infinitely merciful, protects the fool and does not condemn people for the worst sins when we really don't understand that what we are doing is a sin or if we can't control our base passions and obsessions. It is also only He who Atones for our sins. No man can take that job away from Him. That is the G-d of Israel that we learn from the Torah. He atones and He forgives sin.

He still loves you no matter what you are or do, even though He might not like the sins that you do. G-d loves 'gays', Nazis, terrorists, Amalekite/Islamite Jihadists in Gaza, and even our beloved serial pederasts who give their child victims AIDS over and over again to the mantra 'Sorry I didn't mean it', 'Sorry I didn't mean it', 'Sorry I didn't mean it', and mean this with all the sincerity of their hearts or even callously and with no hope for mercy or repentance. But still G-d loves them and will have mercy and forgive, especially if we repent. That is all He wants form us; to return to Him, to come closer than we wee before, no matter how far we were. If this statement makes you want to explode in angry judgment, as it may to many, then just relax and feel comfort in that G-d also loves us when we sin our level. For a person on a higher level a bad thought may be just as bad as a serial murderer and may cause more damage to the world too as we learn in many of the Torah books.

The Torah says in two sources that we sin because of our 'being like youth' and that we sin only when 'the spirit of folly over comes us' so the excuse "I didn't mean it', as the body count rises daily, has a source in Torah. In Hebrew the word for youth (naar) means 'empty of understanding'. He judges us based on our level and that is the level some people are holding on. As my father likes to say, when someone asks him what he does: "If I knew what I did I wouldn't do it". This is a classic answer that has a deep truth in it. If we really knew that what we do is wrong then we would not do it. This may excuse our worst sins in my opinion because G-d does not judges us on what we don't really know or understand is wrong. Where G-d will draw the level to our responsibility for our actions we really don't know. That's to say: how far does the 'I didn't know' or 'I didn't really mean it' excuse go? We don't really know 'what's going on' (a song with an important message by Marvin Gay), who's who and what the true truth is without a Sanhedrin or Messiah king to teach us. In any case, again, only G-d really Knows the full truth or any persons situation (past, present and future lives) and the real judgment.

Instead of turning to Christianity, Islam, Atheism, materialism, pleasures, Yolo (You Only Live Once), someone can just as easily turn to Hashem, get real credit for doing what commandments he can, find comfort in that Hashem is a loving-kind-forgiving-understanding-merciful G-d. This can help the person get over or deal with his problem with prayer to Him and continually trying to repent. He will help even if it takes ten years, even a lifetime, or even if it takes many lifetimes. Try, pray, try again, and pray again, and He will be there for you. You don't need Christianity; it just hurts, it doesn't really help. Turn to Hashem. He will help; real help. You don't want to find out the hard way in the next world. It's better to fix your self now.

My book on the Messiah shows that Isaiah 53 holds true for the Messiah. If you look carefully at the basic simple details of the verses of Isaiah 53 you will see that Jesu the Nazarene does NOT fulfill Isaiah 53, although the real Messiah does, especially the later verses of Isaiah 53 where the Messiah lives and succeeds in many ways, such as having children and wealth.

The inventors of Christianity warped and perverted the meaning of the scriptures of the Prophets and deceive many innocent, good people. For example, everyone knows that Christianities' scriptural 'source' for the virgin birth, Isaiah 7:14, is based on a total mistranslation of the scripture there. The real text of Isaiah 7:14 does not say 'virgin' birth but 'young woman' birth and is not even taking about the Messiah. There are numerous examples of such misinterpretations, mistranslations, perversions of the texts, and just simple basic perversions of the meaning of the scriptures. Christianity is based on perversions of the meaning of the scriptures. Many good, well intentioned people have been deceived into believing in it. Its time to grow up, be a man and accept the real G-d and His Torah and Noahide laws as explained in my book on the Messiah. The Noahide laws and Covenant is what the Gentiles are supposed to follow and the Jewish people the 613 commandments of the Torah. That is when we will have real Redemption of Man with a real Messiah.

Many of the Rabbis, even the very Holy Chabad Lubavitch Rebbe, who had some real Messianic qualities himself, recognize that most real Christians are basically good people who will go to Heaven. But, unfortunately they were tricked and deceived into believing in a false man made Roman religion that Rome invented, for all sorts of motives, some good, some not so good.

By the Mycenaean council of 325CE under Caesar Constantine I, 'Christianity' was abused by Edom/Rome, 'the forth beast', in order to manipulate and control people, for power, sex and money, *and* anti-Semitism, and to deny G-d's true law-the Torah so that they cold be 'free' (from the Torah and Noahide laws). Christians must be warned that the Anti-Semites amongst them are also part of the fourth beast, modern Edom/Rome, are against Hashem and the real Messiah, and thus are really part of the real 'Anti-Christ' system. You must turn them back from their evil and compel them to accept Hashem and the Noahide Covenant if they are Gentiles, and the 613 Torah commandments if they are Erev Rav Jews, or Hashem may purge some of them from the earth and man them to hell with the rest of the unrepentant sinners as the prophets teach us. Others may repent and receive real Mercy and Grace from Hashem. By turning to Hashem they will truly be saved and be on the side of the G-d of Israel, Hashem, and can earn eternal reward in Heaven.

Remember the adage 'the devil can quote scripture for his own purposes'. The 'beast', now lead by America, now also uses especially Atheism, but sometimes Christianity, Islam, and even 'Judaism' as well to manipulate, control, dominate and rule over people all over the world, including Americans. The Jewish people also have infiltrators of false leaders amongst us from this side as well, and these are not just Christians, but some who pass themselves of as 'Jewish Rabbis' as well. Reform 'Rabbis' is an example of this.

We will succeed and be blessed when we go by the wisdom and advice of the Holy Sinless Righteous Orthodox Rabbis which comes from the Holy Torah- the real Word of G-d Almighty and All Merciful. Those who go against the Torah, Christianity, as well Atheism, Islam, Buddhism, Hinduism, etc., are all really satanically incited cults filled with people who have been lured in to and deceived by Satan to go against G-d, the Holy Torah, the Rabbis and the Noahide Covenent. Although mostly inherently good people, some of these people may just basically be really evil souls, like Amalek (may their memory be erased) who are marked for perdition for the Glory of G-d as the will rise high and be brought low before all to see on TV and the Internet internationally. Be careful; 'the devil can quote scripture for his own purposes'

Every time a Christian, Muslim, Gentile or Jew advises a Jew to return to his true faith of Torah Judaism, or a Gentile to the Noahide Covenant, he gets serious credit with Hashem and he will see the reward at sometime in his existence in this world or the next (Heaven), or at least will way on the scales of Heavenly justice in his favor. He may go the Heaven for this good deed, or, at least give him less time in hell, after which he goes to Heaven hopefully.

There is a small but strong and growing movement of Gentiles today, including many Christians, especially in America, today's leader of the nations of the world, who believe in the Noahide laws and Covenant, which ensures them, according to the Torah, that they will 'go to Heaven if they keep the seven' ('Do the seven and go to Heaven'- the seven Noahide laws), even though some may unfortunately still believe in Jesu as the Messiah. You can join their groups on the Internet. Buy the book 'The Path of the Righteous Gentile' by Chaim Clorfene and Jacob Rogalsky for details on the Noahide Covenant and seven Noahide laws which is the proper path (and set of G-d given laws) for Gentiles. It's a great, Holy and important book for every Gentile to own and live by under the advise of righteous orthodox Rabbis. You should also be in touch with your local orthodox Rabbis.

Based on my understanding of Torah and personal logic, I am still not sure that if some beliefs of Islam and Christianity that contradict Torah are permissible to Gentiles, since partnership idol worship is permissible to Gentiles. The fact that these man made religions may be interpreted by some to deny the authority of and undermine the belief in the Torah and Rabbis may lead them to throw off the yoke of the Noahide Covenent and by such sin. Beliefs against the Torah are defiantly not permissible to Jews. Leniencies may apply to Gentiles, but Jews, on the other hand, are obligated to believe in and abide strictly by the 613 Torah laws, to reject Jesu, and accept the real Messiah, that is described in this book.

In any case, Hashem understands all people and is VERY Merciful and forgiving, especially when your heart is with the right intention to do good, and when you turn to Him. He is very Merciful and Forgiving to people who really mean to do good, even if they make some mistakes and fall to sin for various reasons. We are only Human. Hashem understands. 'The righteous fall seven times and get up'. G-d Created us, Loves us all, Forgives us, has Mercy on us, and only wants the best for us, including the best for us in this world and eternal life in Heaven. May everyone who reads this book on the Messiah merit these blessings. Spread the word.

Redemption: A Real Peace Plan for the 'Palestinians' as a Part of Israel

Today there is difference of opinion by the right and the left in Israel regarding what to do with the Palestinian issue. The right wants to annex the West bank Yehudah and Shomron territories and the left wants to make a Palestinian State. Both sides are adamant about their opinion. Both sides' policies really don't see nor rectify the roots of the problems that cause the conflict. Both sides don't have a real, viable, practical solution. Both sides' policies would have tragic, destructive and deadly consequences since they are without true Daas Torah that maybe only a Sanhedrin can see, and we don't have a Sanhedrin yet. They haven't even sought the advise of the big Rabbis to see what to do. This is a problem that leaves them both deadlocked in failure. It seems that the right and the left both need to see each other's points of truth in order to have a more balanced and objective judgment of policy. Both sides believe points of Torah that the Torah supports, but there is no balance since both sides only see their own extreme side without recognizing the other side's points of truth. Although they both have truth in what they are saying, they are both missing the most essential points that are the real root causes of the Palestinian-Israeli conflict.

There are a number of root causes of the war between the Israelis and Palestinians. These must be rectified for Israel to make peace with the Palestinians. To rectify the root causes of the war we must 1) all live by the Torah laws, 2) uphold righteous judgments between Palestinians and Israelis, 3) relentlessly pursue peace with the Palestinians by respecting them and being friendly to them (while at the same time always being strong in order to keep the peace), 4) teach the Palestinians the Noahide laws, and 5) establish the Sanhedrin. Right now, the most important action needed to be taken is to do is to relentlessly pursue peace with the Palestinians by respecting them and being kind to them. This will pave the way to peace between the Israelis and Palestinians that, when followed up by the other steps in this plan, will eventually bring the Palestinians into wanting, and agreeing by their own will, to be well behaved and respected citizens of Israel with the same responsibilities and opportunities afforded all Israelis. I am respectful and friendly to Arabs and three of them have told me that 'if all Jews were like me then there would be no war'.

The chapter in the beginning of this book titled 'the Divinity of Torah' proves that the Torah is the law of G-d and the absolute truth by which we all must live. The biggest mistake ewe Jews are making, and also the Palestinians, is not living by the Torah. The Torah promises that "*If you will follow My laws and observe My commandments and perform them, then I ... will provide rains in their times and the land will give its produce... you will dwell securely in the land......I will provide peace in the land ... and the sword will not pass through your land*" (Leviticus 26:3-6). G-d promised peace as a reward for living by the Torah commandments. If we want peace then we must make peace with G-d by living by His Torah. Then G-d will give us peace. This goes for the Jews and Palestinian Arabs, many of whom the previous chapter in my book has shown are also Jews.

The Torah teaches us that G-d gave the land of Israel to the Jewish people for an eternal heritage and that the land of Israel can only prosper with Jews living in the land according to the Torah. Otherwise the land is barren and fallow. If the land was given to 'Palestinians' then it will only be waste and desolation. The land must be inhabited by Torah Jews for it to flourish, prosper and thrive.

Just as a historical reminder for those who don't know, the Jewish people were exiled from our land by Rome circa 135CE and Rome called the land of Israel 'Palestine' in order to spite the Jews. None the less, since then the land has always been the property of the Jews, even though we were exiled by force by the ancient Roman Empire, which eventually fell. Gentiles, particularly Ishmaelite Arabs, came to live in the land of Israel, but never made a legally purchase of the land from the true owners, the Jews. They stole the land from the true Jewish owners. The land of Israel, called 'Palestine' by the Romans, is still the property of the Jewish people.

In light of the 136 countries (totaling 5.5 billion people) recognition of a Palestinian State, the May 13, 2015 Pope Francis's recognition of a Palestinian State, and the recent US President Barak Obama's recognition of a Palestinian

State, I would like to remind them that Gentiles who take the land of Israel away from Jews are punished by G-d. Its is written: "*Therefore said the Lord Hashem: I have spoken in the fire of My vengeance against the remaining nations and against all Edom, who have arrogated My land (the land of Israel that G-d gave to the Jewish people) to themselves as a heritage, with the joy of all their heart, with contempt of soul, because of expulsion and scorn*' (Ezekiel 36:5). Many different groups of Gentiles with various ideologies and religions have claimed the land of Israel for themselves. In particular these Gentiles include Islam, the Arabs, Edom, Christianity, Democracy and Communism. These groups and the anti-Semites along with them committed scorn and expulsion against the Jews from the land of Israel and shall be punished by Hashem for taking the land of Israel from the Jewish people. We saw an example of this prophesy of Hashem punishing Edom for taking part of the land of Israel away from Jewish people when the USA and Europe coerced Israel to expel 10,000 Jews from their homes in Gush Katif, Gaza, in August, 2005. Some 10,000 men, woman, children, elderly and sick were forced out of their homes and communities in Gush Katif. Their businesses and all that they built up were destroyed. Many people, entire families, were left without work and became homeless refugees. Just as soon as Gush Katif was totally evacuated and destroyed as a settlement, Hashem punished Europe with heavy storms, floods and fires that killed many people and caused billions of dollars in damage. In addition, shortly thereafter, Hashem hit the USA Edom with a massive hurricane 'Katrina' that wiped out New Orleans killing some 10,000 people there, the same number of people who were expelled of the Gaza strip. The number of those hit in each case was ten thousand thus showing the measure for measure nature of Hashem's Retribution. If there is a State of Palestine, Palestinian extremists will be blamed for terrorist activities against the United States; rightfully so; and will then be bombed by the US armed forces as they did to Iraq and Dayash (ISIS). Palestinian towns will be turned into waste and rubble. It will be a horror for all to witness. The State of Palestine will be the Palestinian's worst imaginable nightmare come true. My book on the redemption goes into a comprehensive coverage of the prophesies that happen in the end of days final redemption. This grievous sin of making a Palestinian State without the agreement of the Rabbis puts all those who are responsible in the hands of Satan to prosecute them and their supporters in the Heavenly court with harsh measures including death in all sorts of merciless ways and hell damnation. Expect more 'natural disasters' in all the responsible countries. All this is because people didn't go to the Rabbis for advice on what to do and they didn't listen to the Rabbis, who are the people who know what the Torah wants us to do in any situation in life. On May 15, 2015, I sent this paragraph, and chapter as a file attachment, in an email to about fifty Rabbis, US Christian leaders and Bible belt radio stations as a warning of what will happen is there is a Palestinian State, so as to avert it, or at least to sanctify Hashem's Name in the case of the likelihood that people still don't listen and the State is made, where after it will then be destroyed along with the rebels who made the state without asking the Rabbis first. As it goes now, the Palestinians are digging their own grave. Many smart ones may decide to jump ship and join Israel.

One of the Torah commandments is for the Jewish people to live in the land of Israel. There are different opinions on how to achieve this, but, after all opinions are considered, the Rabbis take the stringent path, and see that it is a Mitzvah to acquire and settle the land by peaceful means (Talmud Bavli Ketuboth 111). The Zionists achieved this Mitzvah. It is also forbidden by the Torah for Jews to incite hatred or antagonize Gentiles as per Jewish law (Shulhan Aruch as per the Talmud) so we must acquire the land by peaceful means, such as purchasing land if it owned by someone else; through the agreement of the Gentiles who live there, if Gentiles live on a particular piece of land. It is now forbidden to kick Gentiles out of the land as we did in the time of Yehoshua Ben Nun by the Tzav of Hashem. If no Gentile lives on a particular piece of land, then we are allowed to reclaim it. In this peaceful means of acquiring the land we are allowed to use force to defend ourselves from attack, which the Ishmaelite Arabs tend to do by their murderous nature. After the Zionists purchased lands in Israel, many Arabs attacked them in an effort to steal back the land and the Zionists defended themselves and their rightfully owned property that they bought from the legal Arab land owners.

In recent times, most of the Arabs (a mixture of Ishmaelites and assimilated Arabized Jews as shown in my book) living in the land of Israel believe in Islam, whose Koran teaches them to kill, convert by force, and terrorize all non-Muslims, and to steal their land. A major part of the root cause of the Arab –Israeli war is Islam's preaching of violence against non-Muslims and the violent nature of Ishmaelite Arabs. At least since fifteen years ago there have been 'Jihad' (Islamic holy war) summer camps, under the direction of varied terror groups such as Hamas, that teach and train Palestinian children in the

West Bank and Gaza to kill non Muslims, using all the available terrorist and military tactics. Other aggravating factors include: the wicked nature of Ishmael, a long history of corruption and violence and being cursed by poverty as Gentiles living in the land of Israel, which is not theirs. Part of the Arabs Israeli conflict stems from the conflict between Western imperialism and colonization and the Arabs, where the Zionist are viewed as Western invaders to the Arabic culture and their Muslim conquered lands (which they never really acquired ethically; the Arabs stole the lands and claimed them as their own). Since the Jews who founded the country of Israel came from the West, part of the problem is Western feelings of arrogance and superiority by the Westerners who settled the land of Israel. There is a war of cultures between the Ishmaelite Arab Islam and the Eisavian Western culture. This is a war between Eisav and Ishmael; a war between Ishmaelite Jews and Eisavian Jews (see chapter on the mixed multitude). This is part of the Arab Israeli conflict. Western arrogance also incites many Arabs living in the land to be violent against the Western Israelis. The history of conflict, tit for tat revenge strikes, between the Arabs and Jews has lasted for a few hundred years. Each side believes that it is defending its own rights and the other started it and is to blame.

I have found that most of the people on both sides of the 'Palestinian' and Israeli conflict, though, have good intentions. They both think that they are doing the right thing. They both believe that they are defending their rights from the other side who started the conflict. They don't mean to do bad and have no bad intentions. Since most of the Palestinians come from Jews, as well as the Israelis, there are a vast amount of good people on both sides in spite of the violent terrorist extremists, the overwhelming majority of whom come from the side of the Arabs. By fostering mutual respect and understanding we can not just bring peace, but can eventually incorporate the Arab Palestinians into Israel as citizens for both of our benefits.

G-d only allows special, good people who He loves to have merit to live in His Holy land of Israel. I have found that most all people living in the land of Israel today; Jew, Arab, Gentile, Muslim, Christian; are really friends of G-d and have some kind of merit to live in the land. As we are all friends of G-d, it is a Mitzvah to respect each other, everyone, to see the good in each other, as well as in ourselves, and to put our differences aside. Instead of blaming others for the problem, both sides must take a good look in the mirror and fix ourselves in what we are doing wrong instead of blaming others for our problems. The Gentiles and Jews living in the land have both endured much hardship and suffering in the land as it is written that the land of Israel is only acquired by travails (the Talmud). We should only be nice to each other. There's enough room here for everyone. Selfish extremist nationalist ideologies have no place here. They are causing senseless murder. We should work together for success instead of killing each other. War is a waste of money, energy and man power. We need to build. Build together. We both need to repent fully for our sins and beg G-d for Mercy, guidance to do the right thing in His Eyes, whatever that is, and success.

If Palestinians thought about it, they would realize that their life under the state of Israel is much better than they have ever been able to achieve on their own. On their own the Palestinian have had only poverty, illiteracy, boredom, lack of plumbing and electricity, lack of roads, bloodshed and sickness. Under Israel, they have economic opportunity, education, entertainment, lack of plumbing and electricity, roads, law and order and health benefits in Israeli hospitals. Under Israel they are far better off then they have ever been. Having their own state would be a disaster for them. It would severely degrade their standard of living that they now have under Israel. They would suffer immensely in poverty. They should be included in Israel for the sake of both our interests.

The main reason that certain reckless and irresponsible tyrants among the Arabs want to make a country 'Palestine' is to vent their hatred and use it as a political tool and military terror base against Israel. They are willing to kill all the Arabs and destroy their higher standard of living under Israel in order to carry out their evil plans. All they seek is war and destruction, and not peace and construction. The Palestinian Authority (PA) was formed from the Palestinian Liberation Organization (PLO) terror group. Just as the leader of the PLO, Yassir Arafat, stole all the money given for the Palestinians, so does the PA steal all the money given for the Palestinians. The PA leaves the Palestinians impoverished with barely enough food to eat and no hope for development. The other vying contender for power over the Palestinians, Hamas, is a puppet of Iran and is used as a proxy of Iran's attempt to take over the region and recruits Palestinians for its Jihad 'holy' war against Israel. Hamas is 'better' than the PA in that it gives charity, but gives it to terrorists. The Palestinian Authority and Hamas are tyrants who murder any Palestinian who speaks out against them. These tyrants of mutual destruction must be banned from the discussion at any level. They are from Satan. All they know how to do is rob, murder, steal and destroy. We now all need to heal and build, not murder and destroy. They get support from the Arab's self righteous hatred, anger and rage that many Arabs have for the Jewish Israelis. The Islamic Koran that preaches murder to all non-Muslims supports them. If there to be a new country called 'Palestine' as proposed by some very 'intelligent' people, it would be a backward, impoverished, uneducated, nightmare of a country with no hope for success or wealth. It would be a terror base that recruits its desperate citizens to throw them selves as cannon fodder in the Jihad against Israel, only to find themselves as pawns being thrown to their deaths by Arab tyrants who have robbed them of all their money and woman. The State of Palestine would be a torturous nightmare for the Palestinians (May G-d have mercy). This would be a punishment for them, not a redemption. If there is a State of Palestine, Palestinian extremists will be blamed for terrorist activities against the United States; rightfully so; and will then be bombed by the US armed forces as they did to Iraq and Dayash (ISIS). Palestinian towns will be turned into waste and rubble. It will be a horror for all to witness. Only a fool among the Jews, with no foresight nor Faith, would support such a thing. We need to heal, mend our misunderstandings, build economy and unify; not destroy, murder and divide, which is all that the Palestinian state idea is really all about. If you are a Palestinian reading this, wise up and work with Israel. It's better for you. Read on and know that there are many Jews like me who care about you, want to help you and will help you if you respect us too.

The question is: how do we Israeli Jews make peace with all these hate filled, angry Palestinian Arabs with their self righteous extremist Islamic beliefs? There are a number of things that must be done to rectify this situation, including: righteous and merciful judgments between Palestinian Arabs and Israeli Jews, to relentlessly pursue peace with the Arabs, and teach the Arabs the Noahide laws.

Righteous judgments

As we saw in previous chapters of this book, justice is the foundation of peace.

Righteous judgments between Arabs and Jews, without political nor economic bias to either side, makes peace between us, and thus makes a national peace in the land of Israel. This is the basis for peace; just settlements of our conflicts. As we learn from king David, mercy and charity is also part of justice. This averts the sword of war, terror, crime, and domestic violence in the land, whether between Jew and Arab, Jew and Jew, or Arab and Arab. Justice is the foundation of peace. Injustice incites more war, terror and violence. Righteous, fair, just judgments makes peace between people and pacifies anger. It demands respect between people; or else the law strikes. These righteous judgments include not only fair, timely, affordable trials for everybody, but also having no tolerance for incitement of violence by anybody for any reason, including the Koran's incitement to murder Israeli Jews, or Jews inciting from our amei haAretz in their low, street level, gang mentality, selfish nationalistic 'Torah'. In our reaction to Islam's wicked ant-Semitic murder and heinous terror, we Jews must also not say things that incite violence against the Arabs, to attack random innocent Arabs or to voice reactionary threats to 'kick them all out of the land' or to 'kill them all'. This is a sin, and a not so wise sin at that, for it incites Goyim to shed Jewish blood (Has ViShalom). In Israel today there is a law against 'incitement'. It must be applied to everybody, including those who use the Torah or Koran to do so.

We also have to remember that in addition to being fair, merciful and righteous, we must also be strong with the Arabs otherwise they will step all over us.

Ideally, all conflicts and disputes should be settled with the assistance of the Rabbinic judges, or, if necessary, then in the Beith Din; the Torah court of wise, fair Rabbinic judges (Dayaneem). But, today we don't have that, so we must relay on the Israeli courts, who in my opinion are doing a pretty good job of being merciful with the murderous Arabs, everything considered, despite the fact that they are not a Sanhedrin, which is needed to judge the real law, which is the Torah law, properly. The Rambam says that any court that does not judge by Torah law is not true justice. Despite this statement, I find that the Israeli court system does seem pretty just to the Arabs in how they judge the Arabs for their crimes. In any case, it is impossible to know what the true Torah law is without a Sanhedrin to sit together and judge specific cases. Rav Yosef Karo said this five hundred years ago, and the Rabbi who I believe is the real Gadol haDor, Rabbi Avraham Stern Shlita, said the same thing.

In my opinion the current Israeli justice system is now more balanced in that it does not allow extremist's violence on both sides; Arab or Jew. They have a tough job, because there is a lot of this in this land. This is not Scandinavia.

For example, on June 12, 2014, three Israeli youths; Naftoli Frankel (of blessed memory), Gilad Shaer (of blessed memory) and Eyal Yifrah (of blessed memory); from settlements in Judea and Sameria were kidnapped, murdered and found burned (the burning was not reported in the media), by Palestinian Arab youths. In a random revenge attack, terror against terror, a Palestinian youth; Mohamed Abu Khdeir (of blessed memory); was then also subsequently murdered and burned; allegedly by Jewish youth. Israeli Prime Minister Benyamin Netanyahoo publicly condemned both murders by the youths and had the police system apprehend and punish all those parties responsible for the murders in an even handed, unbiased, fair, righteous meeting out of justice for all. His government then put the memory of the Arab youth Mohamed Abu Khdeir (of blessed memory) on the Israeli monument of terror victims. In my opinion, the Israeli government's recent 2015 decision to put an Arab victim of reverse terror on the monument of terror victims, mostly comprised of Israeli Jewish victims of Arab terror, was a progressive and fairly balanced judgment of justice that moves peace forward. I'm sure it appeased many Arabs as well as Jews who want fair treatment of Arabs in spite of their thousands of atrocities and war crimes against Israelis over the past decades. I was pleasingly surprised and impressed by the Israeli justice system. I saw this as a light unto the nations (Isaiah 49:6, 42:6).

It made me feel good. We can have peace, but we must speak peace to have it. We are now moving forward in the right direction.

There are Arab towns in the land of Israel that have Arab youths who throw rocks at Israeli cars driving by on the neighboring highway with the intent to kill the drivers and their families. The Arab parents are too afraid to attack the Israelis themselves, out of fear of being punished, so they incite their children to attack the Israelis. The parents are responsible for the attempted murder attacks. The Israeli government now responds to these attempted murder attacks by interrogating the whole town involved, which often involves arrests. This is good solid investigatory police work. But, in addition to the police action, I would suggest that Israel would have an 'Israeli Peace Corps' that would go to these towns to make peace with the residents in order to rectify the root of the problem, so that it doesn't happen anymore. Lets be smart about this. This may involve giving charity, showing sympathy and understanding for them, but not condoning the terror attacks, and being basically kind and understanding and respectful of them, in order to make peace. Teaching them the Noahide laws is also important to rectify one of the roots of the problem: the Islamic Koran that incited them to commit these atrocities and war crimes. The Israeli police action is needed to stop Arabs terror, but a relentless initiative on our part to make peace with each of these Arab villages is also needed.

Pursue peace with the Arabs

The Talmud teaches us that 'to save one life is to save an entire world'. Killing is a horrible thing and never good under any circumstances. It is always a tragedy, even when justified by Torah. When the Sanhedrin would execute a person they would drug him so as not to feel the pain, maintained his human dignity and respect when they killed him, and fasted to atone for their sins that caused the death of a person due to their negligence in not educating the people to behave properly. They accepted responsibility for the death as well.

It is a big Mitzvah to pursue peace and resolve this misunderstanding with all people at all times when there is conflict between people. In Hebrew a 'pursuer of peace' is called a 'Rodeif Shalom'. This saves peoples lives, saves entire worlds.

In laws of kings, chapter six, the Rambam brings that we are commanded to pursue peace whenever there is a possibility of war so as to make our maximum efforts to avoid the tragedy of war and thus save the needless shedding of blood on all sides. G-d loves all His creations and never wants us to shed the blood of another when we can avoid it. The Mitzva to pursue peace is of the highest forms of Mitzva justice and those who do this are considered as partners in Creation (Talmud Bavli Shabbos 10). Since there is always the possibility of war between the Palestinians and Israelis it is therefore always a Mitzva to be Rodeif Shalom, at all times. This Mitzvah is a matter of pikuah nefesh that can save lives, save worlds. Since many Palestinians are really Jews, the war between the Palestinian and Israelis its really often times a case of Jew against Jew; Ishmaelite Jew against Eisavian Jew (see previous chapter citing Even Shleima).

It is forbidden for Jews to incite hatred or antagonize Gentiles (or Jews) as per Jewish law (Shulhan Aruch as per the Talmud). By not being friendly and respectful to Gentiles this can antagonize them and incite their hatred to shed the blood of Jews since a Jew did not respect them. Although it is true that the land of Israel is really the property of the Jews, it is forbidden to say this to Arabs because it can incite them to shed Jewish blood. Instead of saying "This is MY land", which incites war and terror, we should both be saying, with a Higher Divine understanding, that "This land is G-d's land and there is enough room for both of us here".

I find that being friendly and respectful to Arab makes peace with most of them. Instead of fighting fire with fire, we must fight fire with water, to put out the fire. This is the way of the wise. We must be kind, sympathetic and understanding to the Arabs. The Shulhan Aruch laws on Tzadka says that it is a Mitzva to give goyim Tzadka to encourage Shalom. I do this by being respectful, friendly and kind to Arabs. I give them candy and Tzadka to make peace with them as we learn to do so in the Shulhan Aruch. This is the Torah law in this situation. Many Arabs have told me that if all the Jews were like me there would be no terror. One Arab confessed to me that he regretted things he had done. The Israeli government gives many Arabs free electricity, land, water, benefits and more. This is a deeply wise policy as king Solomon has said: if your enemy is hungry then feed them.

If we want respect and peace with the Arabs in Israel and in general, then we Jews must show more respect to the Arabs and be friendly and kind to them; not necessarily to be 'friends', since Jews are not allowed to be friends with goyim (so as to avoid intermarriage), but to be friendly, kind, fair and respectful with them. Then many of them will be more respectful to us as well. This is basic human nature. This kindness and respect to the Arabs must come from a place of strength though, as the wicked among the Arabs will attack us if we are weak, as is the nature of the wicked, especially Amalek and Ishmael among the Arabs. Yes, we must be strong, friendly, respectful, fair and kind, all at the same time, in the right balance. The youth need to learn this. This will help save lives.

The peaceful relations between Israelis and Arabs have been improving in time. With our further efforts, the vast majority of Arabs and Israelis will live in peace, mutual respect and even more economic cooperation than there already is. This is what is the trend now by the progressive people on both sides. It is mostly only the spiritually frustrated, impoverished, selfish nationalistic, extreme right wing, especially the youth, who are making problems with inciting words, aggression, violence, terror and return terror. The Jewish kids doing this are not listening to the big Rabbis like Rabbi Stern Shlita who teaches peaceful ways by example, as the ways of Torah are ways of peace. The

Arab youth are violent largely due to the bad Islamic teachings that preach terror and violence against all non Muslims. This must stop. It is incitement to murder. The Israelis are reacting to this by an 'Iron Fist' policy and at times reverse terror by the youth. The Muslims must learn that it is a sin, not a Mitzvah, to kill non-Muslims, and the proper way is the Noahide laws. We Jews are responsible for teaching them this. There is much bitterness and revenge on both sides, each one thinking the other side started the conflict and deserves revenge. The way to deal with this is to pursue peace aggressively and relentlessly. Since it is not the nature of the Arabs to do this, therefore, we Jews have to make the first steps towards reconciliation and peace by showing the Arabs kindness and respect, and by being friendly to them, not arrogant and disrespectful, which is demeaning to them and it is understandable why they would hate us, the 'chosen people', for treating them like that. This is a Hilool Hashem. We must be a light unto the nations (Isaiah 49:6, 42:6) by a nation of priestly ministers (Exodus 19:6) and show them love and respect. This is a Kidoosh Hashem (Sanctification of G-d's Name) as a nation of priestly ministers to the Goyim. Until then we will be viewed as a despised nation of Ghetto Jews living by the ways of the exile.

We must show all people love and respect. We must empathize with the Palestinian's poverty and disadvantage and help them achieve a descent humane standard of living that is blessed by their living by the Noahide laws. The Palestinians who are Jews must live by the Torah. We must love them, respect them, pursue peace, teach them the Noahide laws and cooperate in our mutual economic success, working together. It is possible. But, again, we must also remember that any war against us is a punishment for our sins. So if we want peace, we must make peace with G-d by living in His Torah ways, so that He does not punish us with war using the Gentiles as a means by which He punishes us.

Since the Arabs will not pursue peace with us, we Jews must make the initiative to relentlessly pursue peace with the Arabs.

Many years ago when I was on the left wing, on a secular in kibbutz called Maagan Michael, which was a founding hub of the Israeli military since before the state of Israel. Thinking that the left was too merciful to the terrorists, I called for their demonization, labeling them 'terrorists' in order to protect Israel from their atrocious Jihad. This policy took hold in Israel and America and is now the status quo policy in the military in the West (Edom).

After reevaluating and reexamining the situation, with more Torah wisdom and life experience, I now recognize that although there are terrorists among them, in any case the Arabs of the land of Israel are human beings, whether Jew or Gentile, and must be treated with respect and human dignity, and are required to treat us Jews the same. If we pursue peace with them as described above and teach them the Noahide laws, and they accept them, then they can be invited to live in the land of Israel with full human rights, as citizens of Israel, under the Jewish leadership alone, as Noahides and reconverted Jews, with all the responsibilities that go along with that, which includes behaving as responsible human beings who respect the rights of others. Those who don't behave as responsible human beings who respect the rights of others, will fall under the jurisdiction of the judicial system and be removed from society as criminals as any normal society must do to those who commit crimes against others; for what ever reasons or self righteous rationalizations that they may entertain. I hope the 'Palestinians' join us Jewish Israelis in our Jewish Torah country of Israel and live in the respect and a respectable standard of living that they deserve as human beings, and work together with us to add to the success of the Israeli economy, which they are not capable of doing on their own. Again, a Palestinian State in reality would be a monstrous nightmare for the Palestinians. They should be smart and join Israel.

We must teach the Noahide laws to the Arabs

The Koran teaches that all people who are not Muslims must be killed, burned, terrorized, crucified, dismembered and beheaded. It teaches that all lands must be conquered for Islam and any land that was conquered is forever Islam's. This includes the land of Israel in their opinion. This is a big part of the problem; belief in the Koran as G-d's law, and not the Torah and Noahide laws. If an Arab Muslim tells you that the Koran is about 'peace' then you can Google sources online where the Koran teaches violence and terror. You will see that the Arab Muslim lies to you.

The Rebbe said that we must leave behind our ghetto mentality and go out and teach the goyim the Noahide laws, and of course this means with respect and love for them.

Our negligence to teach the Arabs the Noahide laws has allowed Islam to fill the vacuum and wreak avoidable violence and murder as a result. Part of the problem to the Israeli-Arab conflict is Islam, and the solution to the problem is teaching the Palestinians the Noahide laws. As the Arabs in the land of Israel revert to their ancestral Noahide laws they will accept Jewish sovereignty over the land and live in the land of Israel, as citizens of Israel, in peace with the Jewish people who they as Noahides will recognize as the sovereign power. In time they will accept them. We must make the first steps of a concerted educational effort now. Some people in Israel, particularly Chabad, have already started to do this. They are online.

According to the Rambam, it is permissible for Gentiles to live in the land of Israel if they swear before the Sanhedrin that they will keep the seven Noahide laws. It is our hope that the Jews among the Arabs living in the land of Israel; 'the Palestinians'; will return to Torah Judaism and the Arabs and any Gentiles who so want will live in the land as Noahides and be good citizens of Israel, soon with G-d's help to be under the leadership of the Sanhedrin, maybe Elijah too, and eventually the righteous Moshiah as king, who is fair to all, including the Arabs. This is the real peace plan with the Arabs and maybe even Iran. All Arabs and Gentiles are welcome to live in the land of Israel, but we must repent and start to live by Hashem's Holy Torah as it is written that 'we were not exiled from the land for any other reason other than our sins'.

As the chapter in my book titled 'Most 'Palestinians' Come from Jews and Many May Still be Jewish' shows, many Palestinians who are really Jewish but have no proof of such may choose to come back to being Jewish by conversion and regain their Jewish identity. The Beith Din will rule on these conversions.

Sanhedrin to appoint the Messiah

The Jewish people are only really fully redeemed from the subjugation of the goyim with the coming of the Messiah (Rambam laws of kings 11, Talmud Bavli Brachot 34). There will only really be peace with the Messiah as king in Israel. As the chapter in my book titled 'Sanhedrin is needed to bring the Messiah in Our Time', the next step to making that a reality is for the majority of the Rabbis to make a Sanhedrin that includes the biggest Rabbis of the generation; the Gidolei haDor. Even before the Messiah is appointed king, and certainly after, will be the judicial body in recent modern history that provides timely, affordable, fair, unbiased, true, righteous and merciful justice, in the right balance. Sine justice is the basis of peace, we can only really have full peace with the Sanhedrin, and eventually the Messiah as king. May that time be soon.

The Jewish Kingdom of Priestly Ministers Loves and Respects All People

As part of our mission as 'the light unto the nations' (Isaiah 49:6, 42:6) and a 'kingdom of priestly ministers' (Exodus 19:6) is to love the goyim, be kind to them and to point out the good in them so as to connect them with G-d. We are also responsible to teach them the Noahide Covenent and the seven categories of laws. See the chapter on the Noahide Covenent. This will elevate the goyim from their current man made religion sin which they are subjugated. We must free them with love and education as we must do to all out fellow Jews. This light comes from our living by the Torah commandments properly in public for all to see so as to sanctify Hashem's Name in public. G-d's power and love through our Torah observance can win the world for the good of all mankind. Let us all rise together through love and light.

This Noahide education may also help the Jewish people, by converting Muslims, Atheists and Christians who are Gentiles, to Noahides, who will then stop proselytizing, oppressing, slandering, persecuting and terrorizing Jews by their man made religions. This will help stop the subjugation and anti-Semitic attacks of these religions against the Jewish people, and bring the Jewish people to their proper place of respect and nobility that is viewed by the Gentiles as 'the light unto the nations' (Isaiah 49:6, 42:6), a 'kingdom of priestly ministers' (Exodus 19:6), chosen by G-d to be a 'kingdom of priestly ministers' who teach the Gentiles their Torah laws, and are a guiding light to them, not a subject of derision; 'a despised nation' (Ezekiel 36) as we are now to many Gentiles and even self hating Jews (may Hashem have Mercy).

The blessing '*the elder (Eisav) shall serve the younger (Jacob)*' (Genesis 25) means that Eisav (and his descendents) serves Jacob (and his descendents) if Jacob lives righteously by the Torah commandments, like the USA helping Israel, otherwise Eisav (and his descendents) attacks and even kills Jacob (and his descendants) (Rashi on Genesis 27:40) like in the holocaust and crusades. Righteous Eisavians defend and fight for Israel.

As a note about the Arabs and the goyim in general I want to say that it is written:" Who is respected, he who respects G-d's Creations" (Ethics of the Fathers. This means that we must respect all of G-d's Creations including all peoples of the world, including the Arabs. It is forbidden by the Torah fro a Jew to incite enmity or antagonize a Gentile or to take the land of Israel by force (Talmud Bavli Ketuboth 111). It is a Mitzvah for Jews to acquire the land of Israel by peaceful means only; as the left wing Zionists did as a matter of policy. This is the proper way in our times according to my opinion. I may be wrong. There may be other opinions that have solid Torah supports upon which to rely. I'm not sure, but I do have an opinion.

In addition to Islam's preaching of violence against non-Muslims, and the violent nature of many Arabs, which is due to many reasons, including poverty and a long history of violence, part of the problem that incites the Arab-Israeli conflict is Western feelings of arrogance and superiority by the Westerners who settled the land of Israel. This Western arrogance incited many Arabs living in the land to be violent against the Western Israel; the arrogance and the Israeli Western culture which they feel is evil, in addition to Islam not allowing for Muslim settled lands to be taken by non-Muslims. If we want respect and peace with the Arabs in Israel and in general, then we Jews must show more respect to the Arabs and be friendly and kind to them; not necessarily to be 'friends' since Jews are not really allowed to be friends with goyim, but to be friendly, kind, fair and respectful with them. Then many of them will be more respectful to us as well. This is basic human nature. This kindness and respect to the Arabs must come from a place of strength, as the wicked among the Arabs will attack us if we are weak, as is the nature of the wicked, especially Amalek and Ishmael. Yes, we must be strong, friendly, respectful, fair and kind, all at the same time, in the right balance.

It is forbidden to incite hatred or antagonize goyim (Gentiles) as per Jewish law (Shulhan Aruch as per the Talmud). By not being friendly and respectful to goyim this antagonizes them and incites their hatred to continue, where being friendly and respectful this makes peace with most of them. Instead of fighting fire with fire, we must fight fire with water, kindness and understanding, and put out the fire.

As we know "All of Hashem's Ways are Pleasantness" and "his paths are of Peace" this is the way we should be with all people so as to Sanctify His name as His ''Nation of Priestly Ministers' to the goyim as they need us to do since we Jews are their Divinely ordained nation of priestly ministers. Would you want to respect or listen to a priest who shows you hatred or arrogance? No; of course not. We must be respectful and friendly to the goyim, and all Jews too for that matter. It's good to remind goyim that G-d loves them and to point out the good in them. That is the job of a priest. We should not to bear a grudge for past crimes of goyim and even atrocities many of their ancestors committed against us (holocaust, Jihad, terror strikes, etc.). It is *wiser* to forgive and move on and when there is anti-Semitism and hatred, to pacify this fire with words of peace, not to fight fire with fire, but to fight fire with water, and to put out the fire. This is the way of the wise and will help build a better future for us all and will help the Jewish people embrace our destiny as the beloved and respected 'kingdom of priestly ministers' who are a light unto the goyim, and not a despised nation anymore. This starts with love, kindness and respect for all Goyim, including the Arabs, and especially those living in the land of Israel, may of whom are really Jews, as shown in the chapter 'Most 'Palestinians' Come from Jews and Many May Still be Jewish'.

Let us all rise together through love and light with us Jews leading the way as G-d's kingdom of priestly ministers and light unto the goyim.

I want you to know that while I was writing this book my identify was being defamed by authorities while concurrently scum from the Zionist Erev Rav regime were trying to kill me through the abuse of the system. I asked they and all those with them if need be, including whole wicked families of Israeli hate filled, lying, thieving, immoral, haughty, murderous scum who would seek evil vengeance if they could, and their political parties which hearted these monsters, all these little Israeli Hitlers be killed with no mercy just as we killed the Nazis even though the Nazis were justified in killing evil scum like this, and many Jews were Nazis for this reason, including Herman Georing (z'l). And yes, we learn from the Bible the story of the children who mocked Elisha and were eaten be bears. This shows that there can be wicked children who deserve death. Where was G-d? G-d sent Hitler to kill the wicked who refused to repent and listen to the Rabbis like me. That's were G-d was. G-d killed them; its totally justified. Moshiah is here and his detractors will bleed. The Jews will now learn the lesson I hope; the lesson to be good and only good, or else.

In the bigger picture, for what they did to me, Moshiah Ben David, these Erve Rav Zionist little terds will be flushed down the toilet of Jewish history with the rest of the little Erev Rav terds.

I still believe that love can conquer though; but not all. I am not naïve; just realistically idealistic.

For these reason I know, from Ruah HaKodesh, that the State of Israel, including the vile Mosad (who are largely responsible for this, motivated by ripping off my music copyrights in New York and denying payment, and molesting children, as part of the Zionist child molester rapist state of the fake Eisavian 'Israel', will literally all go to hell), will fall, and me and the House of David will stand now and forever as the true kings of Israel.

The Messiah son of David 'Kills' Armilus

As explained in full detail in my book on the war of Gog and Magog, in the end of days and anti-Semitic, anti-God, multi national coalition force attacks Israel with the intent to destroy Israel, establish Armilus as king and force mankind to worship Satan instead of God. Armilus is an anti-Semitic demonic war Golem formed by the enemies of Israel through black magic. He and Gog lead the attack against Israel in the war of Gog and Magog.

The Rabbis learn out through the oral transmission that the phrase in Isaiah 11 "*The Messiah slays the wicked with the breath/spirit of his lips*" means that the Messiah slays Armilus; in addition to other wicked.

Since Armilus is not a human being, rather a being created by black magic, normal means can not kill him as with a human and the Messiah son of David must use Kabalistic methods, probably from the sefer Yitseera (that is Hebrew for 'Book of Creation'), to spiritually de-activate Armilus. My book on the war of Gog and Magog explains in more detail who is this Armilus and how the Messiah slays him.

Other than the Midrashic sources quoted fully in my book on the war of Gog and Magog, the most notable authoritative Jewish source on Armilus is found in 'Emunoth viDaoth', chapter six, by Rav Saadia Gaon (Zt'l). There he says that '*Then, if it (control of the land of Israel and the world) be in the hand of Armilus, he (the Messiah son of David) will kill him (Armilus) and take it (control of the land of Israel and the world) from him… and he (the Messiah son of David) will to those who are to be redeemed encourage them and heal their breach and console their souls… and G-d will bestow upon His people distinction and honor and glory*'.

The 'Days of the Messiah'

Rambam (laws of kings chapter 12) says the 'days of the Messiah' starts during the war of Gog and Magog. Talmud Bavli Sanhedrin 99 onward discusses how long will be the Messianic Era.

The Rambam (laws of kings chapter 12) describes the 'days of the Messiah' as "*when the kingship of the Messiah is established in Israel everyone will accept his Holy Spirit that rests upon him as he will identify the pure Cohaneem and Levieem and who is from which tribe. The main point of the Jewish people's lives will be to occupy themselves with learning Torah and wisdom of Hashem so that they will merit the world to come (going to Heaven). There won't be hunger, war, jealousy nor competition. The good things and delicacies will be abundant and the whole world will occupy itself with knowing Hashem. Therefore Israel will be recognized as the priests and great wise men of the world and the knowledge of Hashem will fill the world as the waters fill the oceans*".

As part of this wisdom of Hashem and living in accordance with the Torah in the proper way, not the fake 'proper' way, prophesy and Holy Spirit (in Hebrew 'Ruach HaKodesh') will be abundant amongst mankind. As Rav Saadia Gaon in 'Emuna and Deoth' points out, this prophesy will be used to identify hidden Jews lost amongst the Gentiles (Jews considered to be Gentiles), whereby they will be returned to the land of Israel.

Prophesies of the "Days of the Messiah'

There are many prophesies which tell what the days of the Messiah will be like. Among them are the following:

'Arise and Shine! For your light has arrived and the Glory of Hashem shines upon you. ... Nations will walk by your light and kings by the brilliance of your shine. ... the affluence of the West will be turned over to you and the wealth of the nations will come to you...I will glorify the House of My splendor...the sons of foreigners will build your walls and king will serve you... the nation that does not serve you will perish... Hashem will be an eternal light for you and your G-d will be your splendor...Your people will all be righteous, they will inherit the land forever' (Isaiah 60).

'Foreigners will stand and tend your flocks and the sons of the stranger will be your plowman and your vineyard workers. And you will be called 'Priests of Hashem', 'Ministers of our G-d' (Isaiah 61).

'Nations will perceive your righteousness and all the kings your honor... Then you will be a crown of splendor in the Hand of Hashem and a royal diadem in the palm of your G-d' (Isaiah 62).

'Behold I am recreating Jerusalem as 'gladness' and its people as 'joy'.... It will be that before they call I will answer, while yet they speak I will hear' (Isaiah 65).

'They will bring all your brethren as an offering to Hashem...from them too I will take as Cohaneem (Jewish Priests who can serve in the Temple) *and Levites* (Jewish Ministers to the Priests who can serve in the Temple)' (Isaiah 66).

The 'Coming of the Messiah'

The Rambam (laws of the king chapter 11:4) says that building the third Temple proves that someone is certainly the Messiah. But, even when the Messiah finally builds the third Temple many people of Israel may still doubt him and that the complete redemption has really arrived. "*When the king Messiah comes he will stand on the roof of the Holy Temple and he will let it be heard, learn our rabbis a the time for you and for Israel and say 'humble ones, the time of your redemption has arrived, and if you don't believe me, see my light that shines on you' as was written 'Rise and Shine because your light has come and the honor of Hashem is radiating on you, and on you exclusively, on not on the idol worshippers as it is said that the darkness (before Redemption) will cover the world'. At that same time, the Holy One blessed be He cleaves the light of the king Messiah and of Israel and they all go together to the light of the king Messiah ...* "(Yalkoot Shimoni Isaiah Perek 60). When the Jewish people feel the inner light then they feel the redemption has arrived. This is what most people would believe is the 'coming of the Messiah' since it is the marking point that proves that the full and complete redemption has arrived. Other points that one might consider as the 'coming of the Messiah 'would include his being born, his moving from Edom to the land of Israel, his winning the war of Gog and Magog or his building the Third Temple, which according to Rambam may seem to define the 'coming of the Messiah'.

The phrase *'and if you don't believe me'* shows that even when the Messiah is standing on the roof of the third Temple (that he built) that there are some people who still may not believe that the redemption has come and that he is the Messiah. This shows that even though building the third Temple proves that someone is certainly the Messiah according to the Rambam, and the full redemption has come, the people of Israel will only accept that he is the Messiah when they feel the light of Messiah and Israel, which are two of the seven kinds of light according to the Zohar. From here we see that the people of Israel will only really feel that it is the complete redemption when they feel the inner light of the Messiah and Israel.

Worthy Charities and Jewish Organizations to Support

Giving charity in the right way to the right people helps bring the Messiah and the final redemption. It can also save your life if you are in danger of loosing it. The codes of Jewish law, Shulhan aruch, laws of Charity, tell you what the rules are regarding to whom to give and to whom not to give, and who are the priorities. I like giving to poor orthodox Jewish Torah scholars who are clean of transgression as one of the most elevated forms of charity. You can see your local orthodox Jewish Rabbi for assistance. The following organizations are recommended to support:

To save babies from abortion (murder) in Israel
https://www.efrat.org.il/english

Preparing brides and grooms for marriage and
providing orphans weddings and homes
http://www.lovingkindness.com

To convict and publicize rapists and child molesters in the Jewish
Community and tell your story and healing for victims and perpetrators
http://www.jewishcommunitywatch.org

To replace negative inner beliefs with positive inner
beliefs and become the possible you
http://www.thepossibleyou.org

Conclusion

This book series shows that there are many points of misunderstanding regarding the issues of the Messiah, the final redemption and the ten tribes and the war of Gog and Magog. I hope this book on the Messiah according to Judaism clarifies the issues for you regarding what the Messiah really is, so that the truth be known, as truth is one of the pillars upon which the world rests and depends for success.

In addition, I hope that this book brings people closer to G-d and to serve Him better and for those who did not believe in G-d or the Divinity of Torah that the chapters in this book that address these issues bring you to realize that the Torah and Noahide covenants are Divine and that we must live by them. May you be successful and blessed for good and merit the best of this world and the world to come and do what you must do to attain that which means being perfectly righteous and may we all merit coming of the Messiah, the full redemption and building of the third Temple speedily hastened in our time. Amen!!!!!

To Contact the author to purchase the books 'The Final Redemption and the Ten Tribes' or 'The War of Gog and Magog', public appearances, questions or comments:

ArielBenYaakov3@hotmail.com

http://themessiahblog.blogspot.co.il
check blog to confirm that email address is current

Biography of the Author

The author of this book, Ariel Ben Yaakov, was born in Newton Center (near Boston), Massachusetts, by the American name Eric Irving Spiegelman on September 29, 1962, which is Rosh HaShana 5723. His parents are Joel Warren Spiegelman (January 23, 1933- present) and Gail Carroll Voelker (of blessed memory July 18 1933-June 17 2013, Tamuz 9, 5773), both of Buffalo, NY. As a Maestro, his father was a keyboardist, classical music orchestra conductor, experimenter in early synthesizers, composer, Professor of music at Brandeis and Sarah Lawrence Universities and recording artist. His mother was an elementary school teacher in Boston, Scarsdale, NY and New Haven, Connecticut, also in Chabad.

Raised as assimilated Jew in Bronxville, Yonkers and Scarsdale, NY, the author learned war, martial arts, sports and music from the age five. Being small and innocent, thus attacked by big bullies and wicked anti-Semites on many occasions, he learned to fight well, with HaShem's aid, and *Hashem beat them,* through him, in many fights as a matter of self-defense. This theme of Hashem protecting him and fighting his enemies would play out all of his life. At age ten he started learning classical, folk guitar, jazz and blues and became a semi guitar virtuoso by seventeen.

He studied in high school at the British preparatory school then called the Franklin School, now called the Anglo-American School in Manhattan. At sixteen, he became interested in religion, started learning for his Bar Mitzvah with Cantor Ira Fein, accepted upon himself observance of the Sabbath and other Mitzvoth as a modern conservative-orthodox Jew and received his Bar Mitzvah at age seventeen. At sixteen he accepted the idea that the world can be saved by music; later to find out that this can be achieved by a great Tzadik (Rav Nahman of Breslov Likootei Aitzoth perek Mangina). In 1980 he went to study pre-med and the humanities study of power and authority at SUNY at Purchase until1982 whereupon he decided to transfer to study electrical engineering at the Technion in Israel. During college he was an activist to save Soviet Jewry and the environment. In the summer of 1982 he moved to Israel and went to work and learn Hebrew in the Kibbutz Ulpan programs of kibbutz Beerot Yitzchak, Maagan Michael and the Sdot Yam and was called Arik Shpiegleman. During that period his Torah observance decreased as he was more attracted to the secular Zionist movement in Israel due to their military prowess and achievements in building the country of Israel. He attended Ohr Sameah Yeshiva in Jerusalem for a few months where he learned with Rabbi Dr. Bonchek and Rabbi Kordoza. In 1983 he then commenced his university studies at the Technion electrical engineering department and graduated in 1987. During his studies at the Technion he wrote and recorded songs and performed them.

Upon graduating the Technion in 1987, he returned to the United States to recruit support for Israel and embark on a music career to gain support for Israel where he supported himself with a day job as an electrical engineer. He went to work as an electrical engineer at Mini Circuits Labs in Brooklyn, NY, and used the money he saved to build a recording studio to develop his music production abilities. In 1988 he took a higher paying engineering job at Anritsu America in Bergen County, NJ, where he began singing lessons with Judy Hages of Park Ridge, NJ. From there he began to develop his style as a music artist as well as his singing, song writing and production skills. In 1990 he went to work as the quality control test engineer at the defense sub-contractor Electro Miniatures Corporation (EMC) in Moonachie, NJ. While living in Ridgefield, NJ, in 1990 he started performing in the NJ/NY Metro area as a solo country artist by the stage name Eric Alrich, playing in live Jam sessions through out the NY Metro area and developed his writing, singing, guitar playing and studio production abilities to a professional level.

The author saw that the United States was falling due to the deterioration of morality and ethics and saw the Mitzvah to save the USA as he felt it was a great country worthy of being saved and it was important to do so for the sake of the many great Jews and Gentiles there, the world, the Jewish people internationally and Israel. Indeed Rabbi Moshe Feinstein (zt'l) called the United States a 'kingship of kindness' and said that is important to show gratitude to the USA and other modern nations that are good to the Jewish people. The author affirms that "We must pray for these nations" and he does so by praying for the welfare and benefit of the nations every day.

From 1991 he took upon himself to be active to right any wrong or injustice, where ever he saw it, and became active in upholding human rights, Israel's rights as a country to sovereignty over the land of Israel while respecting Arab's rights who live there, animal rights, the environment and children's rights, often personally intervening to resque children from all the sorts of abuse they endure. He endured suffering from the conflicts that ensued from these interventions, even death threats and being framed to the government, which brought Divine wrath upon the sinners involved in these scenarios. At that time he boycotted tuna that lead to Dolphin safe tune and made a petition for the US and United Nations to stop the Serbian holocaust of Croatians in Yugoslavia by air strikes and war crimes trials. Both the boycott and petition were successful. In 1992 he returned to a commitment to keep the Torah commandments as an orthodox Jew. In 1992 he sent his "Regrowth Redemption' demo tape by his band 'Covenent' to record companies and by 1993 major label record companies were interested in signing him as an artist under his stage name Eric Alrich. The goal of saving the world by teachimg Torah through music awakened in him and he started an independent record company called ClearVision records paying homage to Moses' ClearVision as a prophet of Israel and the world. He also recorded a CD called 'Jew lost in exile' which was later renamed 'Return to Hashem' in 2008 in Tsfat. He wrote over eighty copyrighted songs and six CDs named: 'Covenent' (1998), 'Return to Hashem' (1998/2008), 'Heart of Love' (sung in Hebrew) (2002), 'Rise and Shine' (2006), 'The New Messiah' (2006) and fighting the evil within (2013). He recorded wrote, engineered and produced his music in his home recording studio on 571 Art Lane, Ridgefield, NJ, exclusively using a Stratocaster guitar and Marshal Amplifier. He later found out that the Gematria of Stratocaster and Marshal equals '571' which equals Moshiah Ben Yosef' with an added 'heh' which according to the Kabala has a meaning.

After witnessing the crime and murder of the Mafia in the NY Metro area and their connection with the US government and wealthy corporations that bribe the government as part of the system of crime, in 1994 he decided to fight the Mafia and exposed the criminal activities he witnessed. At the time. Everyone who fought the Mafia was killed, with out exeption. He attributes his being protected by Hashem to his total trust in Hashem (Bitachone in Hebrew) and his merit of being committed to keep the Torah commandments. He felt this was a prophetic mission to defeat the 'all powerful' wicked who everyone feared and to reveal the G-d is really king. He felt that the Mafia murder of police and a Rabbi were a Hillul Hashem (Desecration of G-d's Name) that he felt compelled to risk his life fighting for as a Kiddush Hashem. At the time he was moser nefesh many times to save Israel and the world from this crime that would destroy the world and Israel if not stopped. He also saw the downward spiral of immorality, desecration of Hashem's Name and corruption in America leading to another holocaust there if not stopped and rectified. Others felt the same. Midrash Raba on Parshat BiHolatheicha says that if someone is moser nefesh for Israel he merits Ruah HaKodesh and siata diShamya. At this time the author received Ruah HaKodesh and has had it ever since, at times on a monthly and sometimes even daily basis. This assisted him in his war against the Mafia, Edom and the enemies of Israel as part of his wars for Hashem. Hashem also sent help to him through many righteous brothers in the Mafia who protected him and even adopted him into one of the five Mafia families, who protected him in the way the Mafia protects people in grave danger, since he was part Italian on his mother's side (Livorno Italy from where great Rabbis like the Hida and Ohr HaChaim came).

In 1994 he filed civil law suits against record companies for copyright infringement of some of his approximately one hundred copyrighted songs that he wrote, but the cases were dismissed along with all the other eighteen cases against record companies that were filed in the Southern District court of New York. The record companies are known to have pain over a million dollars in 'gifts' to the government parties at the time. Four music artists an done record company president died of mysterious causes and murder that year. In the fall 1995 he filed a civil rights suit against these corporations and the US federal justice department, FBI, US Attorney, Warner Brothers Records, SONY, et al, alleging numerous well documented criminal activities such as bribery and abuse of power to pervert justice in the Southern District of New York (SDNY), the second circuit appellant court and Supreme Court and federal justice system headquarters in Washington, DC. He was moser nefesh (risked his life) liShem Shamayim (in the name of Heaven) for the desecration of the Name of Hashem and His commandments of Justice in the area and warned people, even in official court documents, that there would be Divine Retribution unless people heeded the Torah and repented, especially regarding the greed motivated injustice in the federal justice system and US establishment. He was and still is grateful for all of Hashem's salvations from grave danger and what many felt was certain death by the Mafia during this period of life, but, Hashem Saved many times.

As a witness to the rampant crime and systematic corruption in the area, epicentered in Manhattan and covering the entire East coast right down to Washington, DC, the author bears testimony that the Oklahoma City Federal building bombing (which occurred right after the federal court denied the author justice in the SDNY federal courts and he warned of Divine retribution for taking bribes as is documented in court papers), the 911 world trade center bombings, hurricane Katrina which wiped out New Orleans, hurricane Sandy (epicentered in Manhattan and covering the entire East coast right down to Washington, DC), and all other acts of G-d hitting the USA in these times, including AIDS and now possibly Measles, are Retribution from G-d Almighty for the US peoples' unrepented sins in the areas being struck by the Mighty hand of G-d, particularly the sins of immorality and iniquitous gain, among others, that is part of the institution of the Western establishment (Edom) as all educated people know as it is well documented internationally, including all Foreign Intelligence Services and Amnesty International. As part of the author's personal experience, he writes this book in part in an attempt to save as many people in Edom, especially the USA, especially Jews and righteous Gentiles there, before the whole system falls and may kill (Heaven Forbid) many, by many dangers that loom overhead (May Hashem have Mercy). That is why the book includes kiruv rihokeem (bringing people closer to G-d and His Torah Mitzvoth) and the real life musar (moral) of warning people of this real life story that recently happened where people in America sinned in the New York Metro area and got hit hard by G-d for it. This is a warning to help motivate people to repent and save their lives and souls. This is an appropriate statement for a book on Moshiah. May G-d have mercy and G-d Bless America. We hope for the best.

In January of 1996 he moved to an orthodox Jewish community in Monsey, NY, until he returned to live in Brookline, Massachusetts where he worked as a senior engineer at Raytheon missile systems division until 1997 when he decided to return to Israel to study rabbinic studies in Jerusalem. Before returning to Israel he released his CDs titled 'Covenent' (a blend of Hard Rock, folk rock and country), 'Jew Lost in Exile' (pop, folk rock and country) by his stage name Eric Alrich and a CD recorded by his friend Michael Avraham HaLevi (formerly Michael Frank) titled 'Mafia'. It was at that time when Hashem revealed to him a novel, almost miraculous, anti-missile system patent that he meant exclusively for Israel.

In 1998 he returned to Israel and learned Torah in Jerusalem at Machon Meir, the Diaspora Yeshiva, Bircas Torah, Tifereth, and eventually the Mir Yeshiva. There he wrote and distributed many Torah essays and in addition to his Yeshiva studies of Talmud, Midrash, Tanach, Shulhan Aruch and Halacha. He began to research the issues of the Messiah, the redemption, the ten tribes and the war of Gog and Magog in depth as part of his learning seder (schedule). At the time Hashem revealed to him through inspiration (Ruah HaKodesh) who was from which tribe and he observed repeated facial profiles, psychological profiles and personality patterns among the Jewish people which he believes represent the thirteen tribes of Israel, which according to the Rabbis, the Gaon of Vilna and the Malbim, are still among us, as his book 'The Final Redemption and the Ten Tribes' shows. He did kiruv in person to IDF personal over the Internet by targeted emails, and publicized crime in the US system on his web page. In 2005 he taught the subjects of the Moshiah, redemption and war of Gog and MaGog in Mea Shaareem, Jerusalem, in English and Hebrew, at the Mir Yeshiva and Yeshivas Hovavoth Livavoth. Being an activist to restart the Sanhedrin, he was asked to be on the New Sanhedrin but declined but hopes that in the future there will be a Sanhedrin in Israel including all the Gidolei haDor (biggest Rabbis in the generation). He is still working on that project to this day, and is affiliated with the biggest Rabbis of the generation who are Sanhedrin level, and believes they are fit to make a Sanhedrin as per Rambam hilcoth Sanhedrin 4:11, but needs major mega bucks funding to accomplish and market that goal, which is the next stage needed to bring the Messiah in our day as his book on the subject shows.

In 2006 he moved to Tsfat and learned Torah at Breslov's Nahal Novea Makor Chochma. There he continued his work in 'kiruv rihokeem' (bringing people closer to G-d) with thousands of personnel in the IDF ranging from privates to generals on a personal basis and over the Internet to all the university students in Israel. In 2007 he received a bracha (blessing) letter of approbation by Rav haTzadik Dov Kook haCohen Shlita to be a Rosh Yeshiva. In Tsfat in 2009 he wrote and recorded his CD demo 'Rise and Shine' and performed original songs on guitar at Ascent and Ohel Avraham.

In 2009 he returned to live in Jerusalem where he lived in Shaarei Hesed and then Beitar where he continued to learn Torah and produce music. In 2012 he wrote the first revision of the book "The Messiah, Redemption and the war of Gog and Magog" until 2015 where he is on the thirteenth revision and dividing it up into a three book series called 'The Moshiah According to Torah' (also called 'The Messiah According to Judaism'), 'the final Redemption and the Ten Tribes', and 'the War of Gog and Magog'. The deputy head of the Mosad, David Kimche, who he knew through is father, recognized him as 'the leader of the Jewish people' for his leadership roles behind the scenes; as opposed to a popularized leaders of what most Rabbis view as 'the Erev Rav' regime currently in power for th etiem being until Moshiah comes. Rosh Yeshiva Mir Nathen Tzi Finkel (zt'l) recognized him as the Gadol haDor on matters of the Moshiah. This book shows an important point that 'Chezkath Moshiah' of the Rambam can only possibly be achieved after the Sanhedrin makes Moshiah king which he believes is needed for ahishena.

In 2013 his mother (zt'l) passed away. Now he learns Torah, tries to make peace with the Arabs by being respectful and friendly (but not friends) with them. He is also working on teaching them the Noahide laws as well as bring 'Messianic Jews' closer to G-d by teaching them Torah so that they can live by the Torah properly. This can save jewish lives. The author is still single and would like to marry a kosher orthodox Jewish girl who is Yirath Shamayim and hagoona, and have children together and raise a family in Israel (biezrath Hashem).

Printed in the United States
By Bookmasters